LOVE AFFAIRS
OF
SOME FAMOUS MEN

Rev. E. J. Hardy.

LOVE AFFAIRS
OF
SOME FAMOUS MEN

Rev. EDWARD JOHN HARDY

Essay Index Reprint Series

BOOKS FOR LIBRARIES PRESS
FREEPORT, NEW YORK

First Published 1897
Reprinted 1972

Library of Congress Cataloging in Publication Data

Hardy, Edward John, 1849-1920.
    Love affairs of some famous men.

    (Essay index reprint series)
    Reprint of the 1897 ed.
    1. Biography. I. Title.
CT105.H26 1972   920'.02   72-4514
ISBN 0-8369-2948-9

PRINTED IN 1r. : UNITED STATES OF AMERICA

THE LOVE AFFAIRS OF SOME FAMOUS MEN

I AM NOT A FAMOUS OR EVEN AN INFAMOUS MAN, BUT I
HAVE HAD A LOVE AFFAIR WITH MY ONLY WIFE, IN
SUNSHINE AND SHOWERS, FROM THE DAY WHEN
I FIRST SAW HER TWENTY-EIGHT YEARS
AGO, AND THEREFORE TO HER I
DEDICATE THIS BOOK

PREFACE

THE problem of the union of man and woman must always remain the supreme and central question of society; and this book is a small contribution to its elucidation.

There is a greater desire just now to have details about celebrated men than to become acquainted with and understand their work. Shelley's amours, for instance, are known to many who have never read even his *Ode to the Skylark*. We hope that we are not pandering to this love of gossip by perpetrating a treatise on the love affairs of some famous men. This depends upon the spirit in which it was written, which, we trust, was that of Bolingbroke, who said of Marlborough, when some one spoke of his avarice, 'He was so great a man that I forgot he had that defect.'

If I were to say that all love affairs not quite proper have been omitted, my book would be little read. The biographies of men of genius are by no means all like moral tales, nor are the conjugal chapters in such biographies always the pleasantest to read. Shakespeare, Milton, Dante, Byron, are not easily to be surpassed as poets, but as husbands they did not amount to much.

What will be found here are the love affairs of some famous men, not chosen for being either good or bad, but such as came, as it were, self-directed in the course of ordinary reading. This is why some are omitted which those who will honour and help to sell my book by abusing it may think ought to have been inserted, and vice versa.

'I can make a hundred nobles at any time,' said Louis XIV., 'but I cannot make one man of genius.' The same sort of consideration has made me exclude the so-called love affairs of kings, princes, and people of this kind. They are generally made to order, and, therefore, uninteresting. In a book about famous men when one who is very famous is mentioned, people say, 'We all know him, and are a little tired of him'; when another not so famous is introduced to their notice they ask, 'Who cares for the love affairs, or anything else, concerning him?'—this made selection a difficult task.

The fact that in a limited book on so large a theme everything cannot receive equally full treatment, may excuse the tit-bit style of some of it. One of the best arguments against vegetarianism is that if we were bigoted vegetarians we would have to eat too much. Our brother, the ox, and our sister, the cow, are good enough to consume cart loads of grass and hay, and give them to us in the form of concentrated food. On the same principle a writer deserves some little credit who browses over acres of books, in order to serve up a dish of steaks which may prove nutritious and not tough.

E. J. HARDY.

CONTENTS

The Love Affairs of Some Famous Men

CHAPTER I

GENIUS AND MATRIMONY

THERE are two species of husbands difficult to live with —the genius and the fool. Perhaps the chances of happiness are greater with the fool ! Certainly it is more satisfactory to investigate as little as possible the private lives of those whose genius we especially reverence, and yet the love affairs of famous men is a subject so attractive that we are all drawn towards it. If the most commonplace wooing of the most commonplace people possesses an irresistible interest, what shall be said when the loves on which we look are the loves of the immortals. When the several parts of our bodies are in perfect health, we do not feel them, or, indeed, notice them at all; but the moment something goes wrong we feel, and cry out, 'Oh, my tooth !' 'My poor head !' 'My leg !'

So it is with matrimony.

When husband and wife pull along happily together they forget themselves and each other, and do not speak about their happiness at all. Thus one unhappy alliance makes more noise than a hundred that are happy. A shriek of pain is heard far more easily than a hum of satisfaction. Matrimonial failures strive and cry in the streets, whereas the successes enjoy domestic felicity at their own firesides and say nothing about it. Is not this the reason why we hear more of the matrimonial misery of great men than of their felicity? And when men of genius are unhappy they cry louder and gain more attention than do less distinguished people.

There was a time when the possession or supposed possession of 'genius' was held to justify a man being irritable and everything that a husband should not be. Now, however, we have come to the conclusion that men of intellect ought to have a law in their lives not less but even more than stupid people.

If they turn day into night and night into day; if they drink too much; if they are more partial to the society of other men's wives than of their own; if they fling away money 'generously' and cannot meet the just claims of butcher and baker—if they act in such ways as these we feel that they at least cannot claim a fool's pardon.

Goldsmith, who 'wrote as an angel and talked like poor poll,' was probably thinking of himself when he said, 'The conversation of a poet is that of a man of sense, while his actions are those of a fool!' 'I love my family's welfare,' said Montesquieu, 'but I cannot be so foolish as to make myself the slave to the minute affairs of a house.' Even a fire was considered a 'minute affair' by another author. He was deeply occupied in his library when some one, rushing in, announced that the house was on fire. 'Go to my wife,' he replied; 'these matters belong to her.'

To do it justice, however, genius is now putting aside this affectation of being above mundane matters, and a man with the divine afflatus will not unfrequently, if properly handled, make as good a husband as the stupidest plodder in existence. Certainly some time ago an essayist compiled a great array of testimony, which went to show that for a good family man warranted to stand bad weather, to love his wife, and to bring up the children respectably, there is no man like a poet. In our own time the two greatest masters of song in this country have been conspicuous for their conjugal felicity. It is the same in America: Longfellow, Lowell, Whittier, were all unexceptionable husbands. 'Men do not make their homes unhappy because they have genius,' says Wordsworth, 'but because they have not enough genius; a mind and sentiment of a higher order would render them capable of seeing and feeling all the beauty of domestic ties.' One thing, to be sure, is necessary, if a genius is to be happy, though married, and that is that his wife should not be a genius. A man of genius only needs a wife of sense; more than one genius in a house is too much. The wife of one of our most celebrated literary men said not long ago, 'It is a great mistake for brainy people to marry brains, and, happily, few of them do it. Put two geniuses together in matrimony, and you have two cats in a bag—nervous, fretful creatures, with no patience and less common sense, who will be always worrying each other, and tugging in opposite directions at the matrimonial chain. What a clever man wants is a clear-headed, sensible wife, who will forget his vagaries in remembering his brilliancy, and remain a constant shield between his sensitiveness and disagreeable things; something, in fact, like one of those cushions that sailors put down the side of a vessel to keep it from jarring too roughly against the dock. Look at me, for instance. I never wrote a word for publication, painted a picture, composed music, or did anything clever in all my life; but I make my husband just the sort of wife he needs.' But though she should not be a genius herself the wife of a gifted man should be able to appreciate his talents. Mrs Poet should not despise poetry and call it 'stuff' because it is less remunerative than paragraphs and puffing. The man of science should not be goaded by the taunts of his wife from the composition of works that would in time do the world good, to writing shilling shockers, or penny dreadfuls, for immediate pot-boiling purposes. The painter should be allowed to pursue his ideals without being pestered to make paying portraits of fashionable beauties. The true wife of a soldier or sailor would object, even if he wished to do so, to his tying himself to her apron-strings at home instead of going to the big or little wars.

Nor will a wife, if she be the right sort, ever feel jealous of the work that makes her husband great. She will be unlike the lady in the famous poem, who felt annoyed with her life partner, and—

> Complained that after noon
> He went to pore on books too soon.

Probably jealousy was at bottom the reason why the wife of Confucius so interrupted the studies of her husband that he had to dismiss her, and why that other philosopher of antiquity would not raise his eyes for three years, lest they should rest upon a woman. In a fit of jealous rage a wife has torn the canvas from the easel where her husband was at work. Another, with grim determination, always chose the time when her husband was striving to finish a sonnet, to practise her scales or pound at some terrible sonata.

After all, men of genius must submit like others to the chances of war, and not 'think the doom of man reversed for them.' Genius may possibly be a factor towards success in life, but it is never a substitute for the prudence that makes a wise matrimonial choice and the common sense that rightly uses marriage.

In a speech upon woman's rights, a lady orator exclaimed, 'It is well known that Solomon owed his wisdom to the number of his wives.' This is too much; but it is an undoubted fact that the success or failure of most men depends to a very large extent upon the kind of woman they marry. And this we think is especially true in reference to men of genius. An intellectual life, however successful, requires the softening influence of a happy marriage to prevent its becoming sour and cynical. Tom Moore spoke for a large number of men of genius when he said that, having experienced the emptiness of applause and popularity, he found in his home something better than the world could either give or take away.

> And one dear home—one saving ark,
>   Where love's true light at last I've found,
> Shining within, when all was dark,
>   And comfortless, and stormy round.

CHAPTER II

SHOULD AUTHORS MARRY?

A FAMOUS author, resident in Virginia, inscribed upon the gravestone of his wife, 'The light is gone from my life.' Time not only modified his distress but suggested a renewal of conjugal bliss. A neighbour had the bad taste to banter him on his engagement, and to express surprise that he had so soon forgotten his words of lamentation. 'So far from forgetting them,' he replied, 'I remember and repeat them now, as originating and confirming the intention that you are pleased to criticise. I declared that the light was gone from my life, and it is for this reason that I propose to strike another match.'

So far are some authorities from thinking that literary men should marry early and often that they would deny them the consolation even once. They believe that matrimony tends to extinguish rather than illuminate literature.

'Minerva and Venus cannot live together,' said one old scholar. Montaigne expressed an opinion to this effect: 'Might I have had my own will, I would not have married Wisdom herself, if she would have had me. But 'tis not to much purpose to evade it, the common custom and usage of life will have it so. The most of us are guided by example, not by choice.'

An amusing skit in *The Book-Buyer* records the establishment of a 'Society for the Protection of Genius.'

The conclusions reached by the first meeting are best stated in its own formal document :—

'WHEREAS—There seems to be a concerted effort in certain quarters to discourage marriageable girls from forming alliances with literary men; and WHEREAS—This prejudice, now widely diffused, tends to perpetuate an absurd and erroneous theory that literary men make disagreeable íhusbands ; and WHEREAS—This theory, if allowed to go unrefuted, will work great and everlasting injury both to individuals and to society at large ; THEREFORE—*Resolved*, that a committee of three be appointed to draw up a Constitution and By-laws to govern an association to be called the 'Society for the Protection of Genius'; and *Resolved*—That the general objects of this society shall be the extermination of the impression, now held by many young women, that irritability always accompanies genius; and, *Resolved*—That we each and all pledge ourselves to do whatever we can in our writings to prove the falsity of this impression.'

Probably there is nothing in literary work more antagonistic to domestic felicity than there is in other occupations; the trouble is that it is done at home and not put out, so to speak—and one of the necessary conditions of peace in a house is that the master should be absent from it for at least six hours a day. Very often men of letters, like clergymen, artists, and others who work at home, do not appreciate their homes as much as those do whose work takes them away from them for days at a time, or at least for several hours each day.

Sterne wrote very beautifully to Maria, but he did not talk so beautifully to his wife. Just in the middle of a sublime paragraph, just as he is catching a sentence perhaps that will immortalise him, in comes Mrs Sterne, as women will do at the most unseasonable times. She has come to tell him that, owing to a little difficulty, dinner will have to be put off for an hour or two. He had forgotten all about dinner, and Mrs Sterne brings him down from glorious heights of imagination to the kitchen. This was why Sterne was of the character of his name to his wife, and not to Maria. He had never seen Maria; he had seen his wife : he had never had to pay Maria's bills; he had to pay Mrs Sterne's. No doubt it was for the same reason that when Lady Byron used to knock at her husband's study door and ask, 'Do I disturb you, Byron?' the noble poet would reply in one word—'Damnably.'

And if an author does not value his home as much as do those who have less domestic life, the honour which he himself receives there is on a par with that which a prophet has in his own country. More than likely his wife thinks of him as did the spouse of the French author who used to exclaim, '*Mon Dieu, que les gens d'esprit sont bêtes !*' Especially is this the case if the guineas he earns resemble angels' visits. The accumulation of MS., and the usual vapourings about neglected genius, are poor substitutes for a satisfactory income in the eyes of a practical housewife. They are not readily convertible into dresses, bonnets, and artistic furniture. Posterity is too remote, while neighbours are inconveniently close and critical. One is not surprised, therefore, when the wife looks with unsympathetic eyes upon elaborate preparations for a *magnum opus*, and occasionally breaks out into a state of hostility.

The temperament and ways of literary men are often very irritating to those with whom they live. The artisan can work at all times, but genius does it in fits and starts; and in these tempestuous moments of cerebral excitement, the home life must be hushed into a fearful silence, lest inspiration should be disturbed. Then there are days when sombre silence pervades the house and the temper of the master at the dinner-table is more than usually nasty. It is because on the study table lies a parcel 'Declined with thanks.' And what shall we say about the operation of 'finishing a book'? According to the wife of a certain man of letters, it is worse than another event of the highest domestic interest.

No! genius in undress is seldom as attractive as genius with its singing robes about it, and speaking with a voice which comes from those higher realms to which we have no access save by its aid.

Domestic felicity or infelicity depends upon the wife as much as upon the husband, and the elder D'Israeli scarcely exaggerated when he said that 'The wives of many men of letters have been dissolute, ill-humoured, slatternly, and have run into all the frivolities of the age.'

'How delightful it is, on the other hand,' remarks the same writer, 'when the wife of a literary man is disposed to, and capable of, helping her husband!' And he mentions an instance—that of Budæus. His wife left him nothing to desire. The same genius, the same inclinations, and the same ardour for literature, eminently appeared in those two fortunate persons. The wife, far from drawing her husband from his studies, animated him when he languished. 'Ever at his side, ever assiduous and ever with some useful book in her hand, she acknowledged herself to be a most happy woman.' Scholars are warned, however, not to allow literary enthusiasm to influence too much the choice of a wife by the case of Francis Philelphus, an eminent scholar of the fifteenth century. He was so desirous of acquiring the Greek language in perfection, that he travelled to Constantinople in search of a Grecian wife. Alas! the lady proved a scold, and the words with which her husband became most familiar were abusive ones inharmoniously pronounced.

There are and have been many authors who, but for their wives, would never have written at all, or never would have written as well as they did.

The French writer, Alphonse Daudet, had determined to remain a bachelor, because he was afraid that if he made a wrong step in marriage he might dull his imagination; but, on being introduced to Mademoiselle Julie

Allard, who loved literature, and was a charming writer and critic herself, his fear was removed. The union proved a very happy one, and the picture of the two at work is an attractive bit of biography. 'She has been,' says his brother, 'the light of his hearth, the regulator of his work, and the discreet counsellor of his inspiration. There is not a page that she has not revised, re-touched, and enlivened; and her husband bore witness to her devotion and indefatigable collaboration in the dedication of *Nabob*, but she would not allow this dedication to appear.' Once, it is related, he had a sentimental and dramatic scene with his wife, concerning which he remarked, 'This seems, my dear, like a chapter that has slipped out of a novel.' 'It is more likely, Alphonse,' was the reply, 'to form a chapter that will slip into one.'

And with all this Madame Daudet excelled as a housewife. There was no Bohemian irregularity in her home. Daudet's visitors, when they left, have often been heard to exclaim, 'What a capital wife he must have !'

Fenimore Cooper became a novelist through his wife's challenge. One evening, while reading a novel, he threw it down saying, 'I believe I could write a better book myself.' 'Let me see you do it,' said his wife, with a smile. In a few days he had written several chapters of *Precaution*, which, when finished, he published at his own expense. The novel attracted little attention, but it gave Cooper an inkling of his capacity for story-writing, and the *Spy*, his next novel, appealed so strongly to the patriotic sympathies of his countrymen that it became a great success. Hawthorne, too, was induced to write the *Scarlet Letter* by a remark of his wife, and he acknowledged that but for the domestic environment which she supplied he could not have produced his contributions to American classics. Like Mrs Carlyle and some other wives of literary men, Mrs Hawthorne kept house so well that the digestion and temper of her husband were not unnecessarily disturbed.

And then how appreciative was this good wife ! She credited her husband with so much goodness that he could hardly help being good.

Here are two glimpses, given in letters to her mother, of her feeling for Hawthorne. Nathaniel had been discharged from being a surveyor, in 1849, when she wrote:—

'You take our reverse of fortune in the way I hoped you would. I feel "beyond the utmost scope and vision of calamity" (as Pericles said to Aspasia) while my husband satisfies my highest ideal, and while the graces of heaven fill the hearts of my children. Everything else is very external. This is the immortal life, which makes flowers of asphodel bloom in my path, and no rude step can crush them. I exult in my husband.'

In 1851, when times were less adverse, she wrote :—

'I am glad you can dwell upon my lot "with unalloyed delight," for certainly, if ever there were a felicitous one, it is mine. Unbroken immortal love surrounds and pervades me; we have extraordinary health, in addition to more essential elements of happiness; my husband transcends my best dream, and no one but I can tell what he must be, therefore. When I have climbed up to him, I think I shall find myself in the presence of the shining ones, for I can only say that every day he rises upon me like a sun at midnoon. And, then, such children ! and now the prospect of means to buy bread, and a little cake, too.'

It might be thought that an 'autocrat of a breakfast table' could not be a married man : but this Oliver Wendell Holmes was for forty-eight years. A friend thus describes the sharer of his home : 'Mrs Holmes was not a literary woman, but she was a woman of education and refinement, and no one who has ever visited the author's home will forget the gracious charm of his wife's presence. She was a small, dainty woman, with manners of old-fashioned cordiality; and yet, with all her gentleness, she stood as a breakwater between her husband and the prying, pushing world.'

Mrs Haggard and Mrs Thomas Hardy gave much literary help to their husbands. The latter urged Mr Hardy to forsake architecture for literature as a profession. When he had written his first novel, *Desperate Remedies*, his wife copied out the entire work from his manuscript, and sent it to the publisher. As part of her work, she keeps herself well posted up in the literature of the day, and her husband constantly draws upon her knowledge.

The works of Max O'Rell (Monsieur Paul Blouët) were written first in French and then translated into English by his wife, who is the daughter of a Devonshire shipowner. When a girl Madame Blouët learned French with great care, little thinking how useful the language would be to her afterwards. She is an excellent cook and a model hostess.

In recalling the story of his life, Mr Sala relates how marriage helped to wean him from the idle and unprofitable ways of his early Bohemianism. The references to his wife are few and unobtrusive, but he tells of the great change that came over him when he had to work for somebody else besides himself, and when his toil was requited by the devotedness and love of a charming and worthy partner. 'It was my great good fortune,' he says, 'to espouse a pious, charitable, and compassionate young woman, and she did her best during a union of five-and-twenty years to weed out of me my besetting sin of selfishness, and to soften and dulcify a temper naturally violent and unreasoning. When I married my life seemed to put on an entirely different and radiant hue.'

These are only a few of the many examples that might be brought forward pointing to the same conclusion as that to which the eminent writer, Mr James Payn, arrives. 'I have known,' he says, 'a great many brethren of the pen, both married and single, and my experience is that there is no class which derives so much benefit from the wedded state as they do.'

CHAPTER III

POETS IN LOVE

POETS are said to learn in suffering what they teach in song; but many of them, it would seem, have considered it necessary to make their wives suffer also. True, as Johnson remarks, 'Many qualities contribute to domestic happiness upon which poetry has no colours to show;' but on the other hand, the domestic surroundings of our poets must greatly colour their productions. To say that misery always awaits women who marry poets would be a rash generalisation. It would be nearer the truth to say that they play a game of double or quits. Poets, like other men of genius, make either singularly good husbands or husbands of the most disastrous kind. So much, too, depends upon Mrs Poet. If, when her husband is in 'the brightest heaven of invention,' she pay a visit to the kitchen and see that a dinner which may in some degree satisfy his intense longings (for making poetry is hungry work) is in preparation, there may be peace and happiness even in the house of poetry.

No more beautiful love of man for woman is on record than that of Dante for Beatrice. It was not joyous, thoughtless, sensual love : it was a love full of sadness; tormented by the sense of, and the aspiration towards, an ideal it was unable to reach. Far different from the love which has deserved the name of *l'égoïsme à deux personnes*—a jealous passion which narrows the sphere of our activity, and causes us to forget our duties to others—the love of Dante did not dry up the other affections ; rather, it fostered and fertilised them, strengthening the sense of duty, and enlarging the heart. He says in the *Vita Nuova*, 'Whensoever she appeared before me, I had no enemy left on earth; the flame of charity, kindled within me, caused me to forgive all who had ever offended me.'

Dante seems to have seen Beatrice, whom he met first in 1274, when he was nine years old, only once or twice, and she probably knew little of him. Nevertheless, when she married he fell seriously ill; and when she died, as she did shortly after, his life was in danger, and he became 'a thing wild and savage to look upon.' He so far recovered from the shock of his loss that two years afterwards he married Gemmadé Donati. He had seven children, and although he does not mention his wife in the *Divina Commedia*, and although she did not accompany him into exile and had a temper of her own, there is no reason to suppose that she was other than a good wife, or that the union was otherwise than happy. Dante, however, always felt that the death of Beatrice had imposed new and solemn duties upon him; that he was bound to strive to render himself more worthy of her. In his love of every form of beauty, in his incessant yearning after inward purity, Beatrice was the muse of his intellect, the angel of his soul, the consoling spirit sustaining him in exile and in poverty, throughout the cheerless wanderings of a storm-beaten existence. The spiritual Beatrice in Dante's song was a nymph dwelling on the same heights of the Christian Parnassus that were trod by our Milton when he transformed Lady Alice Egerton into an ideal of purity, the Lady in *Comus*, and shaped her innocence into an allegory of man's duty in the using of the gifts of God.

On the 6th of April, 1327, happened the most famous event of Petrarch's history. He saw Laura for the first time. Who Laura was, remains uncertain still. We may, however, reject the sceptical hypothesis that she was a mere figment of the poet's fancy; and, if we accept her personal reality, the poems of her lover demonstrate that she was a married woman, with whom he enjoyed a respectful and not very intimate friendship.

Laura died of the plague in 1347, as did also several other friends of Petrarch.   These losses were the turning-point of his inner life.   The poems written *In Morte di Madonna Laura* are graver and of a more religious tone.   The poet fancied himself in frequent communion with her spirit; he describes her appearing to him in the middle of the night, comforting him, and pointing to heaven as the place of their next meeting.   He blesses the memory of her who, by the even tenor of her virtue, had been the means of calming and purifying his heart.

Chaucer, who wrote,—

> Marriage is such a rabble rout,
> That those who are out, would fain get in;
> And those who are in, would fain get out,

had himself experience of it.   He married one of the ladies of the bed-chamber to the Queen.   In so many of his poems he was satirical about wives that it is supposed he was not happy in his domestic life.   In the *Clerk's Tale*, for instance, wives are ironically urged 'not to let humility nail their tongues, to imitate Echo that keeps no silence, to ever clap like mills, to make their husbands care and weep and ring and waille.'   The fault, however, was most likely not all on the side of Mrs Chaucer, and indeed there are indications that the poet had a passion for another.

Shakespeare's experience told him,—

> Never durst poet touch pen to write
> Until his ink were temper'd with love's sighs.

Accordingly, when he was eighteen and a half years of age, he fell in love with Anne Hathaway, aged twenty-six.   They loved not wisely, and their marriage becoming necessary, the wedding took place when banns had only been once asked in church.   The child that was born was christened Susanna.   The other children Shakespeare had were twins, Hannah and Judith.   Was

the marriage a failure?   The way Shakespeare dwells
upon the evils of jealousy (the *Comedy of Errors*, Act
V., 69-86) and the fact that he left by will to his wife
'the second best bed,' have given rise to the supposition
that it was.   Still, we do not know.   It is possible that
a woman seven and a half years older than her husband
might not be afflicted with the 'green-eyed monster,'
jealousy.   As for 'the second best bed,' it may have been
the bridal one, and this is not a bequest which a husband
who had grown cold and indifferent to his wife would
make.   True, Shakespeare said that Anne Hathaway
'hath a way,' but he may have been only playing on his
wife's name and may not have meant that she was particularly stubborn.

> As the most forward bud
> Is eaten by the canker ere it blow,
> Even so by love the young and tender wit
> Is turned to folly; blasting in the bud,
> Losing his verdure even in the prime,
> And all the fair effects of future hopes.

This is a common consequence of precocious marriages; but we are not, therefore, to conclude that 'the
young and tender wit' of our Shakespeare was 'turned
to folly'—that his 'forward bud' was 'eaten by the
canker'—that 'his verdure' was lost 'even in the
prime' by his marriage.   The influence which it must
have had upon his destinies was no doubt considerable;
but it is too much to assume, as it has been assumed,
that it was an unhappy influence.

In his thirty-fifth year Milton married Mary Powell,
the daughter of a justice of the peace in Oxfordshire.
Being one of a large family, in which there was 'much
company and joviality,' the regulations of the poet's
house were not to her taste.   Four o'clock was his time
for rising in the summer, five in the winter.   The day
began with reading a chapter from a Hebrew Bible,
which was followed by continual study till dinner-time.

Then more study, an hour of walking exercise, organ-playing, and very early to bed. Having 'done' a month in this prison, the bride fled back to her father's house. Here she remained in spite of promises to return, and so enraged her husband that he composed his three pamphlets on divorce. Different reasons have been assigned for the subsequent surrender of the young wife by her relations. D. Johnson thinks it was because the poet had begun to put his doctrine into practice, by courting a lady of great accomplishments. Be this as it may, at one of his usual visits to a relation Milton was surprised to see his wife come from another room, and implore forgiveness on her knees—a scene which the poet afterwards made Eve enact before Adam. With 'noble leonine clemency' Milton forgave and took back his wife. Four children were born, and at the birth of the fourth the mother died, in her twenty-sixth year. Two years afterwards the poet married Catherine, daughter of Captain Woodcock, of Hackney. She died within a twelve-month at the birth of her child, but her memory is kept fresh, generation after generation, by her husband's sonnet beginning,—

Methought I saw my late espoused saint.

After remaining a widower for five years, as he wanted 'a domestic companion and attendant,' Milton married Elizabeth Minshul, a woman he had never seen, and who, it would seem, was rather a shrew. The Duke of Buckingham called her a rose. 'I'm no judge of colour,' said Milton, 'but it may be so, for I feel the thorns daily.' Soon after his third marriage, it is said that Milton was offered at the Restoration the continuance of his employment as Latin secretary, and being pressed by his wife to accept it, answered, 'You, like other women, want to ride in your coach; my wish is to live and die an honest man.' This third Mrs Milton survived her husband· for no less than fifty-three years, not dying

till 1727. If we are to believe Dr Johnson's summing
up of Milton's matrimonial experiences, marriage was
not in his case a success. 'The first wife left him in
disgust, and was brought back only by terror; the
second, indeed, seems to have been more a favourite,
but her life was short. The third oppressed his children
in his lifetime, and cheated them at his death.

The poet Waller (1605-1687) inherited £800 a year
and became richer by marrying Mrs Banks, a City heiress. She died at the birth of her first child and left
Waller a widower of about five-and-twenty, gay and
wealthy. He set his affections on Lady Dorothea
Sidney, eldest daughter of the Earl of Leicester, the
'Sacharissa' of his poems. She, however, disdained
his suit, and married the Earl of Sunderland. In her
old age, meeting Waller, she asked when he would again
write such verses upon her. 'When you are as young,
Madam,' said he, 'and as handsome as you were
then.'

When a young man Wycherley, the comic poet,
married the Countess of Drogheda, but their marriage
was anything but a happy one. At the end of his life
he again entered what certainly was not to him a holy
estate, for he wedded only to spite and punish his
nephew and heir. He declared that he was not going
to leave the world without paying his debts, and that he
would *die* married, although he could not endure living
so. Accordingly, about ten days before his death, he
espoused a Miss Elizabeth Jackson.

When Pope wrote the lines,—

> Born to no pride, inheriting no strife,
> Nor marrying discord in a noble wife,

he is supposed to have had in his eye the marriages of
Dryden and Addison. The former married Lady Elizabeth Howard, daughter of the Earl of Berkshire, 'with
circumstances not very honourable to either party.'

She once rebuked her inconsiderate partner by the remark that if she had been a book, he would have shown her more attention. To this the great satirist replied, that he wished she were an almanack, for that was a book he could change every year.

Young also married a lady of rank. She was daughter of the Earl of Lichfield, and widow of Colonel Lee, to whose two children the poet was tenderly attached. The death of this lady, which was followed, though at considerable intervals, by that of the two children, produced a powerful impression on Young's mind, and had, it is probable, a great influence in suggesting the tone and subject of his last and greatest work, the *Night Thoughts*.

The fatal facility with which the 'Ploughman Bard,' Robert Burns, captured the hearts of rural maidens, was due to his personal charm rather than to his poetical gifts. When he was fifteen, 'Handsome Nell' (Nelly Fitzpatrick), aged fourteen, a fellow field-labourer, attracted his attention. Mary Morison, who occasioned so many songs, has been identified with Miss Ellison Begbie. In 1786 the poet exchanged Bibles, as a testimony of lasting love, with Mary Campbell—'Highland Mary.' Next year he was in the 'full career of friendship' for Misses Margaret Chalmers and Charlotte Hamilton.

He had met her eighteen years before, but it was not uutil 1788 that, for the sake of the respectability of herself and prospective twins, he married Jean Armour. Of her he wrote,—

> She is a winsome, wee thing;
> She is a handsome, wee thing;
> She is a bonnie, wee thing,
> This sweet, wee wife of mine !

and yet, two years after he got legal possession of the winsome, handsome, bonnie, sweet wee wife, he had a daughter by a certain Anna Park. In 1794, Chloris (Mrs Whalpdale) claimed Burns's wandering fancy—

but enough of the unedifying catalogue. The bare enu-
meration of his victims is the poet's condemnation.

Hogg, the 'Ettrick Shepherd,' says, 'Never was poet,
now or of yore, who was not tremulous with love-lore.'
He himself 'always liked women better than men,' and
his sweetest songs echo his own experience. He gave a
happy and playful turn to this admiration when he
wrote,—

> Could this ill world ha'e been contrived
>   To stand without mischievous woman,
> How peacefu' bodies might ha'e lived,
>   Released frae a' the arts sae common !
> But since it is the woefu' case
>   That man maun ha'e this teasing crony,
> Why sic a sweet bewitching face?
>   Oh, had she no' been made sae bonny !

The poet was fortunate in drawing a prize in the
matrimonial lottery, his wife being a handsome and
estimable woman, much above his original rank in life,
and he showed his appreciation of a happy fireside by
being a faithful and devoted husband. The lady who
won his affections was Margaret Phillips, and turning
a deaf ear to numberless suitors, she remained constant
to him during an engagement of ten years. Patience at
last was rewarded, and as the wedding drew near it was
not the bride only who was anxious about her attire on
the eventful occasion. 'I would have you dressed,'
Hogg writes, 'in white muslin, with a white satin Highland bonnet, with white plumes and veil.'

The following, which the poet Thomas Campbell wrote
to Lord Jeffrey, shows the sort of husband he was :—

'I received your letter, my dear Jeffrey, this morning
at the time when I was agitated with the feelings of past
joy and present anxiety. I have got a son, and my wife
is doing as well as possible; but at this critical state of
her health I feel an anxiety about her—I cannot describe
how uneasy—I may lose all that is my comfort in existence, in a few days; at least, so my thoughts at certain

hours forebode. I have not slept an hour to an end for
four days and nights, and my tongue and throat are
parched with incessant feverishness. I have much to do,
but cannot compose my thoughts to do anything of consequence.' When some twenty years after this his wife
did die he thus wrote : 'I have gone through the melancholy task of searching poor Matilda's depositories.
What sensation a knot of ribbon or a lace cap can now
excite ! . . . When I looked at the Berlin black metal
necklace, it was not, God knows, its intrinsic value—for
that is not much—that made me feel as if I were tearing
a string from my heart to part with; but the remembrance that my poor Matilda had kissed me so often,
and so tenderly, when she put it round her neck, and
thought it so good a mark of my taste, in knowing what
would please *her* elegant taste. . . . I did not think
I had been made of such shivering stuff.'

Coleridge 'ought not to have had wife or children;
he should have had a diocesan care of the world; no
parish duty.' Unfortunately he did marry at the age of
twenty-three, and prolonged his honeymoon in a seques-
tered cottage, amid beautiful scenery, until the necessity
of supplementing the ambrosia of love with the bread
and cheese of mortals compelled him to re-enter the
world. He had no other prospect of support than a
promise to be paid liberally for all the poetry he would
write. The children came faster than the poetry, however, and the poor man had even to contribute to the
support of his wife's relations. The unequal struggle
went on for six years or more before he confessed defeat.
Mrs Coleridge's faults might have been virtues in some
other adjustment of the marriage tie, but to her husband
they were torture. A threatened separation seems to
have made her serious, for in a letter to Southey Coleridge writes, 'She promised to set about an alteration
in her external manners and looks and language, and
to fight against her inveterate habits of puny thwarting
and unintermitting dyspathy. . . . I, on my part,

promised to be more attentive to all her feelings of pride, etc., etc., and to try to correct my habits of impetuous censure.'

Probably De Quincey was right when he said, 'Neither Coleridge nor Byron could have failed to quarrel with *any* wife, though a Pandora sent down from heaven to bless him.'

The former thought that he could have been happy even with a servant girl if she sincerely loved him, and gave it as his opinion that the ideal union would be that between a deaf man and a blind woman. The servant girl would have to have loved very sincerely indeed to have been happy with a man who had contracted the habit of laudanum-drinking with its 'pleasurable sensations,' as an antidote to pain. What a cheerful companion to live with must he have been who in the daytime was always haunted with

> A grief without a pang, void, dark, and drear,
> A stifled, drowsy, unimpassioned grief;

who was wont to remark, 'Conceive whatever is most wretched, helpless, hopeless, and you will form a notion of my state. . . . Conceive a spirit in hell, employed in tracing out for others the road to that heaven from which his crimes exclude him,' and who at night was visited by horrible dreams !

Mrs Coleridge was not blind, so she saw that her husband's face had become sallow, his eye wild, his nerves shaken, and his steps tottering, not because he was a genius and wrote poetry, but because he had become a slave to opium.

In his better nature Coleridge loved his children and respected his wife, but his better nature was drugged, and he left his wife and children to be mainly supported by friends, and allowed his son Hartley to be sent to college on alms collected by Southey. So indifferent did he grow, that he never wrote to his wife or children, or even opened a letter from them. With the freedom of a bachelor he lived apart, taking his opium and dreaming his dreams.

Coleridge married Miss Sarah Fricker, on October 4th, 1795, and five weeks after, his friend and brother poet, Southey, led to the altar Edith Fricker, Mrs Coleridge's sister. He parted from her at the church door, not because there was much insanity in the Fricker family (which would have been a very good reason), but because the gains of his poetry did not at the time enable him to set up a house. Indeed, he was at a loss how to pay the marriage fees and buy the wedding-ring ; for often during previous weeks he had walked the streets dinnerless.

Southey went for some time to Lisbon, and then came back for his wife. When they returned to England their prospects brightened, and making a home at Keswick, they managed matrimony much better than did the Coleridges.

It must indeed have been irritating for Mrs Coleridge to see her brother-in-law maintaining a bright and happy home by orderly and conscientious work, while her own husband spent his time in dreamy inactivity and far-reaching schemes, or plunged into literary enterprises, so injudiciously planned and so irregularly conducted, as only to lose money and end in failure. If one poet could finish his poems and pay his tradesmen's bills, why could not another? Nobody could have appreciated a home more than did Southey. He says, 'Oh dear, oh dear ! there is such a comfort in one's old coat and old shoes, one's own chair and own fireside, one's own writing-desk and own library—with a little girl climbing up to my neck and saying, " Don't go to London, papa; you must stay with Edith !"—and a little boy whom I taught to speak the language of cats, dogs, cuckoos, jackasses, etc., before he can articulate a word of his own. There is such a comfort in all these things, that *transportation* to London for four or five weeks

seems a heavier punishment than any sins of mine
deserve.'

Sorrow, however, will enter the best regulated home,
and the Southeys had to endure the loss of two much-
loved children. Then came the mental illness and death,
after a union of forty years, of Mrs Southey, from which
her husband never recovered. True, he married again;
but it was as a nurse rather than as a wife that he chose
the poetess Caroline Bowles.

CHAPTER IV

MORE POETS IN LOVE

A FRIEND was talking to Wordsworth of De Quincey's
articles about him. Wordsworth begged him to stop;
he had not read them, and did not wish to ruffle himself
about them. 'Well,' said the friend, 'I'll tell you only
one thing he says, and then we'll talk of other things.
He says your wife is too good for you.' The old poet's
dim eyes lighted up, and he started from his chair,
crying with enthusiasm, 'And that's true ! There he's
right !' his disgust and contempt visibly moderating.

The maiden name of this good wife was Mary Hutchinson. She was the poet's cousin. He had loved her from
childhood, and scarcely exaggerated when he said,—

> She was a phantom of delight,
> When first she gleamed upon my sight.

She was not beautiful, but 'she exercised all the practical fascination of beauty, through the compensatory
charms of sweetness all but angelic, of simplicity the
most entire.' And she believed in her husband when all
the world despised his poetry. 'Worse and worse,'
Jeffrey said, when a new poem came out; 'Better and

better,' said Mrs Wordsworth.   And what did you see?
one was asked, who had been into the lake country' and
had gone to Wordsworth's home.   'I saw the old man,'
he said, 'walking in the garden with his wife.   They
were both quite old, and he was almost blind; but they
seemed like sweethearts courting, they were so tender to
each other and attentive.'   So, too, Miss Martineau, who
was a near neighbour, tells us how the old wife would
miss her husband and trot out, to find him asleep,
perhaps, in the sun, run for his hat, tend him, and watch
over him till he awoke.

Just after leaving Eton, Shelley fell in love with his
cousin, Harriet Grove, the parents on both sides approv-
ing.   The views, however, which he expressed about
religious and social matters, so alarmed her that with the
advice of her parents she broke off the informal engagement into which she had entered.   Some of the poet's
biographers think he suffered a lifelong sorrow from this
early mischance, and there is no doubt that his first
unhappy marriage was contracted while the wound
remained unhealed.   The name of Harriet Westbrook
and something in her pretty face reminded him of
Harriet Grove ; it is even still uncertain to which
Harriet the dedication of *Queen Mab* is addressed.
Harriet Westbrook was a school friend of Shelley's
sister.   With great earnestness he preached to her
freethought, and had the satisfaction of forming his
pupil—only sixteen years of age—to his views.   She
had for Shelley the charm of a heroine struggling
against tyranny.   'Her father,' so he wrote in a letter
to his friend Hogg, 'has persecuted her in a most
horrible way, by endeavouring to compel her to go to
school. . . . I advised her (of course) to resist.   She
wrote to say that resistance was useless, but that she
would fly with me, and threw herself upon my protection.'   The young people eloped to Edinburgh, and were
married according to the formalities of Scotch law.   The
age of the bridegroom was nineteen; that of the bride

sixteen. By the time the coach reached York, a night and a day after leaving London, the bridegroom had to realise that this harsh and tyrannous world has an ignoble desire for cash in return for hotel accommodation. 'A slight pecuniary distress' is Shelleyan for hard up,' and the modest request that Hogg should send him £10 shows that the extremity was real enough.

Harriet was the daughter of a coffee-shop keeper, and Shelley's father considered that marriage with her was a *mésalliance* for his son; so for a considerable time he stopped all supplies, as did also ' Jew Westbrooke,' the girl's father. However, after allowing the rash pair to suffer a good while from impecuniosity, both parents relented, and both gave them £200 a year.

The young people lived for a time in the 'lake district' and then in London. Shelley took no thought for sublunary matters, and Harriet was an indifferent housekeeper. Dinner came as it were by chance; and when there was no meat provided for the entertainment of casual guests, the table was supplied with buns, procured by Shelley from the nearest pastry-cook. He had abjured animal food and alcohol. When he was walking in the streets and felt hungry, he would dive into a baker's shop and emerge with a loaf tucked under his arm. He could not understand how any one should want more than bread. 'I dropped a hint,' says Hogg, who lived with them, 'about a pudding.' 'A pudding,' said Shelley, dogmatically, 'is a prejudice!'

Why did Shelley desert her whom he married to protect? It is said that he suspected her faithfulness to him, but the real reason seems to have been because he had fallen in love with Mary Godwin. Her lips had touched his 'tremblingly,' her dark eyes had soothed his dream of pain.' At the time his mind, according to Peacock, was 'suffering like a little kingdom the nature of an insurrection. His eyes were bloodshot, his hair

and dress disordered. He caught up a bottle of laudanum, and said, ''I never part from this.''

When the guilty lovers eloped together, the deserted
wife drowned herself in the Serpentine. The following
lines, which Shelley wrote the year after, seem to
allude to the tragic event :—

> That time is dead for ever, child,
> Drowned, frozen, dead, for ever !
>   We look on the past,
>   And stare aghast
> At the spectres wailing, pale and ghast,
> Of hopes which thou and I beguiled
>   To death on life's dark river.

Meeting a lady at a ball, Walter Savage Landor determined on the instant to marry her. Not long after he
had done so, Mrs Landor came to think that a conversation with her husband was incomplete without a quarrel,
and generally ended with the remark that she should not
have married a man so many years older than herself.
She never was aware that more can be said in one
minute than can be forgotten in a lifetime.' Even in
the honeymoon she wounded the poor man's vanity.
Landor was reading some of his own verses to his bride—
and who read more exquisitely?—when all at once the
lady, releasing herself from his arm, jumped up, saying.
'Oh, do stop, Walter ! There's that dear delightful
Punch performing in the street. I must look out of the
window.'

After enduring as long as he thought he could the
headaches which his wife's tongue inflicted upon him,
Landor walked across the island of Jersey, where the ill-
mated couple were living, and embarked in an oyster-
boat for France. A reconciliation took place, but it was
only temporary. We have given Landor's account of
the matter; but in fairness it should be acknowledged
that it was small reproach to any woman that she did
not possess sufficient charm, tact, and intelligence to

suit a man who admitted having 'an affection of the brain.' Landor demanded beauty in women, but was not submissive to its influence; and while he was intolerant to folly, he would have been impatient of any competing ability.

His brother wrote of him in 1815, when travelling with him and his wife : 'He is seldom out of a passion or a sulky fit excepting at dinner, when he is more boisterous and good-humoured than ever. Then his wife is a darling, a beauty, an angel, a bird. But for just as little reason the next morning she is a fool. She is certainly gentle, patient, and submissive. She takes all the trouble, indeed is too officious, and would walk on foot willingly if he wished it, and she were abl . If he loses his keys, his purse, or his pocket-handkerchief, which he does ten times in an hour, she is to be blamed, and she takes all very quietly.'

The final rupture with his wife, in 1835, took place in consequence of words spoken by her in the presence of his children. Their home was then in Florence, which place he left, never, he thought, to return. He wrote as though the only creature he loved on earth had been rent from him. Yet this extraordinary man was by no means inconsolable. His friends did their best to get at least the two elder children entrusted to his care; but Landor himself, after writing a few heart-broken letters, interested himself no further in the project. He spent the next twenty years at Bath, in very good spirits, as a rule, pre-occupied with literary work. His little Pomeranian dog, it is impossible not to feel, compensated for the loss of his children.

Scott said of Byron's countenance that it 'is a thing to dream of,' and there is from all sides similar testimony to the personal beauty which led the unhappiest of his devotees to exclaim, 'That pale face is my fate!' 'Dear Childe Harold,' exclaims a German critic, 'was positively besieged by women.' His rank and fame, the glittering splendour of his verse, the romance of his travels, his picturesque melancholy and affectation of mysterious secrets, combined with the magic of his presence to bewitch and bewilder them.

At the age of fifteen he fell in love with Mary Anne Chaworth, in spite of his age and her treatment of him as a mere schoolboy. This affair 'darkened many an after year with vain longing and yearning protest.'

Then the poet went to travel. At Athens he stayed with Theodora Macri, widow of the English vice-consul. The eldest (Theresa) of her three beautiful daughters is immortalised by him as the 'Maid of Athens.'

In 1813 Lord Byron's thoughts turned seriously to marriage, and he told a friend that he was going to propose to Miss Milbanke, only child of Sir Ralph Milbanke. The friend suggested the name of another lady and agreed to write a proposal for him. An answer containing a refusal arrived one morning as the friends were sitting together. 'You see,' said Byron, 'that after all Miss Milbanke is to be the person. I will write to her.' He did so, and his friend, who was still opposed to the choice, took up the letter, and reading it over, observed, Well, really, this is a very pretty letter. It is a pity it should not go.' 'Then it *shall* go,' said Byron, and in so saying, sealed and sent off this fiat of his fate. On the 10th of January, 1815, Byron wrote to Moore : 'I was married this day week. The parson has pronounced it; Perry has announced it; and the *Morning Post*, also, under the head of "Lord Byron's Marriage," as if it were a fabrication, or the puff direct of a new staymaker.'

Miss Milbanke was 'the paragon of only daughters,' to use his own words, and had been for some time attached to him, which he had not known. When he offered, he had not seen her for ten months; perhaps when he did see her, especially with all the odious preliminary of settlements on his hands, the charm was broken. The morning of his marriage he awoke with a heavy heart, and became more dejected on glancing

at his wedding suit laid out before him.   His feelings
at the ceremony have been described by himself :—

> I saw him stand
> Before an altar with a gentle bride;
> Her face was fair, but was not that which made
> The starlight of his boyhood.

Nevertheless, in the very early days of that inauspicious
marriage, Byron wrote : 'Swift says, no wise man ever
married; but for a fool, I think it is the most ambrosial
of all possible future states.   I still think one ought to
marry upon *lease*;   but am very sure I should renew mine
at the expiration, though next term were for ninety and
nine years.'

Alas ! his term was soon ended.   A year afterwards
we find Byron 'at war with all the world and my wife.'
To see why he was at war with his wife we need not
believe the story told by Mrs Beecher Stowe of an
incestuous intrigue between Byron and his half-sister.
The fact is, Lord and Lady Byron were quite unsuited
to each other.   Byron's valet is reported to have said
that 'Any woman could manage my lord except my
lady.'   What could her placid temperament conjecture
of a man whom she saw, in one of his fits of passion,
throwing a favourite watch under the fire, and grinding
it to pieces with a poker?   Or how could her conscious
virtue tolerate the nine executions for debt which took
place in her husband's house during the year she lived
with him?   And there were worse things—vices which
gave Lady Byron no choice but to separate from her
husband.   On the other hand, it must have been trying
to a poet to be asked by his wife, impatient of his late
hours, when he was going to leave off writing verses;
to be told that he had no real enthusiasm;   or to have
his desk broken open, and its compromising contents
sent to the persons for whom they were least
intended !

To describe the love affairs which Byron had with Countess Guiccioli and others, after abandoning all hope of reconciliation with his wife, would require a volume; and, after all, those of us who have none of his temptations are scarcely fair critics.

Goethe is another poet who abused the fatal gift of personal beauty. His fickleness in love affairs is a common-place of remark. His numerous attachments all ring changes on the same theme—the vagaries of an essentially cold heart, of which a timely utterance in song or story is at once the deliverance and the recantation.

Speaking of his early fondness for natural history, Goethe says: 'I remember that when a child I pulled flowers to pieces to see how the petals were inserted in the calyx, or even plucked birds to observe how the feathers were inserted in the wings.' He treated women in much the same way.

We can only mention some of the women-birds from whom he plucked feathers, many or few. There was Gretchen, Anna Katharina, Charity Meixner, Emilia and Lucinda, the last two his dancing-master's daughters. Poor Frederika had almost all her feathers plucked, and Goethe confessed as much—'Gretchen had been taken from me; Annchen had left me; but now, for the first time, I was guilty.' He soon relieved himself of these remorseful feelings by giving his affections to Charlotte Buff (Werther's Lotte); then, 'constant to a constant change,' he transferred them to Anna Sybilla Münch. There was a passing affection for Anna Elizabeth Schönemann (Lili) before the great one with Baroness von Stein began. She, as is well known, is the original of the charming countess in *Wilhelm Meister*. She was the mother of seven children when she first met Goethe, but was more perilously fascinating than at any period of her life. The poet was three nights sleepless in consequence of Zimmermann's description of her, and he is said to have written more than a thousand letters to her.

Goethe's motto, however, was 'From beauty to beauty, and in time another reigned in her stead. Still, though he may have broken the heart of the Baroness, he attended to her stomach, and constantly sent her from his table (a table at which he was sitting with the rival woman) portions of any dish that pleased his own palate. The rival woman was Christiane Vulpius. She was handsome, though 'globular' in form, but of inferior social position, and addicted later on to intemperate habits, which destroyed her beauty and caused serious domestic troubles. After living with her some years without marriage, Goethe married her in his fifty-eighth year. Ten years afterwards Christiane died. People said it was a 'happy release,' but in spite of her faults the poet was very sorry to be thus released. He had loved her and she had been devoted to him for twenty-eight years. We must refer those who wish to know about 'the child' love of Bettina Brentano to Lewes's *Life of Goethe.*

In the seventy-fourth year of his age the widower fell, not into the grave, but into love with a Fräulein von Lewezow, and she returned the compliment. Only the remonstrance of his friends, and perhaps the fear of ridicule, prevented him from marrying her.

We have one more captive, but happily only one, to mention. This was Madame Szymanowska. She was 'madly in love' with the 'old man eloquent.'

Mathilde Mirat, a beautiful, uneducated, unintellectual, yet infinitely charming and loyal Parisienne, became the wife of Heine, and was his good angel in his later years. She did not understand him, but she loved him; he was not the great poet, the famous author, to her—she could not even bring herself to read his verses when she accidentally discovered that he *was* a poet—but only the witty, perverse and lovable Henri. It is touching to read of the playfulness of Heine, who was a great sufferer, on his 'mattress grave.' Once he expressed a wish that his wife would marry again after his decease. Why? Because he was anxious that at least one man should lament his death! 'Have your jest, *mon ami*, but you know you cannot do without me,' was Mathilde's sensible answer.

In his will Heine left everything to 'my wife, Mathilde Crescence Heine, *née* Mirat, who, as true and loyal as she is beautiful, has cheered my existence.' And yet the poet had to complain that 'Nonotte,' as he called her, sometimes lavished more caresses upon her parrot than upon her Henri; or sat up all night to apply poultices to a cat which had scratched its ear, a sacrifice no human creature could have drawn forth. Heine never resented his beloved Nonotte's sanguine faith in his recovery; on the contrary, her invincible cheerfulness was an unmistakable factor in what went to enable Heine to maintain his long struggle against death. When one day he was seized with dreadful spasms of coughing, he thought the end was at hand; but when the physician assured him that they would not hasten his death, he ironically panted out, 'Do not tell my wife this : she has enough to bear already !'

Heine used to beat his wife, but not as his friend Weill humorously alleged, like 'any coal-heaver.' He would say to Weill, 'My wife must be beaten again'; and the day of beating was usually Monday. Without minding Weill, he would draw down the blinds, and with his poor sick hands would pat her on the shoulders, saying, 'This is for such and such a fault.' Although three times as strong as he, she would suffer it and cry, 'Did you ever see a man beat his wife? Help me, Weill; you would not beat your wife.' Heine patted away with bursts of laughter. Suddenly she would fall crying on the floor, and pulling him down by the feet, would roll him over on the carpet.

Racine had been religiously educated, and when he was at the height of success as a play-writer he took it into his head that plays did harm and resolved to write no more of them. He determined to enter the austere order of the Chartreux; but his confessor, more rational than himself, advised him to marry a woman of a serious turn, and that little domestic occupations would withdraw him from the passion he seemed most to dread, that of writing verses. The lady he chose was Catherine de Romanet, of a good family but with few personal attractions. She was a good sort of woman, but no one could have been more capable of mortifying the passion of literary glory, and the momentary exultation of literary vanity. She had neither seen acted, nor ever read, nor desired to read, the tragedies which had rendered her husband so celebrated throughout Europe; she had only learnt some of their titles in conversation. And she was as insensible to fortune as to fame. One day, when Racine returned from Versailles with a purse of 1,000 louis which Louis XIV. had given him, he hastened to embrace his wife and show her the treasure. But she was full of trouble because one of the children had not learnt lessons for two days. 'We will talk of this another time,' exclaimed the poet; 'at present let us be happy.' She insisted, however, that he ought instantly to reprimand the child, and continued her complaint; while Boileau, in astonishment, paced to and fro, exclaiming, 'What insensibility ! Is it possible that a purse of 1,000 louis is not worth a thought !' This stoical apathy did not arise in Madame Racine from the grandeur but the littleness of her mind. Her prayer-book and her children were the sole objects that interested this good woman. Domestic sorrows weighed heavily upon Racine. When the illness of his children agitated him, he sometimes exclaimed: 'Why did I expose myself to all this? Why was I persuaded not to be a Chartreux? He was an excellent father, however, and delighted to join in the sports of his children. When absent he wrote to them, not merely as a father but as a wise friend.

A lady, whose name was Birch and who possessed considerable property, when past the bloom of youth became passionately enamoured of the poet Lamartine from the perusal of his *Meditations*. For some time she nursed this sentiment in secret; but learning the embarrassed state of his affairs, she wrote to him, tendering the bulk of her fortune. Touched with this proof of her generosity, and supposing it could only be caused by a preference for himself, he at once made an offer of his hand and was accepted.

It is related that when the poet Scarron espoused Francoise D'Aubigné the notary enquired what dowry the bride possessed, when the future husband replied : Two large eyes, a beautiful figure, a pair of lovely hands, and plenty of wit.' When he asked again what settlement Scarron would make upon the lady, the poet replied in the single word 'Immortality.'

Thomas Moore and Thomas Hood were as happy in domestic life as some of the other poets we have mentioned were miserable. It is true that the enemies of the former said that he preferred the company of aristocrats to that of his wife, but this was a calumny. Whatever amusement he might find in the grand society in which he mixed, he always returned to his wife (his Bessy) and children with a fresh feeling of delight.

On the 5th of May, 1824, Hood married Jane Reynolds, daughter of a master at Christ's Hospital. She was a woman of literary tastes, and, in spite of all the sickness and sorrow that formed the greatest portion of the afterpart of their lives, the marriage was a happy one. The poet had so much confidence in his wife's judgment that he read, and re-read, and corrected with her all that he wrote. Many of his articles were first dictated to her, and her ready memory supplied him with references and quotations. In his last years her time and thoughts were entirely devoted to him, and he seemed restless and unable to write unless she were near. To her he addressed some of his sweetest songs, as for instance : *I love thee, I love thee, 'tis all that I can say,* and the less known *Birthday Verses* :—

> Good-morrow to the golden morning,
>   Good-morrow to the world's delight—
> I've come to bless thy life's beginning,
>   Since it makes my own so bright.

When away from home in search of health this husband-lover wrote most touching letters to his wife. One of them ended in these words of enthusiastic tenderness: ' Bless you, bless you again and again, my dear one, my only one, my one as good as a thousand to your old unitarian in love, T. H.'

Hood enjoyed playing off little harmless practical jokes on his wife. Once, when staying at Brighton, he gave her a few hints on buying fish, and concluded by saying, ' Above all things, if the fish you are buying is plaice, beware of any having red or orange spots, as they are certain to be stale.' When the fisherwoman came round, it happened that she had very little except plaice, and Mrs Hood observed that they all had the red spots against which she had been warned. She hinted to the fishwife that they were not fresh, and upon being assured that they were not long out of the water she observed: ' My good woman, it may be as you say, but I could not think of buying any plaice with those very unpleasant red spots !' The woman's answer, which Hood heard with delight from behind the door, was a perfect shout : ' Lord bless your eyes, Mum ! who ever see'd any without 'em ? '

When, as often happened, the playful husband used to tease his wife with jokes and whimsical accusations, her only answer was, ' Hood, Hood, how can you run on so ? '

Perhaps you don't know,' he said, on one occasion, to some friends, that Jane's besetting weakness is a desire to appear in print, and be thought a Blue ? ' His wife coloured and gave her usual reply; then observed, laughingly: ' Hood does not know one material from another. He thinks this dress a blue print.' It was really a pretty blue silk.

Edgar Allan Poe acted foolishly when in 1836, he married his young cousin, Virginia, because she was consumptive; and the girl was not less foolish in accepting as a husband one who was idle and dissipated. The result was sickness and extreme poverty and the death of the cousin-wife eleven years after her marriage. It was the last event that suggested that 'most musical, most melancholy' dirge—*Ulalume*.

Referring to the obscurity of much of Browning's poetry, Wordsworth said, when he heard that the poet was going to marry the poetess, Miss Barrett, 'I hope they'll understand one another.' Certainly Mrs Browning did think that she understood her husband, for she wrote to a friend: 'Nobody exactly understands him except me, who am in the inside of him and hear him breathe.' If it is a risk to marry any poet, it seemed to Miss Barrett's friends a tempting of Providence and a doubling of this risk for two of the irritable profession to wed. Contrary to the expectations of all, the result was exceptional happiness. Mrs Kemble, who saw a great deal of the Brownings in Rome, remarked that 'Mr Browning was the only man she had ever known who behaved like a Christian to his wife.' There are those who talk of the chains of matrimony, but Browning literally kissed these chains. After returning to London from abroad, he would go to the church where he and his wife had got themselves secretly married, and kiss the paving-stones in front of the door. Until she married, in her thirty-fifth year, Miss Barrett was an invalid, imprisoned to her sofa and silence' in a darkened room,' but the soul-cure of happiness raised her almost from death to life.

Very touching and weird is the history of the first volume of Dante Gabriel Rossetti's poems. On the day of his wife's funeral he walked into the room where the body lay, carrying in his hand the MS. of his poems.

'Regardless of those present, he spoke to her as though she were still living, telling her that the poems were written to her and were hers, and that she must take them with her. He then placed the MS. beside her face in the coffin, leaving it to be buried with her in Highgate Cemetery.' The existence of the buried treasure was mentioned with reverence and sympathy and with something of awe. Seven years later Rossetti, upon whom pressure to permit its exhumation had constantly been put, gave a reluctant consent. The Home Secretary's permission was obtained, the coffin opened, and the MS. withdrawn and printed.

It has been said that 'of all the great literary figures who have loomed upon the latter part of the nineteenth century, Lord Tennyson has been the most fortunate in his married life.' In 1850 he married Miss Emily Sellwood, the daughter of a solicitor. The young couple lived for the first two years at Twickenham. Their first baby died; but in 1853 there was another a year old, 'crazy with laughter and babble, and earth's new wine.'

CHAPTER V

PROSE WRITERS NO LONGER PROSY

ALMOST all we know of Margaret Stretch, the first wife of Sir Richard Steele, is that she was a widow from Barbadoes. To Mary Scurlock, who became his second wife, he wrote upwards of four hundred letters, and these have been published. The lady was a 'cried up beauty,' and probably this is why at first she refused to marry Steele. After being wooed a month, however, she accepted him, saying that he 'was as agreeable and pleasant as any in England.' Then, feeling shy at his sudden conquest of her, she erased the dates from their letters, that in showing them to a friend it might not appear she was so rapidly won.

The love letters of Steele are playful, pretty, tender, admiring. They are masterpieces of ardour, of good sense and of earnestness. Swift's *Journal* is to some extent a similar unfolding of private thoughts and feelings, but Steele was exempt from the limitations imposed upon Swift by his relations to his correspondents.

Sir Richard Steele tells Miss Scurlock in one letter what was saying a good deal : that the vainest woman upon earth never saw in her glass half the attractions which he saw in his 'Prue.' In another he says that he has not a moment of quiet out of her sight; 'and when I am with you, you use me with so much distance, that I am still in a state of absence, heightened with a view of the charms which I am denied to approach. In a word, you must give me either a fan, a mask or a glove you have worn, or I cannot live; otherwise you must expect that I'll kiss your hand, or, when I next sit by you, steal your handkerchief. You yourself are too great a bounty to be secured at once; therefore I must be prepared by degrees, lest the mighty gift distract me with joy.

'Dear Miss Scurlock,—I am tired with calling you by that name; therefore, say the day in which you will take that of, Madam, your most obedient, most devoted, humble servant, RICH. STEELE.'

One more specimen. 'Madam,—It is the hardest thing in the world to be in love and yet attend to business. As for me, all who speak to me find me out, and I must lock myself up, or other people will do it for me. A gentleman asked me this morning, "What news from Lisbon?" and I answered, "She is exquisitely handsome." Another desired to know when I had been last at Hampton Court. I replied, "It will be on Tuesday come se'nnight." Pr'ythee, allow me at least to kiss your hand before that day, that my mind may be in some composure. O love !

A thousand torments dwell about me !
Yet who would live to live without thee ?

Methinks I could write a volume to you; but all the language on earth would fail in saying how much and with what disinterested passion I am ever yours, RICH. STEELE.'

At the time of his engagement Steele shared Addison's lodgings, and wrote these love letters whenever he found himself alone. Nor were his letters to the lady after he married her less loving. He assures his 'loved creature' that she has his heart 'by all the ties of beauty, virtue, good-nature and friendship'; that this heart aches when she speaks an unkind word, and that the inequality of his behaviour gives him real sorrow. He subscribes nearly all the letters, especially when he has mentioned some folly of which he was guilty, 'Your most obliged husband and most obedient, humble' (sometimes adding 'obsequious') 'servant.'

Steele lived in a chronic state of impecuniosity, owing to his careless habits, and tried too often to relieve the anxiety of this condition—this 'pain in his pocket'—by drink, while his poor wife was battling with abusive creditors. His best nature, however, always came out when he thought of 'Prue,' and remorse would cause him sincere grief for having wronged that 'best of women.' At such a time, by a frank acknowledgment of his faults, and by his constant expression of affection, he would try to disarm censure. Here is one of these little flags of truce. 'Dear Prue, Forgive me; I will neglect nothing which may contribute to our ease together, and you shall always find me your affectionate, faithful, tender husband.' However willing a wife might be to find fault, or however necessary it might be to do so, she could not but be softened with the words in which Steele dedicates one of his volumes to 'Prue': 'How often has your tenderness removed pain from my sick head, how often anguish from my affected heart ! If there are such things as guardian angels, they are thus employed. I cannot believe one of them to be more good in inclination or more charming in form than my wife.

The 'guardian angel' was of a colder temperament.
Sometimes, indeed, she resembled a governess rather
than an angel. In the letters of one period Steele shows
signs of rebellion at the way in which his 'dear ruler'
required him to account for every minute of his time,
and for everything that he did. He objected to his wife
being his 'sovereign director.'

When only a child, Richardson was consulted by
girls in their early love affairs, and used to write
amatory epistles for them. 'What shall I write?' he
asked one of these young friends. 'Oh,' she replied,
blushing, 'how can I tell you? But you can't be too
kind in what you say to him.'

When *Pamela* ; *or Virtue Rewarded* appeared it
made a great sensation. In places of public resort ladies
held up the volumes to one another, to show that they
were not behind the fashion. The author received
anonymous letters from six ladies, pressing him to
declare upon his honour whether the story were true
or false, and informing him that they had taken an oath
to keep the secret if he would tell them. He replied
that it was never known, since the world began, that
a secret was kept which was intrusted to six—women.
Richardson 'lived in a kind of flower-garden of ladies;
they were his inspirers, his critics, his applauders, his
chief correspondents. He had usually a number of
young ladies visiting him, whom he used to engage in
conversation on some subject of sentiment, and provoke,
by opposition, to display the treasures of intellect they
possessed.' Poor Letitia Pilkington was one of those
who could scarcely find words to express her admiration : 'What can I pay thee for this noble usage but
grateful praise? So Heaven itself is paid; and you,
truly made in the image of God, will, I hope, accept of
the low but sincere oblation of a thankful spirit.'

Richardson's family had little experience of 'noble
usage.' The arrangements of his home were perfect,
but his wife was made jealous by such friendships as

have been described, and his children stood in awe of him. When Lady Bradshaigh told him that his daughters' letters, beginning and ending with 'honoured sir' and 'ever dutiful,' were cold and formal, he replied, 'I had rather (as too much reverence is not the vice of the age) lay down rules that should stiffen into apparent duty, than make the pert rogues too familiar with characters so reverend.'

Henry Fielding married a Miss Cradock, who was beautiful and not without money. She could scarcely have been very happy with one who was incapable of economy and self-denial, and capable of forgetting every duty and anxiety 'when he was before a venison pasty and a flask of champagne. When she died, Fielding was in despair, but not very long after he married her favourite maid, with whom it had been a relief 'to mingle his tears, and to lament together the angel they had lost.' Contrary to what might have been expected, the promoted woman made an excellent wife and a good step-mother. The novelist erected, in honour of his first wife, the companion of his early struggles, the noblest and most enduring monument that genius ever consecrated to love and grief. This was the romance of *Amelia*, in which the exquisite picture of conjugal virtue and feminine charm in the heroine, the character and even the infidelities of Booth, her husband, are evidently transcripts from reality, and, there is little doubt, faithful copies of his own early history.

In the year 1790, Walter Scott, aged nineteen, offered his umbrella to a young lady of much beauty, who was coming out of church during a shower. The umbrella was graciously accepted, and Scott fell in love with the borrower, who turned out to be Margaret, daughter of Sir John Belches Stuart. This introduction resulted in an intimacy which lasted six years. Regarding the young lady Scott said to a friend : 'It was a proud night with me when I first found that a pretty young woman could think it worth her while to sit and talk with me

hour after hour, in a corner of the ball-room, while all
the world were capering in our view.'

Notwithstanding that she gave such encouragement,
the lady married William Forbes, eldest son of Sir
William Forbes, who proved a good friend to Scott after
his financial downfall in 1825.   However, Margaret
Belches became the heroine of *Rokeby* and of *Woodstock* ; and late in life Scott found that the old emotion
was not dead.   If his heart was not broken it received
a crack which was never quite mended.   When residing
at No. 6 Shandwick Place, Edinburgh, in 1827, he
discovered that the aged mother of his first love was
living close by.   He expressed a wish to Mrs Skene to
renew the acquaintance.   Mrs Skene did so, and a
painful scene ensued.   He wrote in his diary : 'I went
to make a visit, and fairly softened myself, like an old
fool, with recalling old stories, till I was fit for nothing
but shedding tears and repeating verses the whole
night.   This is sad work.   The very grave gives up its
dead' (Margaret, Lady Forbes, had died thirteen years
after her marriage), 'and time rolls back thirty years
to add to my perplexities.'   In *Peveril of the Peak*
(1823), Scott had written : 'There are few men who
do not look back in secret to some period of their youth,
at which a sincere and early affection was repulsed or
betrayed, or became abortive from opposing circumstances.   It is these little passages of secret history
which leave a tinge of romance in every bosom, scarce
permitting us, even in the most busy or the most
advanced period of life, to listen with total indifference
to a tale of true love.'

Six months after the marriage of his 'false love' Scott
became engaged to Charlotte Margaret Charpentier,
daughter of a French refugee.   Pride may have had
something to do with this, or the young man may have
admired the black-haired, brown-eyed, olive-com-
plexioned lady of cheerful and vivacious disposition.
She had £500 a year in her own right, and she herself

was not without value. She may not have been capable
of sharing all her husband's anxieties or participating
in all his dreams, yet she did not lack spirit. Indeed,
she held her own with him in their correspondence
before marriage. In one of these letters she wrote :
'Before I conclude I will give you a little hint. It is,
not to put so many "musts" into your letters. It is
beginning rather too soon, and another thing is I shall
take the liberty not to mind them. You *must* take
care of yourself. You *must* think of me. You *must*
believe me yours sincerely, C. C.

Scott had told her in a letter where he wanted to be
buried. The lively lady thus answered : 'What an idea
of yours was that to mention where you wish to have
your bones laid ! If you were married, I should think
you were tired of me. A very pretty compliment before
marriage ! I hope sincerely I shall not live to see that
day. If you always have those cheerful thoughts, how
very pleasant and gay you must be ! Adieu; take care
of yourself if you love me; for I have no wish that you
should visit that charming and romantic scene—the
family burying-place.

When Jeffrey, having reviewed *Marmion* in the
Edinburgh in that depreciating and omniscient tone
which was then considered the evidence of critical
acumen, dined with Scott on the very day on which the
review had appeared, Lady, then Mrs Scott, behaved
to him through the whole evening with the greatest
politeness, but fired this parting shot in her broken
English as he took his leave : 'Well, good-night, Mr
Jeffrey—dey tell me you have abused Scott in de
Review, and I hope Mr Constable has paid you very
well for writing it.'

In her last illness Lady Scott would always reproach
her husband and children for their melancholy faces,
even when that melancholy was, as she well knew, due
to the approaching shadow of her own death. Ten
days before this took place Scott entered in his diary :

'Still welcoming me with a smile, and asserting she is better.' After she died 'he never wrote glad word again,' and his diary shows how much he missed her who for twenty-nine years had shared his thoughts and counsels, 'who would talk down my sense of the calamitous apprehensions which break the heart that must bear them alone. . . . I can exert myself and speak, even cheerfully, to the girls; but alone, or if anything touches me—the choking sensation !'

Though one of the most hard-working of men, Scott made time to be the companion and playmate of his children. One day, when little Walter came home from school, with his face stained with tears and blood, his father said,—

'Well, Wat, what have you been fighting about to-day?'

The boy replied, with much confusion, that he had been called 'a lassie.'

'Indeed,' said Mrs Scott, 'that was a terrible mischief to be sure.'

'You may say what you please, mamma,' Wat indignantly replied; 'but I dinna think there's a *waufer* (shabbier) thing in the world than to be a lassie, to sit boring at a clout.'

On inquiry it appeared that the *Lady of the Lake* had suggested the ignominious nickname. The same boy was asked why people made more of his father than they did of his uncles. After considering for some moments, the little fellow replied, 'It's commonly *him* that sees the hare sitting.'

In time this boy joined the army, and when he was a lieutenant in the 15th Hussars his father thus wrote to him : 'I wish I heard of you giving some part of the day to useful reading; that is a habit as well as other habits, and may be acquired or lost, and when it is lost, a man cannot escape being a trifler through his whole life.'

Sir Walter always treated his daughters with courteous gallantry, and though there could not be a gentler mother than Lady Scott, they always made him their first confidant.

'I parted from Scott,' wrote Thomas Moore, 'with the feeling that all the world might admire him in his works, but that those only could learn to love him as he deserved, who had seen him at Abbotsford—viz., in the bosom of his family.'

When Jeremy Bentham was a young man he proposed to a lady and was refused. At sixty years of age he made her another offer of marriage with the same result. He could not speak of her without tears coming into his eyes. When eighty years old he addressed this farewell to her : 'I am alive, more than two months advanced in my eightieth year—more lively than when you presented me, in ceremony, with the flower in the green lane. Since that day, not a single one has passed (not to speak of nights) in which you have not engrossed more of my thoughts than I could have wished.'

If Bentham loved till late in life Bryan Waller Procter ('Barry Cornwall') did so very early. In after-life he said that he could distinctly remember being enamoured with a young friend when only five years of age. 'My love had the fire of passion, but not the clay which drags it downwards; it partook of the innocence of my years, while it etherealised me.' Not long after the young lady died. Procter had a more real love affair in after years which came to nothing, and then he married a Miss Skipper, whose brilliant qualities made their home for nearly half a century one of the principal centres of London literary society.

CHAPTER VI

LOVE AFFAIRS OF PROSE WRITERS

LEIGH HUNT married, in 1809, Marianne Kent, with whom he had been acquainted from her thirteenth year. Though not handsome, she had a pretty figure and fine hair and eyes. When first married she was a good house-wife, but when sickness undermined her strength, she became the wretched manager described by Mrs Carlyle, who lived next door to her at Chelsea.

Nor was Leigh Hunt himself more practical. It was said of him that if he saw something yellow in the distance, and was told it was a buttercup, he would be disappointed if he found it was only a guinea. Carlyle, though also very poor at the time, was a kind neighbour. A visitor to him, seeing two sovereigns lying exposed in a little vase on the mantelpiece, asked what they were for. Carlyle looked embarrassed and gave no definite answer.

'My dear fellow,' said the visitor, 'neither you nor I are quite in a position to play ducks and drakes with sovereigns; what are they for?'

'Well,' said Carlyle, 'the fact is that Leigh Hunt likes better to find them there, than that I should give them to him.'

But Leigh Hunt, though he acted foolishly, uttered wise sayings. One of them was that no reasonable person ought to marry who cannot say, 'My love has made me better and more desirous of improvement than I have been.' He wrote his own experience on this point in a letter to his *fiancée*: 'I am naturally a man of violent passions; but your affection has taught me to subdue them. Whenever you feel any little disquietudes or impatiences arising in your bosom, think of the happiness you bestow on me, and real love will produce the same effects on you as it has produced on me.'

The prospect of marriage had also an improving effect upon De Quincey. During his engagement he reduced his daily dose of opium from three hundred and forty grains to forty. The lady to whom he was engaged, and whom he married in 1816, was Margaret Simpson, the daughter of a Westmoreland gentleman. She was very beautiful and was an exemplary wife to a most eccentric husband. Speaking of his early married life De Quincey says: 'Without the aid of Margaret, all records of bills paid, or *to be* paid, must have perished; and my whole domestic economy, whatever became of political economy, must have gone into irretrievable confusion.'

How deep was the affection of the gifted but miserable opium-eater for this charming, long-suffering woman may be seen by the following words which he addressed to her : 'Thou thoughtest not much to stoop to humble offices of kindness, and to servile ministrations of tenderest affections; to wipe away for years the unwholesome dews upon the forehead, or to refresh the lips when parched and baked with fever; nor, even when thy own peaceful slumbers had by long sympathy become infected with the spectacle of my dread contest with phantoms and shadowy enemies that oftentimes bade me "Sleep no more !"—not even then didst thou utter a complaint or any murmur, nor withdraw thy angelic smiles, nor shrink from any service of love.'

No girl ever studied harder for a situation by competitive examination than did Miss Lewin during the two years she was engaged to Grote, the historian. He set her themes on various subjects, and gave her books to read, on which he required her to send him a digest. After waiting two years in vain for his father, the banker, to give consent, George Grote met Harriet Lewin one March morning, in 1820, at a neighbouring church, where they were married early enough for her to take her usual place at the breakfast table. The marriage was kept secret for a month, after which they took lodgings in Chelsea. From these they moved into the banking-house, Threadneedle Street, where Mrs Grote says they lived in two worlds—'the ancient, and the modern'—Plato and Aristotle on the one side, Kant and Bentham and James Mill on the other; yet fortunately the latter world not inhabited by these alone, for Grote shared his wife's tastes for poetry, painting and music, and even played the violoncello himself. Each of these well-suited people gave and took an education. He endowed her mind with a more solid basis; she fashioned, mounted, framed and glazed him.

We may remark that this marriage which turned out so happily, was nearly prevented by the treachery of Grote's own familiar friend. Telling him one day of his love for Harriet Lewin, his friend assured him that 'he knew it as a fact that her heart and hand were engaged to another man.' Fortunately Grote found out in time that this was not true, and that it had been said only because the amiable friend wished the lady for himself.

Charles Lever's father wished him to marry the daughter of a rich tradesman rather than Miss Kate Baker, whom he had loved from childhood. The novelist's early love proved a wise selection, for Kate broke him off many a bad habit and helped him in his work. He read his novels to her in manuscript, and from the day she died he felt as if his right hand had lost its cunning.

Samuel Lover, the author of *Rory O'More, Handy Andy*, and other stories, was a great favourite in society, but he was not one of those who 'hang up their fiddles behind the door' when they come home. On the contrary, he was never more happy and entertaining than when he was at home, with only his wife and daughters about him. Between his writing and painting he had little or no time for reading, so his wife always read the newspapers and new books and gave him a *résumé* of their contents. His first love refused him, but he afterwards got not only one good wife, but after her death a second.

Edward Bulwer, afterwards Lord Lytton, was sitting with his mother at a literary tea-party, when suddenly the latter said to him, 'Oh, Edward, what a singularly beautiful face. Do look ! Who can she be?' The lady was Rosina, daughter of Francis Wheeler, and Bulwer married her in 1827, though his friends tried to convince him that she was unfit to be 'the wife of a man of his exacting disposition and nervous temperament.' She possessed an unrivalled power of virulent satire, and she was likened by Thackeray to that character mentioned by Addison, who appeared either angel or devil, according as it happened to be either light or shadow in which she met your view. So clever was she that it was currently reported by the rivals and detractors of Bulwer that he was indebted to her for important aid in the composition of some of his best works.

Before long the ill-assorted couple separated; but Bulwer, though he set on foot a disgraceful system of espionage, could not find any grounds for a divorce. A full account of the persecution to which she had been subjected was given by her ladyship in a volume entitled *A Blighted Life*, in which Bulwer is depicted as 'false, cunning, cruel and unscrupulous.' Then, when he presented himself as a candidate for Parliament, she made a sudden rush upon the hustings, at the conclusion of his speech, harangued the mob in a strain of coarse invective, and revealed to the world the odious secrets of the prison house.

On the 2nd of April, 1836, Charles Dickens married Miss Catherine Hogarth. They lived very happily together for twenty years when there arose a dark cloud in which they lost each other. The story is thus related by one who was an intimate friend of Dickens : 'His wife was a plain woman, and not an intellectual one. She was a good mother, though, and managed her house well; but as Charles improved and broadened, accumulating more money meanwhile, she failed to grow with him. He entertained largely, and the most charming men and women in England. She did not care greatly for them. Then her sister came to live with them. She was a beautiful woman, and a highly accomplished one as well. She received the distinguished guests, and entertained them. Without doubt she did this partly to conceal her sister's deficiencies, and partly because it was natural for her to assume a prominent position. But by-and-by Mrs Dickens resented most bitterly the attitude which her sister had assumed in her household.'

To say the least, Dickens was very injudicious. He did not hesitate to speak of Mary Hogarth as his ideal in her sister's hearing, and he complained to his friends that he and his wife were not made for each other.' The result was a separation. Dickens allowed his wife £600 a year, and the eldest son went to live with her. The other children and their aunt remained with the novelist.

At the age of twenty-four Thackeray married Isabella Gethin Shawe, who was born in Java in 1818. When at the birth of a third daughter (subsequently Mrs Leslie Stephens) the mental disease from which Mrs Thackeray suffered first made its appearance, her husband clung to her, and waited on her with an assiduity of affection which only made his task the more painful to him.' At length she had to be placed under the care of a lady away from her home. Yet years after, writing to a friend, Thackeray: said 'Though my marriage was a wreck I would do it over again, for behold love is the crown and completion of all earthly good.'

Thackeray was a devoted father, and if his words were satirical his acts were very much the reverse. 'In the week following his death,' writes one to whom the incident happened, 'there appeared some genial memorial lines in the pages of *Punch*. Walking down the then unsavoury thoroughfare known as Bedfordbury, hard by St. Martin's Lane and Covent Garden, my eye caught the open page of the popular periodical, and I stayed to read the graceful tribute to the dead moralist. Turning away at length, a poorly dressed man in working garb said to me : "I knew that man, sir."   "*You* knew Thackeray?" I asked. "Yes, sir. I keep that little baker's shop yonder" (pointing to the other side of the street), "and many's the time Thackeray would come and buy a pound or two of cake of me. I cut it into slices for him, and then, distributing it among a crowd of hungry children, he would walk away and hide in that court over there, that he might have the pleasure of seeing their enjoyment. He didn't know I knew him, but I did. People used to call him a 'cynic,' sir, but it wasn't true, it wasn't true. He loved the children, sir, and no man is a cynic who does *that* !"'

When Charles Reade tried to sell his plays he was snubbed by all the theatrical people' except the actress, Mrs Seymour, who granted him an interview that he might read part of one to her. She remarked when he had concluded :—

'Yes, that's good ! That's plotting. But why don't you write novels?'

Reade looked the disappointment he felt, and Mrs Seymour was sorry for him.

'Hard up, I suppose,' she muttered, 'like the rest of them. Wanted me to buy his play for an old song, no doubt—but of course that's absurd. Still, I don't like to see a fellow of his sort down on his luck, and I'll tell him as much.'

She wrote a letter to this effect, and added that while she could not make him an offer for his play, she begged he would accept the loan of five pounds.

Reade immediately brought back the money to her

and said, 'That is not what I need. But you have unintentionally supplied it.' At the close of the interview that followed, 'each had learnt in a moment to respect the other, and a friendship then commenced which was from the outset considered as sacred.'

We must hope that the connection *was* as sacred and Platonic as it was said to have been. It certainly was a most useful one for Reade, though he had to supply Seymour, her dissipated husband, with money when he turned up. Mrs Seymour found a market for Reade's plays, urged him to write novels, kept house for him, and was in everything his counsellor and helper. When she died he wrote : ' . . . Ah, to think that for five-and-twenty years I was blessed with Laura Seymour, and that now for the rest of my pilgrimage she is quite, quite gone ! Not one look from her sweet eyes—not one smile ! Oh, my heart ! my heart ! I am wretched. I have lost my love of the world. . . . My dogs, and the portrait of my lost darling—they are all I have. Ah, would to God I could add that I have my Saviour ! I believe He is here, and pities me, but from want of faith I cannot feel His presence. Oh, God, increase my faith !'

A little incident narrated by his son shows that Douglas Jerrold was in his home anything but 'cold, cutting and sharp,' as the outside world knew him. 'Returning on one occasion from Ostend he brought back with him a large packing-case. He came eagerly into the house and bade me open the case. He stood over me, his eyes following those of my mother and sister. He was as excited as a child that has bought a present for its mother with its pocket-money. Presently the case was opened, and he lifted out a beautiful work-box of sandal-wood, decorated with fine original paintings—a most exquisite piece of art and workmanship. He placed it before my mother with an intensity of delight that I shall never forget. He looked from one to the other, inviting our enthusiasm. He felt how his heart and soul had been in the business when he had bought this present; how he had watched it across the water; how he had left his luggage behind that he might bear it with him to his home.'

'Upon the female soul as well as upon the female body is bound an eternal corset.' This is the protest of Jean Paul Richter against the conventionality by which the weaker sex is trammelled; yet many of his lady admirers, and their name was legion, made bold to throw off all restriction, and address him in terms of open admiration while he was yet a stranger to them.

Caroline Myer, the daughter of one of the most distinguished Prussian officers, was a refined, intellectual, noble girl, with almost unlimited resources within herself, devoted to her family and to every good. Paul had met women who dressed more elegantly, who were more sparkling in conversation, who were more beautiful, but they did not satisfy his heart. In his thirtyeighth year he had found a character that seemed perfection. He wrote, 'Caroline has exactly that inexpressible love for all beings that I have till now failed to find even in those who in everything else possess the splendour and purity of the diamond. She preserves in the full harmony of her love to me the middle and lower tones of sympathy for every joy and sorrow in others.'

Her love for Richter was nearly adoration. Several months after their marriage she wrote her father, 'Richter is the purest, the holiest, the most godlike man that lives. Could others be admitted, as I am, to his inmost emotions, how much more would they esteem him!' Richter also wrote to his best friend, Otto, 'Marriage has made me love her more romantically, deeper, infinitely more than before.' At the birth of their first child, he wrote again to Otto, 'You will be as transported as I was when the nurse brought me, as out of a cloud, my second love, with the blue eyes wide open, a beautiful, high brow, kiss-lipped, heart-touching.

God is near at the birth of every child.' On Caroline's first birthday after their marriage, he wrote, 'I will be to thee father and mother ! Thou shalt be the happiest of human beings, that I also may be happy.'

When Balzac, the French novelist, was travelling in Switzerland, he arrived at an inn just at the moment the Prince and Princess Hanski were leaving it. Balzac was ushered into the room they had vacated, and was leaning from the window to observe their departure, when his attention was arrested by a soft voice at his elbow, asking for a book which had been left behind upon the window-seat. The lady was certainly fair, but appeared doubly so in the eyes of the author when she intimated that the book she was in quest of was the pocket edition of his own works, adding that she never travelled without it, and that without it she could not exist ! She drew the volume from beneath his elbow and flew downstairs, obedient to the screaming summons of her husband, an old gentleman, who was already seated in the carriage.

Upon this a literary correspondence commenced, and was kept up between the author and the princess for fifteen years. At length, instead of a letter containing criticisms upon his writings, a missive of another kind, having a still more directly personal tendency, reached him from the fair hand of the lady. It contained the announcement of the demise of her husband, the prince —that he had bequeathed to her his domains and his great wealth—and, consequently, that she felt bound to requite him in some measure for his liberality, and had determined upon giving him a successor—in the person of Balzac. It is needless to state that the author waited not a second invitation.

Another foreign author whom we must mention is the American, Nathaniel Hawthorne. Like the poet Browning, he had become attached to a chronic invalid. Sophia—for that was her Christian name—had told herself that for one so delicate marriage was not to be thought of. She loved Hawthorne, but she was none the less resolved never to marry him. He understood and accepted the situation. Writing to Sophia's sister some months later, he says : 'She is a flower to be worn in no man's bosom, but was lent from Heaven to show the possibilities of the human soul.'

But day by day their love deepened; to each life seemed incomplete without the other, and Hawthorne pressed his suit with passionate ardour. Sophia, who had long ago secretly surrendered, raised one last barrier; she would promise to marry Hawthorne if she should recover from her twenty years' ill-health—not otherwise. She did recover, for love and happiness are good physicians, and the marriage took place in the year 1842.

How perfect were the relations between husband and wife, the following lines, written six years after their marriage, show : 'Oh, Phoebe' (his pet name for her), 'I want thee much. Thou art the only person in the world that ever was necessary to me. Other people have occasionally been more or less agreeable, but I think I was always more at ease alone than in anybody's company till I knew thee. And now I am only myself when thou art within my reach. Thou art an unspeakably beloved woman.'

And Hawthorne was as good a father as he was a husband. He delighted in his children and was their constant companion. One day he took Julian, when a very small boy, for a ramble, in the course of which they came upon an old churchyard. They entered, and Hawthorne read aloud the various inscriptions. It was the age of flowery epitaphs, and little Julian listened with silent awe to the interminable list of the virtues of the departed. Presently he pulled his father's sleeve and whispered : 'But, father, where do the poor wicked people lie?'

CHAPTER VII

DR JOHNSON AND THE LADIES

JOHNSON, we are told by one who knew him, 'had always a metaphysical passion for one princess or other —the rustic Lucy Porter, or the haughty Molly Aston, or the sublimated Methodistic Hill Boothby; and lastly, the more charming Mrs Thrale.' When verging on seventy years of age the great dictionary-maker said : 'If I had no duties and no reference to futurity, I would spend my life driving briskly in a post-chaise with a pretty woman,' but the woman, as he explained on other occasions, would have to be something more than 'pretty'; she would have to be able to 'understand' him, and 'add something to the conversation.'

We know that Johnson was one of the most virtuous of men, but he was too manly not to admire women, as when he seized the hand of that 'very airy lady,' Mrs Cholmondeley, and held it close to his eyes, wondering at its delicate whiteness, while she exclaimed aside, 'I wonder will he give it me again when he has done with it.'

Yet it cannot be said that the sage took women as seriously as some of them even in those days took themselves. When two young women from Staffordshire came to consult him about Methodism, he said: 'Come, you pretty fools, dine with Maxwell and me at the Mitre, and we will talk on that subject.' To the Mitre they all went, and 'after dinner he took one of them upon his knee and fondled her for half an hour together.' Mrs Thrale, having on appeared at breakfast in a dark-coloured gown, wa thus reproved: 'You little creatures should never wear these sort of clothes. What ! have not all insects gay colours?' When Miss Monckton,

· MEN OF LETTERS ·

William Shakespeare.

Geoffrey Chaucer.

Sir Francis Bacon.

John Milton.

L.A.

C

who became Countess of Cork, ventured the remark
that Sterne's writings were 'very pathetic,' Johnson
bluntly contradicted her. 'I am sure,' pleaded the fair
enthusiast, 'that they affected *me*.' 'Why,' said he,
smiling and rolling himself about, 'that is because,
dearest, you are a dunce.' Miss Reynolds having asked
his opinion of a metrical translation of Horace which a
young lady had recently published, he replied : 'They
are very well for a young miss's verses—that is to say,
compared with excellence, nothing; but very well for
the person who wrote them.' He said that a woman's
preaching is like a dog's walking on his hind legs. It is
not well done, but you are surprised to find it done at
all. He would not admit that women excelled, even
in their own province. 'Women,' he said, 'can not make
a good book of cookery.' They could not, in his opinion,
dress themselves nicely, for they are 'the slaves of ordeı
and fashion.' He denied them the power of moral
judgment. 'Ladies set no value on the moral character
of men who pay their addresses to them; the greatest
profligate will be as well received as the man of the
greatest virtue, and this by a good woman—by a woman
who says her prayers three times a day.' He thinks
that women are less vicious than men, but it is 'not
from choice but because we restrict them and they have
a perpetual envy of our vices.'

Johnson liked flattery as much as any man, but when
it was administered injudiciously he could be quite rude,
even to a lady. When Hannah More was introduced to
him she began singing his praises in the warmest manner, and talking of the pleasure and instruction she had
received from his writings. For some time he listened
to her encomiums in silence. Then she began them
again, and peppered still more highly, until, at length,
Johnson turned suddenly upon her with a stern and
angry countenance, and said : 'Madam, before you
flatter a man so grossly to his face, you should consider
c whether or not your flattery is worth his having.'

That women are fascinating, however, the sage never doubted. 'Nature,' he says, 'has given women so much power that the law has very wisely given them very little.' Indeed, Johnson could sometimes be just to the fair sex. Of one lady, Mrs Fitzherbert, he said she had the best understanding that he ever met in any human being, and of a contemporary scholar he remarked that he understood Greek better than any one he had ever known 'except Elizabeth Carter.'

When a young woman confided to Garrick's brother that Johnson was 'a very seducing man,' she was probably alluding to the pretty compliments he could pay. The year before his death Mrs Siddons, the actress, paid him a visit. When she came into the room there was no chair for her, which, when he observed, he said, with a smile, 'Madam, you who so often occasion a want of seats to other people will more easily excuse the want of one yourself.' When he was an old man, he once, at an evening party, asked an 'amiable, elegant, and accomplished young lady' to sit down by him, which she did; and upon her inquiring how he was, he answered, 'I am very ill indeed, Madam. I am very ill, even when you are near me : what should I be, were you at a distance?' Then there was the young lady, who, having just handed him some coffee, remarked that the coffee-pot was 'the only thing she could call her own.' 'Don't say so, my dear,' entreated the Doctor; 'I hope you don't reckon my heart as nothing.'

And women were always ready to meet the advances of the sage at least half-way. He was the fashion, but there was also an attraction in himself in spite of his ungainly appearance, which caused all the ladies in any assembly where he was to cluster round him. The beautiful Duchess of Devonshire, then in the first bloom of youth, was seen 'hanging on the sentences that fell from Johnson's lips, and contending for the nearest place to his chair.' When he went behind the scenes at Drury Lane and Covent Garden, as he pretty often did, there would be quite a flutter amongst the theatrical queens. Even on his tour in the Hebrides, the formidable visitor was more than well received by the simple Scotch dames. Boswell reveals the fact that 'one of our married ladies, a lively, pretty little woman, good-humouredly sat down upon Dr Johnson's knee, and being encouraged by some of the company, put her hands round his neck and kissed him.' The Doctor was equal to the occasion. 'Do it again,' said he, 'and let us see who will tire first.' It was a game of give and take on both sides. 'I am much pleased with a compliment from a pretty woman,' owned the sage. 'I love to sit by Doctor Johnson; he always entertains me,' simpered the famous Kitty Clive, giving the opinion of most of the other fashionable beauties of the day.

Even when a schoolboy Johnson was attached to several ladies. There was a Quakeress, Olivia Lloyd, and a Miss Hickman, to both of whom he wrote poetry. Miss Lucy Porter, the daughter of his future wife, was also admired by him. His first serious affair of the heart, however, was with a sister of his friend Hector. She became the wife of a clergyman called Careless, but Johnson never forgot her. When talking of her on one occasion, in his old age, to Boswell, he said, 'If I had married her it might have been as happy for me.' In his correspondence with her brother he invariably alludes to her as 'dear Mrs Careless,' and sometimes asked for her prayers. Describing a subsequent meeting with her at the house of some friends, he says, 'Mrs Careless took me under her protection *and told me when I had tea enough.*'

During a visit to Lichfield, Johnson remarked in confidence to Boswell: 'Forty years ago, sir, I was in love with an actress here, called Mrs Emmet.' Of this lady scarcely anything is known. Then there was Molly Aston, who solved for Johnson, when a young man, a not very difficult problem, which, strange to say, had long puzzled him: 'Why the interest of money is lower when money is plentiful?' On one occasion Thrale asked him what had been the happiest period of his past life. He answered, 'The year in which I spent one whole evening with Molly Aston. That, indeed, was not happiness, it was rapture; but the thoughts of it sweetened the whole year.'

And when, owing to his physical infirmities, he was precluded from offering ladies those attentions which it is the privilege of younger and more agile men to bestow, he did his best in this respect. When Madame de Boufflers, who had visited him in his chambers in the Temple, left in company with Boswell, they heard a noise like thunder. This was occasioned by Johnson hurrying down the staircase in violent agitation, to open the door of the lady's carriage.

But it was to women overtaken by poverty and weakness that the best side of Johnson revealed itself. He made a home in his house for Mrs Williams, the blind friend of his deceased mother; for Mrs Desmoulins, the daughter of his godfather; for her daughter, and for the slatternly 'Polly' Carmichael, and tolerated their complainings and endless quarrels. Mrs Williams might be peevish and exacting, but he never answered her except in kindness, and strove to propitiate her by sending dainties from the cook-shop when he ventured to dine out.

Coming home late one night he found an unfortunate woman lying in the street. He took her on his back and brought her to his house, where she was taken care of until she was recovered in health, and he had procured for her a virtuous way of living.

CHAPTER VIII

JOHNSON AND BOSWELL AS HUSBANDS

AT the age of twenty-six Dr Johnson married Mrs Porter, a widow twenty years older than himself.   Johnson
and his bride travelled on horseback from Birmingham to Derby, at which last place they were to be married. The bride complained that Johnson rode too fast,
and when he slackened his pace she passed him and
scolded him for lagging behind.   Johnson then pushed
on till he was out of sight, and when the bride at length
came up with him she was in tears.   He was not 'to be
made the slave of caprice,' and resolved to begin as he
meant to end.   Johnson attributed this conduct of hers
to the reading of old romances, where she had imbibed
the idea that a woman of spirit should treat her lover
like a dog.

A quarrel on the way to church is not a happy beginning of wedded life; but Johnson proved a good husband, and had great confidence in his wife's judgment.
He read his *Rambler* to her, and she, wife-like, told
him that she had not imagined he could write anything
so good.   Some men would not have cared for this;
but Johnson was much delighted, and said that praise
from a wife comes home to a man's own bosom.

Many husbands and wives are unhappy in their marriage because before that event they were not honest
with each other.   Johnson and the widow acted very
differently. The former told the latter plainly that he
was of humble extraction, that he had no money, and
that one of his uncles had been hanged.   The sensible
woman responded that she had no more money than he,
and that though none of her relatives had been hanged,
she had several *who ought to be !*

Boswell thus writes : 'Miss Porter told me that when he, Johnson, was first introduced to her mother his appearance was very forbidding; he was then lean and lank, so that his immense structure of bones was hideously striking to the eye, and the scars of the scrofula were deeply visible. He also wore his hair, which was straight and stiff, separated behind ; and he often had, seemingly, convulsive starts, and odd gesticulations, which tended to excite at once surprise and ridicule. Mrs Porter was so much engaged by his conversations that she overlooked all these external disadvantages, and said to her daughter, "This is the most sensible man I ever met." '

Nor was Johnson less appreciative. When he was thirty-one and his wife fifty-one he addressed her in a letter as 'My dear girl,' and 'My charming love.'

Speaking of her to Mrs Thrale, he had nothing to complain of but her 'particular reverence for cleanliness.'

Where ignorance is bliss it is folly to be wise. Johnson was short-sighted and love is proverbially blind, so he considered the woman a 'pretty charmer,' who is thus described by Garrick : 'She' (Johnson's wife) 'was very fat, with a bosom of more than ordinary protuberance; her swelled cheeks were of a florid red, produced by thick painting, and increased by the liberal use of cordials; glaring and fantastic in her dress, and affected both in her speech and general behaviour.' Garrick must have seen a good deal of Mrs Johnson, for he was one of the pupils (there were only three of them) who came to the school which Johnson tried to set up after his marriage. Johnson's affection was so grotesquely and oddly shown, that these young gentlemen had no pleasure equal to that of watching their master making love to his wife.

Though, as Johnson assured Beauclerk, his marriage was a 'love-match on both sides,' there was an occasional tiff between the quaint couple. Indeed, we find that on Mrs Thrale's asking him if he ever disputed with his wife, the answer was, 'Perpetually.'

On one occasion, when Dr and Mrs Johnson were travelling together, a gipsy examined the hand of the former, and told him his heart was divided between a Molly and a Betty; but though Betty loved him best, he took more delight in Molly's company. 'When I turned about to laugh,' Johnson said, in telling the story, 'I saw my wife was crying. Pretty charmer, she had no reason.' We have seen that there was a Molly Aston, whom he much admired.

Mrs Johnson was querulous, exacting, and the reverse of beautiful, but when she died her husband was utterly prostrated. He buried himself in hard work in his garret, a most inconvenient room; but he said, 'In that room I never saw Mrs Johnson.' Acute sorrow like this is often short-lived, but it was not so in Johnson's case. A considerable time after his wife's death he said that ever since the sad event he seemed to himself broken off from mankind, a kind of solitary wanderer in the wild of life, without any direction or fixed point of view, a gloomy gazer on the world, to which he had little relation. After recording some good resolution in his journal he was in the habit, since her death, of writing after it his wife's name—'Tetty.' It is only a word; but how eloquent it is! When a certain Mr Edwards asked him if he had ever known what it was to have a wife, Johnson replied, 'Sir, I have known what it was to have a wife, and' (in a solemn, tender, faltering tone) 'I have known what it was *to lose a wife*. I had almost broken my heart.' Nor did he allow himself to forget this experience. To New Year's Day, Good Friday, Easter Day, and his own birthday, which he set apart as sacred days, dedicated to solemn thought and high communion with his own soul, he added *the day of his wife's death*. Her wedding-ring was placed in a little box, and tenderly kept till his death. And, what was far more important, he took care of Mrs Williams, a blind woman, of whom he said, 'She was a friend to my poor wife, and was in the house when she died. She has remained in it ever since.'

When only eighteen James Boswell fell in love with a Miss W.; then he conceived a *grande passion* for a gardener's daughter. After some time he had a love affair, to use his own words, with a 'dear infidel' who had separated from her husband. He brought her to Edinburgh and kept her there, all the time trying to persuade himself and others that he was doing no harm. When he was emancipated from this charmer he began to think seriously of matrimony. There was a Miss Blair, a 'neighbouring princess,' who had 'dominions' adjoining Auchinleck, Boswell's family seat. He proposed to the lady that they should join hands and lands.

'You are very fond of Auchinleck,' he pleaded; 'that is in my favour.'

'I confess I am,' the lady replied, with obdurate candour, 'I only wish I liked you as well as I like Auchinleck.'

She refused him in favour of a richer man—Sir Alexander Gilmour—Sir Sawney, as Boswell called him.

Boswell, who said that the madness of which there were seeds in him was so heightened by love that he was deprived of judgment, had his eyes opened by the refusal. He saw faults in her which he had not seen before, and comforted himself with the thought that no one could tell how fine a woman he might marry; 'perhaps a Howard, or some other of the noblest in the Kingdom.' He even wrote a poetical narrative of the refusal.

> Although I be an honest laird,
>   In person rather strong and brawny,
> For me the heiress never cared,
>   For she would have the knight Sir Sawney.

And when with ardent vows I swore,
Loud as Sir Jonathan Trelawney,
The heiress showed me to the door,
And said she'd have the knight Sir Sawney.

She told me, with a scornful look,
I was as ugly as a tawny;
For she a better fish could hook,
The heir and gallant knight Sir Sawney.

The next girl to whom Boswell made love was a Miss Dick, whom he describes as 'fine, healthy, young, and amiable.' At the same time 'a charming Dutch woman,' called Zelide, is frequently mentioned in his correspondence. She proved a 'termagant and scorched him.' After 'furious Zelide' an Irish beauty appeared on the scene and was perfection in Boswell's eyes. He never before, he said, was in a situation to which there was not some objection, 'but here every flower is united, and not a thorn to be found.' He repeated his passion again and again and 'her little heart beat.' He carved the first letter of her name on a tree and cut off a lock of her hair. In spite of all this he neglected the lady for a time and then was surprised when on renewing his addresses she laughed him to scorn. He told his woes to a cousin, Margaret Montgomerie, and was so touched with her sympathy that he proposed to her. It was an evil day for herself when Margaret accepted him, for Boswell, whatever else he learnt from Johnson, had not imbibed the first principles of marital conduct. He would never settle down, and even during the last illness of his wife, though he did stay with her five weeks at Auchinleck, he was, according to his own acknowledgment, 'repeatedly from home,' and, when neighbours visited him, 'drank too much wine.'

Mrs Boswell did not like Dr Johnson, and when he visited Auchinleck she treated him as an intruding guest. Speaking of her husband's admiration for him, she remarked that she had often heard of a bear being led by a man, but never till now of a man being led by a bear.

That there was nothing of the bear about Johnson except his skin, is shown by the way he returned good for evil to Mrs Boswell. When he heard that her health was failing, he told Boswell to be kind to her, and bring her up to London for a change. He even offered to give her his own rooms. Boswell lightly replied that his wife was not as fond of travelling as were the Doctor and himself, and that she would be unhappy if at a distance from her children. More than content to be alone, he started for London. He had only been there a fortnight when he was recalled by the news that his wife was sinking fast. After a journey of sixty-four hours he found her dead, and wrote as follows to his friend Temple : 'I cried bitterly and upbraided myself for leaving her, for she would not have left me. This reflection, my dear friend, will, I fear, pursue me to the grave. . . . I could hardly bring myself to agree that the body should be removed, for it was still a consolation to me to go and kneel by it, and talk to my dear, dear Peggy.'

Boswell was fond of his wife after his fashion, but he had a wholesome fear of her. He has recorded many of her shrewd and often witty sayings. Here are a couple : Boswell, speaking of a certain horse, said he was a horse of blood. Mrs Boswell remarked, 'I hope so, for I am sure he has no *flesh*.' She disapproved of her husband's inviting to a party at their house a man of ability but of bad manners. 'He is,' said she, 'like fire and water, useful, but not to be brought into company.'

During Mrs Boswell's illness Johnson warned him, 'In losing her you will lose your anchor, and be tossed without stability on the waves of life.' That this was a true prophecy Boswell found to his cost. 'While she lived,' he said, 'I had no occasion almost to think concerning my family. Every particular was thought of by her, better than I could. I am the most helpless of

human beings.' He did not know what to do with the
five children that were left upon his hands. His second
son, however, though only eleven, was 'quite a companion.' He is much of his father—'vanity of vanities.'

Though the loss he had experienced was 'perpetually
recurring,' just a year after his wife's death, the
widower, now fifty years old, took to his old pursuit of
heiress-hunting. He proposed to a lady of fortune in
the North and was sanguine that she would accept
him, because, so he reasoned, she 'had refused young
and fine gentlemen.' The lady, however, was as
little ambitious of possessing the mature charms of
Boswell.

Then came the last of his many marriage proposals.
It was to a daughter of the Dean of Exeter, 'an agreeable woman *d'un certain âge* with £10,000.' In this case
she was not agreeable and Boswell became discouraged.
But indeed it was death and not a second marriage that
was coming to him. He died before he had another
opportunity of seeking earthly treasure in the hand
of an heiress.

CHAPTER IX

MR AND MRS CARLYLE AT HOME

RECENTLY we have seen a contrast drawn between the
domestic virtues of Johnson and the supposed absence
of them in the case of one who in some respects resembled Johnson—Thomas Carlyle. This, then, is the place
to say something about the love affairs of Mr and Mrs
Carlyle. The first thing we remark is that neither of
these people married their first love. At Kirkcaldy
while schoolmastering in 1846, Carlyle had met 'the
fair-complexioned, softly elegant, softly grave, witty and
comely' Margaret Gordon, the 'Blumine' of *Sartor*

Resartus. 'Peculiar among all dames and damsels glanced Blumine, then in her modesty like a star among earthly lights, noblest maiden. . . . One morning he found his morning-star all dimmed and dusky-red. . . . She said, in a tremulous voice, they were to meet no more.' The aunt of this Margaret Gordon had put an end to the intercourse. In a farewell letter the maiden advised Carlyle to cultivate the milder dispositions of his heart; his abilities would be known in time. Genius would render him great. 'May virtue render you beloved! Remove the awful distance between you and ordinary men by kind and gentle manners.' Carlyle met her in Hyde Park twenty years later, when she was Lady Bannerman, wife of the Governor of Nova Scotia, and her eyes seemed to say, 'Yes, yes, that is you.'

And Jane Bailie Welsh, who became Mrs Carlyle, had, before meeting Carlyle, been a pupil and afterwards lover of Edward Irving. 'Had I married him,' she said, 'the " tongues" would never have been heard.' The young divine, however, could not marry her, as he had engaged himself rather hastily to Isabella Martin, daughter of the Kirkcaldy minister. We may remark here that she made Irving as good a wife as probably Mrs Carlyle would have done, though she may have contributed some of that incense of idolatry that clouded the genius of the popular preacher.

Carlyle succeeded Irving as tutor to Miss Welsh, and encouraged her to read German literature. In 1823 she wrote to him : 'I love you. . . . All the best feelings of my nature are concerned in loving you. But were you my brother I should love you the same. . . . But your wife---never, never.' Carlyle replied : 'You love me as a sister and will not wed; I love you in all possible senses of the word, and will not wed any more than you.' But by 1826 they were engaged, Jane Welsh admitting that her affection was simple, honest, serene, 'made up of admiration and sympathy.' So she accepted the heart and hand of Thomas Carlyle, with his then barren and perplexed destiny, and they were married October 17, 1826, he being about thirty-two and she twenty-five.

In one of Carlyle's letters, dated 1822, there is a passage full of interest, in the light of after events as the world knows them : 'These women of genius, sir, are the very d——l when you take them on a wrong tack. I know very well that I myself—if ever I marry, which seems possible at best—am to have one of them for my helpmate, and I expect nothing but that our life will be the most turbulent, incongruous thing on earth—a mixture of honey and wormwood, the sweetest and the bitterest, or, as it were, at one time the clearest sunshiny weather in nature, then whirlwinds and sleet and frost, then thunder and lightning and furious storms—all mingled together into the same seasons—and the sunshine always in the smallest quantity.'

Compare with this a letter which Mrs Carlyle wrote early in life to a girl friend, who had informed her of her approaching marriage : 'Will you think me mad if I tell you that when I read your words, "I am going to be married," I all but screamed? Positively it took my breath, as I saw you in the act of taking a flying leap into infinite space. Congratulation on such occasions seems to me a tempting of Providence. The triumphal procession air which in our manners and customs is given to marriage at the outset—that singing of *Te Deum* before the battle has begun—has, ever since I could reflect, struck me as somewhat senseless and somewhat impious. If ever one is to pray, if ever one is to feel grave and anxious, if ever one is to shrink from vain show and vain babble, surely it is on the occasion of two human beings binding themselves to one another for better and for worse till death part them; just on that occasion which it is customary to celebrate only with rejoicings and congratulations, and trousseaux and white ribbon !'

Having both had 'horrible imaginings' about marriage when at a distance, it is no wonder that as it came near to them Miss Welsh and Carlyle were full of 'present fears.' They strove to encourage each other as if they were mounting a scaffold. Miss Welsh spoke of the wedding preparations as 'horrid circumstances.' Carlyle, from shyness, or a general sense of protection, wished his brother John to go part of the way with him and his bride on the wedding journey in a coach from Dumfries. Miss Welsh, however, drew the line at John. She wrote : 'I prohibit John from going with us an inch of the road.' Carlyle, who had been striving to fortify himself against what Miss Welsh called the 'odious ceremony' by reading Kant's *Critique of Pure Reason*, had turned in despair to Scott's novels, which cheered him somewhat. 'After all,' he wrote, 'I believe we take this impending ceremony too much to heart. Bless me ! have not many people been married before now?' Still he was quite sure that his matrimonial difficulties could never be surmounted without the aid of tobacco. 'I shall only stipulate,' he continues, 'that you will let me, by the road, as occasion serves, *smoke three cigars*, without criticism or reluctance, as things essential to my perfect contentment.'

Highly characteristic is the heading of Miss Welsh's final letter to Carlyle : 'The Last Speech and Marrying Words of that Unfortunate Young Woman, Jane Bailie Welsh.' 'Truly,' answered Carlyle, 'a most delightful and swanlike melody is in them; a tenderness and warm, devoted trust, worthy of such a maiden, bidding farewell to that unmarried earth of which she was the fairest ornament.'

'Except the Newgate Calendar there is no more sickening reading than the biographies of authors.' Did we not know what a good man Carlyle in the main was, these words of his would occur to us about himself, when we read the exaggerated terms in which the sins of omission, bringing up, and temperament—which made him an imperfect husband, to say the least—have been depicted.

When Mrs Carlyle announced to a friend in a letter the conclusion of her husband's book, *The French Revolution*, she added, *Quelle vie !* let no woman who values peace of soul ever dream of marrying an author.'

The thirteen years—1853-65—during which *Frederick the Great* was being written was another period of intense nervous strain and mental absorption, and the sage could not suffer the slightest interruption. The story goes that Mrs Carlyle ventured up to the 'sublime garret,' where the book was composed, with her needle-work one day, but before long her husband drew attention to the noise which she made with her needle. Folding her hands idly upon her lap, she sat motionless; but presently the silence was broken by the voice of the philosopher : ' Jane,' said he, 'I can hear you breathing.' As Mrs Carlyle found it inconvenient to abandon this natural process, she was forced to give up all attempts at keeping her husband company in his study.

When matters went well with Carlyle it never occurred to him that they could be going ill with any one else; and, on the other hand, if he was uncomfortable, he required everybody to be uncomfortable along with him. As an illustration of the latter characteristic Mrs Carlyle used to say that when her husband first grew a beard, all the time he had saved by ceasing to shave he spent wandering about the house, and bemoaning that which was amiss in the universe.

We must not, however, take too seriously all that we find in Mrs Carlyle's published letters about her husband. Like him, she spoke direct from her nerves; the little miseries of life ate into her heart, and she had a Titanesque power of making mountains out of molehills. This we must bear in mind when reading in her letters about the irritability, gloominess, and negative unkindness of her husband.

There were faults on both sides. She was not more

easy to live with than was he, as even her own mother had discovered.   Charming, witty, brilliant, affectionately playful as she naturally was, she had 'a hot temper, and a tongue, when she was angry, like a cat's, which would take the skin off at a touch.'

It was a failing of Carlyle that when he was uncomfortable he could not keep it to himself, and made more of it than the reality justified.   Long before he had terrified his family with accounts of his tortures from dyspepsia, and told them afterwards they should have known that when he cried 'murder' he was not always being killed.   'The truth is,' he used to say, 'we are never right as we are.'   He was fond of a story of an Irish drummer, feeling how well it fitted him. 'Oh, the devil burn it !' said the drummer, flogging his countryman; 'there's no pleasing of you, strike where one will.'

Mrs Carlyle suffered perhaps more than her husband from colds and pains and sleeplessness; when he was dilating upon his own sorrows, he often forgot hers, or made them worse by worry.   It was her experience that 'when the wife has influenza, it is a slight cold—when the man has it, it is, etc., etc.'   Even when at heart he was really grateful for the thoughtful care of his wife, Carlyle's acknowledgments were limited; he was shy of showing feeling, and even those who knew him best, and understood his ways, were often hurt by his apparent indifference.

All this is true, but if Carlyle, in spite of his good resolutions, was occasionally 'a little ill-haired,' we must remember that he was engaged with work into which he was throwing his entire heart and soul.   His wife, instead of allowing her mind to be 'churned to froth,' might, understanding all as she did, have been more ready to pardon, and to admit extenuating circumstances.

And Carlyle was not always the aggressor.   Miss Ella Hepworth Dixon gives the following story which she had

from an intimate friend of the lady who was a witness of
a fracas at Chelsea. This lady, calling one day in Cheyne
Row, met Carlyle on his own door-step, his head bent,
and perplexity and annoyance wrinkling the philosophic
brow. Somewhat to her surprise—for she was an intimate of the house—the sage only bowed, and went on his
way down the dismal little street. The servant showed
the visitor into a darkened room, where were to be seen
the debris of tea and the prostrate form of Mrs Carlyle
on the sofa. 'Did you meet Thomas,' demanded the
wife, in a voice which showed unmistakable traces of a
recent domestic storm. 'Yes. He was going out. I
met him on the door-step, looking very sad. What's the
matter, my dear?' 'The matter!' cried Mrs Carlyle
from the sofa with sparkling eyes; I've been two days
on this sofa with a sick headache, and he's only this
instant come in and asked me what ails me ! And—
well, I've just thrown my tea-cup at him !'

Probably this attack was caused by an unreasonable
and silly jealousy which tormented Mrs Carlyle in reference to an acquaintance formed by her husband with
Lady Ashburton. That a man of genius should enjoy
the society of a brilliant and gifted lady of high rank was
'just and laudable,' as he called it. It was natural, too,
if not laudable, that Mrs Carlyle should not be equally
interested in a person who rivalled her in her own
domain. Carlyle made the mistake of trying to force his
wife into a position which she detested; and every step
which he took in this direction only made the irritation
greater. It was only natural, however, that he should
feel impatient when called on to abandon friends whose
high character he admired, and who had been singularly
kind to him, for a cause which he knew to be a prepos-
terous creation of a disordered fancy, and which, in
yielding, he would have acknowledged tacitly to have
been just. Carlyle was as innocent of any thought of
wrong as incapable of understanding why the domestic
barometer should remain at 'stormy.'

Nothing showed Mrs Carlyle the affection with which she was regarded by her husband so much as his kindness on the occasion of her mother's death. She was staying from home at the time. Carlyle knew what she would be suffering, and sent the following letter : ' My darling ! my poor little woman ! Alas ! what can I say to thee? It was a stern welcome from thy journey this news that met thee. Oh, my poor little broken-hearted wife ! Our good mother, then, is away for ever. She has gone to the unknown Great God, the Maker of her and of us. We shall never see her more with these eyes. Weep, my darling, for it is altogether sad and stern, the consummation of sorrows, the greatest, as I hope, that awaits thee in this world. I join my tears with thine; I cry from the bottom of my dumb heart that God would be good to thee, and soften our tears into blessed tears. The question now, however, is what is to be done. Tell me, would you wish me to come, to attend you forward? to bring you back home? to do or attempt anything that promised to aid you? . . . I can advise nothing, but in everything I will be ordered by your wishes. Speak them out. Oh, that you had but stayed with me ! It would have been something to weep on my shoulder. God help thee to bear this sore stroke, my poor little Jeannie ! It seems cruel to ask thee for advice, and yet thy wishes, dearest, shall be the chief element of guidance for me. As yet, in the wood I am in, all whirls and tumbles; but this question does arise. Ought I not, by all laws of custom and natural propriety, to be there, with or without thee, on the last sad, solemn occasion, to testify my reverence for one who will be for ever sad, dear, and venerable to me?' . . .

It was after this event that Carlyle bought the little birthday present of which Mrs Carlyle thus speaks in a letter to a friend : ' Only think of my husband, too, having given me a little present ! He who never attends to such nonsenses as birthdays, and who dislikes nothing

in the world so much as going into a shop to buy anything, even his own trousers and coats; so that, to the
consternation of Cockney tailors, I am obliged to go
about them.   Well, he actually risked himself in a
jeweller's shop, and bought me a very nice smelling-
bottle !   I cannot tell you how *wae* his little gift made
me, as well as glad; it was the first thing of the kind he
ever gave to me in his life.   In great matters he is
always kind and considerate, but these little attentions,
which we women attach so much importance to, he was
never in the habit of rendering to any one; his up-
bringing, and the severe turn of mind he has from
nature, had alike indisposed him towards them.   And
now the desire to replace to me the irreplaceable,
makes him as good in little things as he used to be
in great.'

Carlyle never forgot her birthday afterwards.   Once
she thought that he had, and she told the story of her
mistake and its correction thus : 'Oh ! my dear husband, fortune has played me such a cruel trick this day !
and I do not even feel any resentment against fortune,
for the suffocating misery of the last two hours.   I
know always, when I seem to you most exacting, that
whatever happens to me is nothing like so bad as I deserve.   But you shall hear how it was.   Not a line from
you on my birthday, the postmistress averred.   I did
not burst out crying, did not faint—did not do anything absurd, so far as I know; but I walked back again,
without speaking a word; and with such a tumult of
wretchedness in my heart as you, who know me, can
conceive.   And then I shut myself in my own room to
fancy everything that was most tormenting.   Were you,
finally, so out of patience with me that you had resolved
to write to me no more at all?   Had you gone to Addis-
combe, and found no leisure there to remember my
existence?   Were you taken ill, so ill that you could not
write?   That last idea made me mad to get off to the
railway and back to London.   Oh, mercy ! what a two

hours I had of it ! And just when I was at my wits' end
I heard Julia crying out through the house, 'Mrs
Carlyle, Mrs Carlyle, are you there? Here is a letter
for you.' And so there was after all. The postmistress
had overlooked it, and had given it to Robert, when
he went afterwards, not knowing that we had been.
I wonder what love-letter was ever received with such
thankfulness ! Oh, my dear ! I am not fit for living
in the world with this organisation. I am as much
broken to pieces by that little accident as if I had come
through an attack of cholera or typhus fever. I cannot
even steady my hand to write decently. But I felt an
irresistible need of thanking you by return of post.
Yes, I have kissed the dear little card-case; and now
I will lie down awhile, and try to get some sleep. At
least, to quiet myself, I will try to believe—oh, why
cannot I believe it once for all—that, with all my faults
and follies, I am "dearer to you than any earthly
creature." '

Whatever the Carlyles were to each other when together they certainly wrote very loving letters on the
rare occasions when they were separated. Carlyle's are
full of the same sort of 'little language' that Swift
made use of in writing to Stella. Bad husbands do not
write love letters such as the following to their absent
wives : 'It is poor Goody's birthday, when she reads
this; and one ought to have said what the inner man sufficiently feels : that one is right glad to see the brave little Goody with the mind's and the heart's eye on such an
occasion, and wishes and prays all good in this world,
and in all other worlds, to one's poor Goody—a brave
woman, and, on the whole, a "Necessary Evil"' (name
by which he often laughingly described his wife) ' to a
man. And now, dearest, here is a small gift, one of the
smallest ever sent. Do not think it cost me any trouble
to buy the thing; once fairly in the enterprise, there was
a real pleasure in going through with it. I tried hard for
a work-box, but there was none I could recommend to

myself. I was forced to be content with a little jewel-box, and there, you see, is the key. Blessings on thee with it! I wish I had diamonds to fill the places with for my little wifie. I knew you had a jewel-box already, but this is a newer one, a far smaller one. Besides, I bought it very cunningly, and " the lady, if she would like anything better, can, at any time, get it exchanged." And so, dear Goody, kiss me and take my good wishes. While I am here there will never want one to wish thee all good. Adieu on the birthday, and may the worst of our days be all done, and the best still coming. Thine evermore.'

To this Mrs Carlyle replied : 'Oh, my darling, I want to give you an emphatic kiss rather than to write. But you are at Chelsea, and I at Seaforth, so the thing is clearly impossible for the moment. But I will keep it for you till I come, for it is not with words that I can thank you adequately for that kindest of birthday letters and its small enclosure—touching little key ! I cried over it, and laughed over it, and could not sufficiently admire the graceful idea.'

The fact is the Carlyles were too like each other. They suffered in the same way from nerves disordered, digestion impaired, excessive self-consciousness, and the absence of children to take their thoughts away from each other. They were, in the fullest sense of the word, everything to each other—sole comforters, chief tor-mentors. After all, however, as their friend Tennyson remarked, it was a good thing that Carlyle and Mrs Carlyle did marry each other, for otherwise there might have been four unhappy people instead of two.

CHAPTER X

SOME PAINTERS IN LOVE

ON the 14th of July, 1494, Albert Dürer married a lady who was very beautiful, but who is said to have been ill-tempered and avaricious. We can find no evidence, however, that proves the painter to have been a hen-pecked husband. As to his being driven to work beyond his strength to provide his wife Agnes with money, it is now shown that she had a marriage portion of 200 florins, and that she received a large sum at her father's death. Indeed, we are afraid that it was Albert Dürer's own love of gain that made him write in a letter to Jacob Heller, for whom he had painted a picture, 'My wife begs for a Trinkgeld.'

Tintoretto married Faustina, the daughter of a Venetian noble, Marco de Vescovi. Their home was a beautifully carved white Gothic house. If it had not been for Faustina, Tintoretto could not have maintained his large household, for he was very imprudent and did not demand or enforce proper payment for his work. When he went out his wife used to find it necessary to wrap up money in a handkerchief for him, and enjoin him to render a strict account of it upon his return. When Tintoretto could not do this satisfactorily, he would say that he had devoted it to the relief of the poor and the prisoners, amongst whom he reckoned himself. Faustina was also very particular about her husband's dress—firstly, that he should always wear the robe of a Venetian citizen when he left home; secondly, that the same robe should be taken care of on rainy days.

Rembrandt did himself well—to use an expressive colloquialism—when he married, in 1634, Saskia Van

Ulenburgh. She belonged to a distinguished family, had a considerable fortune, and was a fortune in herself. She was the model of many of her husband's paintings and etchings. There was nothing Bohemian in the *ménage* of the Rembrandts; it was simple, sober, and regular. Alas ! its able mistress did not last long. Saskia died in her thirtieth year. After enduring a widowerhood of twelve years Rembrandt married Henricktie Stoffelt, and after her death a third wife, Catherine Van Wyck.

Rubens married his first wife, Isabella Brandt, in 1609. In 1630, four years after this lady's death, he married one of the richest and most beautiful girls in all Flanders—Helena Fourment—then only sixteen years of age. She it is whom we recognise in so many of his pictures. By her he had five children.

One day Francesco Giocondo, a rich money-lender of Florence, asked Leonardo Da Vinci to paint the portrait of Mona Lisa, his beautiful wife. The artist stated his terms : 'We shall want a dozen violin players to keep the sitter in a bright humour. If you like, we will add some singers and a few buffoons, so as to vary the monotony of the instruments.' Another way the artist discovered of keeping the fair sitter in bright humour, was to make love to her. Mona Lisa's husband was old, while Leonardo was not more than forty-three, handsome, intellectual, eloquent, and with the prestige of genius attached to him. It is difficult to discover the truth of this matter. All we know is that from the time the great painter had the typical visage of Francesco Giocondo's wife for a subject, he never introduced any other into his important pictures.

In his thirty-second year Hogarth married, on the 23rd of March, 1729, Jane, daughter of Sir James Thornhill. Jane's father, doubting Hogarth's ability to keep her in the style in which she had been brought up, at first disapproved of the match. When the artist, however, had etched 'The Harlot's Progress,' Lady

Thornhill was so pleased with the picture that she got it and advised her daughter to place it in her father's way. One morning it was conveyed secretly into Sir James's dining-room. When he saw it he inquired from whence it came, and by whom it was brought. On being told, he cried out, 'Very well! very well! The man who can make works like this can maintain a wife without a portion.' He designed this remark as an excuse for keeping his purse-strings close; but soon after became not only reconciled, but generous to the young people.

Gainsborough had painted the picture of a young lady of sixteen years of age called Margaret Burr. When it was finished, she expressed her warm appreciation of the artist's skill, and gave him the gentlest possible hint that perhaps, in time, he might become the possessor of the original. He took the hint, and after a short court-ship was rewarded by her hand, and with it an annuity of two hundred pounds. Rumour said that she was the natural daughter of an English prince, and instead of being ashamed, she used to boast of this origin.

George Romney, born 1734, was a good painter but a bad husband. When twenty-two years of age he married a young woman who had attended him through a fever. He then took it into his head that 'a young man married is a man that's marred' and lived apart from her, for fear that married life might in any way interfere with his artistic aspirations and ambitions. No artist was ever more influenced by beauty than George Romney, and it was his fate to meet that most attractive woman, Emma, Lady Hamilton, maid-of-all-work, model, mistress, and pauper. Romney painted her according to some twenty-three, according to others forty-one times, in all kinds of attitudes and characters. So it was that the poor wife in the North was forgotten, while 'the divine lady,' as Romney fondly called Lady Hamilton, was inspiring him with forms of loveliness in Cavendish Square. When, however, the infirmities of age rendered the artist burdensome to his friends and to himself, he remembered the wife whom he had neglected. He returned to her; and in this noble woman found a tender nurse, who had never been irritated 'to an act of unkindness or an expression of reproach by an abandonment of forty years.'

Mulready and his wife need not have come together as soon as they did, for they could not live together, and were separated fifty years. He was only eighteen when he married, and she a year older, and in his nineteenth year the painter became a father.

William Blake, born in 1757, was original in courtship as in all other things. He was describing one evening to a Miss Catherine Boutcher the pains he had suffered from a certain capricious lady.

'I pity you from my heart,' said the dark-eyed Kate.

'Do you pity me?' replied Blake. 'Then I love you for that.'

'And I love you,' said the frank-hearted lass, and so the courtship began.

The artist tried how she looked in a drawing; then described her charms in verse. They were married, and Blake must indeed have been glad that his first love refused him, for Mrs Blake was a most admirable wife. She made herself happy at home and was content with the simplest food and the plainest clothes. The only thing she really cared about was her husband's fame. She coloured with a light and neat hand the impressions of his drawings, and, what is more remarkable, she kept a secret, which he only confided to her, in reference to his method of colouring.

Blake died in his seventy-first year, and almost his last words were, 'I have no grief but in leaving you, Catherine; we have lived happy, and we have lived long.' Three days before his death he was bolstered up in his bed to put finishing touches on his favourite picture, 'The Ancient of Days.' Seeing his wife in tears he exclaimed, 'Stay, Kate ! Keep just as you are. I will draw your portrait, for you have ever been an angel to me.' She obeyed, and the dying artist made a fine likeness.

The Cornish painter, John Opie, born 1761, was obliged to divorce his first wife. To this misfortune he thus alluded when passing the Church of St Giles, late one evening, with a friend of avowed sceptical opinions.

'I was *married* at that church,' observed Opie.

'And I was christened there,' said his companion.

'Indeed!' answered the painter, 'it seems they make unsure work at that church, for it neither holds in wedlock nor in baptism!'

Opie married again, and his second wife, a famous writer in her day, was as good as his first wife was bad.

Thomas Stothard was such an industrious artist that he only allowed himself half a wedding-day. After bringing his bride back from the church he quietly walked down to the Academy, to draw from the antique till three o'clock, the hour at which it then closed. There he sat, by the side of a fellow-student named Scott, with whom he was on intimate terms, and after drawing the usual time, at length said to him, 'I am now going home to meet a family party. Do come and dine with me, for I have this day taken to myself a wife.' In his domestic life he had many trials. One of his sons was accidentally shot, another was killed by a fall from a ladder. The shocks rendered Mrs Stothard a confirmed invalid, but this brought out the goodness and kindness of her husband's heart. He thought of and took care of her health in a way that can only be described as motherly.

About the year 1811 John Constable fell in love with Maria Bicknell, daughter of the solicitor to the Admiralty. In the first letter, however, which she addressed to her lover, the lady was as guarded as a lawyer's daughter should be. It begins 'My dear sir,' tells him that she has consulted papa, *i.e.* taken a lawyer's opinion, and concludes with, 'Believe me, my dear sir, your obliged friend.' In another letter she said that her father's only objection to the suit was on the score of 'that necessary evil, money,' and advised him to apply himself diligently to his profession, and to 'such parts that pay best.' Indeed, in nearly all the letters which this very prudent young lady wrote to Constable, she told him plainly to 'make money before he made love.' Before long Constable became known as a portrait painter and was paid at the rate of fifteen guineas for a head. Then Miss Bicknell allowed herself to marry him, and in spite of, or perhaps by reason of, her want of romance, she turned out a most amiable and devoted wife. When she died, and left her husband and seven children, her loss was irreparable.

The French painter, Horace Vernet, was only twenty years of age when he married Louise, the daughter of Abel de Pujol, and from his charming letters to her we gain our best idea of his character as a man. Very busy as his life soon became, home ties were always the strongest. Wherever his restless spirit carried him, he could always find time to think of those left behind, and to write them letters full of descriptions and of longings for the time of his return.

Turner's chance of domestic happiness was spoiled by the mean conduct of his lady-love's step-mother. This person disliked the match, so she intercepted and kept from her step-daughter all the letters that Turner had written, during an absence from her of two years. Thinking that she had been given up the girl engaged herself to another, and when Turner came back she said that she could not, as an honourable woman, break off the new engagement. There was another young lady, some years afterwards, whom the great painter wished to marry; but he was too timid to propose, and contented himself with wishing that she would 'waive bashfulness, or, in other words, make an offer instead of expecting one.'

Turner was, of course, an admirer of female beauty,

but he was too diffident to make much way with the fair sex. He was once at a party where there were several beautiful women. One of them struck him much with her charms, and he said to a friend, in a moment of unguarded admiration, 'If she would marry me, I would give her a hundred thousand.'

Turner's name suggests that of his great vindicator, John Ruskin, and we may here briefly relate his love affairs—if they can be called by that name. The first was with Charlotte Withers, a 'fragile, fair, freckled, sensitive slip of a girl about sixteen' who was on a visit to his parents' house. 'She was,' says Ruskin, 'graceful in an unfinished and small wild-flower sort of a way, extremely intelligent, affectionate, wholly right-minded, and mild in piety. An altogether sweet and delicate creature of ordinary sort, not pretty, but quite pleasant to see, especially if her eyes were looking your way, and her mind with them. We got to like each other in a mildly confidential way in the course of a week. We disputed on the relative dignities of music and painting; and I wrote an essay nine foolscap pages long, proposing the entire establishment of my own opinion, and the total discomfiture and overthrow of hers, according to my usual manner of paying court to my mistresses. Charlotte Withers, however, thought I did her great honour, and carried away the essay as if it had been a school prize. And, as I said, if my father and mother had chosen to keep her a month longer, we should have fallen quite melodiously and quietly in love, and they might have given me an excellently pleasant little wife, and set me up, geology and all, in the coal business, without any resistance or further trouble on my part. When Charlotte went away with her father, I walked with her to Camberwell Green, and we said good-bye, rather sorrowfully, at the corner of the New Road; and that possibility of meek happiness vanished for ever. A little while afterwards her father "negotiated" a marriage for her with a well-to-do trader, whom she took because she was bid. He treated her pretty much as one of his coal sacks, and in a year or two she died.'

The great writer and art critic met the girl whom he did marry in a ballroom. He admired her as he would the statue of a Greek goddess, but there was no warmer feeling on either side.

One day Ruskin brought Millais to paint his wife's picture. Artist and sitter fell in love with each other. The husband not only forgave, but in order to enable the lovers to marry got a divorce from his wife, and then went to the church where the wedding took place and gave her to Millais.

The first wife of Alma Tadema, a French lady, died in 1869, leaving two daughters. At her death Mr Tadema came to England with his children and took up his residence in London, becoming a naturalised British subject a few years later. In 1871 he married Miss Laura Theresa Epps, whose striking features and wonderful red-gold hair we have admired in so many of Tadema's pictures, and whose clever painting would have made the name of Tadema well known, even if it had not been illumined by the genius of her husband. We may here mention that Mr Tadema does not follow the example of so many husbands and absent himself from his wife's receptions. Mrs Tadema receives in her studio, and, after chatting with her for a while and drinking a cup of tea, her friends move upwards to the larger studio, to talk with their host and to enjoy his work.

CHAPTER XI

'IF MUSIC BE THE FOOD OF LOVE'

LADIES greatly admired Handel, who was very hand-some, but the serenity of the composer seems only to have been ruffled twice by love on his part. His first attachment was to a London girl, a member of the aristocracy. Her parents thought him beneath her in social position, but were good enough to say that if he abstained from writing any more music, the question of marriage might be entertained. It was easier to abstain from their daughter than from his art, and he did so. Years after almost the same thing occurred. Handel and another beautiful pupil of his fell in love with each other, and proud parents gave him the choice between giving up his profession or their daughter. Music, 'heavenly maid,' was chosen.

Bach was twice happily married. His first wife was an excellent house-manager. When, after thirteen years, she died, she was in due time succeeded by a second wife, who also possessed the rare union of an artistic nature and domestic faculties. She copied his manuscripts, listened with delight to his productions, and in many other ways assisted his artistic labours. There must have been plenty of matrimonial music in his home, for he had twenty children.

When Haydn was a boy in the choir of St Stephen's Cathedral at Vienna, he was very fond of practical joking. One evening during service he cut off the queue of one of the other chorister's wigs and caused the congregation to smile. The choir-master, who had often threatened him before, turned him out of the choir-school that night, and, as he had no money and no friends, he had to pace the snowy streets until the morning, when he met and told his woe to a wig-maker named Keller, who happened to know him slightly.

'Since you lost your place by damaging a wig,' said this good-natured man, 'it is but right that a repairer of wigs should take you under his charge.' The poor boy was allowed to sleep in the attic, and a knife and fork were always placed for him at the table downstairs.

Keller had two daughters, and, in process of time, Haydn loved the elder, a girl of a sweet disposition; but she went into a convent, partly, it is said, to escape from the scolding tongue of her sister. Some years passed, and the composer enjoyed a competence and the wig-maker was reduced in circumstances. In order to help his benefactor, Haydn married this younger daughter, and his life afterwards was as miserable as an ill-tempered woman could make it.

She had a mania for priests and monks, and the composer's house was continually filled with them. Their noisy conversation prevented him from pursuing his studies; and, further, in order to escape curtain lectures from his wife, he was under the necessity of supplying the convents of each of these good fathers, gratis, with masses and motets.

At last he separated from her and attached himself to the lovely Boselli, a great singer. He had her picture painted, and nearly emptied his pocket by humoring her whims and caprices.

In after years he had a love affair with Mrs Billington, whose person was as beautiful as her voice was fine. Sir Joshua Reynolds was painting her portrait for him, and had represented her as St Cecilia, listening to celestial music.

'What do you think of the charming Billington's picture?' asked Sir Joshua, when Haydn came to see it.

'It is indeed a beautiful picture,' was the reply. 'It is just like her, but there's a strange mistake.'

'What is that?'

'Why, you have painted her listening to the angels, when you ought to have painted the angels listening to her.'

The first girl whom Mozart loved and wished to marry was Aloysia Weber, who became a rather famous singer. For some time she encouraged his attentions, but when better-looking suitors appeared she began to scorn the diminutive young composer. 'I knew nothing of the greatness of his genius,' she afterwards explained. 'I saw in him only a little man.' Mozart transferred his affections to her younger, less brilliant, and more domestic sister Constance.

The girl, however, had a stern guardian, and he prohibited Mozart from all communication with his charge until the lover declared himself in writing. Mozart, therefore, signed a document, by which he agreed to marry Constance within three years, or, 'in the event of such an impossibility happening as that he should alter his mind,' to pay her a yearly sum of three hundred florins. The guardian, contented with this, having gone away, Constance, 'heavenly girl,' tore up the paper, and fell upon Mozart's neck, exclaiming, 'Dear Mozart, I need no written assurance from you; I believe your word!' And this same faith in the composer was maintained by his wife after marriage. When she heard reports of slight breaches of conjugal fidelity, Frau Constance called them 'chambermaids' tattle' and refused to believe them.

Mozart's father was as unfriendly to the marriage as was the girl's guardian, nevertheless it took place on the 4th of August, 1782. 'When we were joined together,' wrote Mozart, 'my wife and I, too, began to weep; upon which every one, even the priest, was moved, and all who witnessed our emotion wept.'

There was, however, clear shining after the rain. The affection of the young couple was sincere and hearty. Constance was distinguished neither by talent nor

MEN OF ACTION

Sir Walter Raleigh.

Sir Francis Drake.

Duke of Wellington.

Lord Nelson.

education, but her husband praised her common sense. She could play tolerably on the pianoforte, and sang prettily at sight, so that Mozart was accustomed to try new compositions with her—or was it upon her, using her as a foolometer? While the husband composed, the wife sat by him and related to him legends and children's tales to his great content.

One day the Emperor Joseph asked Mozart why he did not marry a rich wife. With dignity the composer replied, 'Sire, I trust that my genius will always enable me to support the woman I love.' Unfortunately it did not. His compositions found few purchasers, for people generally did not comprehend them. So poor, indeed, were Mozart and his wife after their marriage that a friend found them one day, without any fuel in the house, waltzing to keep warm.

Then Constance became delicate from severe confinements, but the trial proved the goodness of her husband's heart. On one occasion, when he was composing beside her as she slept, suddenly a noisy messenger entered. Alarmed lest his wife should be disturbed, he rose hastily, when the pen-knife in his hand fell and buried itself in his foot. Without a word he left the room, a surgeon was called, and though lame for some time, his wife was not told of the accident. If Constance were asleep when he quitted home in the morning he would leave a tender note to greet her waking. Here is one of them : 'I wish you good-morning, my dear little wife. I hope you have slept well, and that nothing has disturbed your repose. Be careful not to take cold, not to rise too quickly, not to stoop, not to reach for anything, not to be angry with the servant. Take care also not to fall upon the threshold in passing from one room to another. Keep all the domestic troubles till I come, which will be soon.'

When Mozart was with his wife he worked hard and was as good as he could be, but whenever he left her he D went more or less to the bad. At the close of the year

1790 he made a journey to Frankfurt, Mannheim, and Munich, and, falling in with bad companions, allowed himself to be carried away by their excesses. When he came to himself he thought of his 'sweet, darling, beloved wife,' as he calls her in a letter promising reformation. 'I shall be delighted to return to you. What an enjoyable life we will lead ! I will work, and work so hard that I may never again get into such a distressing position.' But the night cometh when no man can work. A few months after he was on his death-bed. Amongst his last words were these : 'Must I go, just as I am able to live in peace? Must I leave my wife and my poor children just when I should have been able to provide better for them?'

When Mozart died, his wife in her despair lay in the same bed, that she might take and die of the same illness—typhus fever. Death seldom comes, however, to those who court it, and she lived on with her children for many years in very narrow circumstances, and never rested until she had paid every debt contracted by her husband.

Beethoven's 'immortal beloved,' 'his angel,' 'his all,' 'his life,' as he called her, was Countess Giulietta Guicciardi, but she preferred wealth and unruffled ease to being linked even with a great genius. Then there was Bettina von Arnim, whom the composer admired, but neither of them fell in love. He formed only Platonic attachments. It was enough that his female admirers knitted him stockings and comforters, and made him dainty puddings and other delicacies. Like Dean Swift, Beethoven accepted the adoration of women as a right, and in return condescended to go asleep on their sofas, after picking his teeth with the candle-snuffers, while they pounded away at his sonatas, the artistic slaughter of which deafness mercifully prevented him from hearing.

Spohr had become attached to Dorette Scheidler, who used to play with him beautifully upon the harp at the Court concerts. Driving home from one of these, at which the players had received an ovation from the delighted audience, Spohr asked, 'Shall we thus play together for life?' 'Bursting into tears,' he says, 'she sank into my arms; the contract for life was sealed.' For twenty-eight years they played together harmoniously the game of life, and then the beloved wife died. During her illness she had taken intense interest in his new oratorio, *Calvary*, so Spohr was anxious to complete it as soon as possible. 'The thought,' he says 'that my wife did not live to listen to its first performance sensibly lessened the satisfaction I felt at this, my most successful work.' Two lonely years had barely passed when Spohr found another good wife, who was also a fine musician.

Schubert represented himself as a woman-hater, but he had one great attachment, which could not be gratified on account of difference of social position and age. This was to Countess Caroline Esterhazy. Once the inexperienced maiden asked him why he had dedicated nothing to her. With abrupt intensity Schubert answered, 'What's the use?—to you all my music is dedicated.'

In 1837 Chopin met the woman who exercised the greatest influence on his life. Madame Dudevant, known to the world as George Sand, was unattractive in appearance, but she had a most fascinating manner, to which the young musician fell a victim. Sometimes Chopin felt scruples with regard to his connection with George Sand, and, had she consented, he would have made her his lawful wife. So great was the influence of this woman over him, that she persuaded him to leave Paris and his friends, and go with her to the island of Majorca. From this time his health began to break up and George Sand's love for him to wane. This woman, passionate and loving as she had been to the interesting young musician, the idol of society, the beloved of princes, was not so to the poor, dejected, and helpless invalid. Being a man of innate sensitiveness, he could not but see that she was weary of him; and this thought aggravated his disease. He felt deeply the complaints she would make at having to nurse him, and begged of her not to give up any of her amusements for his sake. Again, his moral sense told him that he ought in some way to atone for having taken this woman unlawfully to himself. She, on her part, was only awaiting an opportunity to break her connection with him. This occurred ten years after their first meeting, and they were permanently separated. About a year after George Sand would seem to have felt remorse for her cruel treatment. They happened to be invited to the house of a mutual friend. A great number of guests were present, and, thinking herself unobserved, she walked up to Chopin and held out her hand. 'Frédéric,' she murmured in a voice audible to him alone. He saw her familiar form standing before him, repentant, subdued, and seeking reconciliation. His handsome face grew deadly pale, and without a word he left the room.

A beautiful singer called Gretchen may have consoled the dismal life Weber lived when he was at Stuttgart, but her influence was not beneficial, for she led him into many extravagances and created in him a taste for playing the cavalier. He steadied down, however, when, at the first performance of his *Sylvana*, in Frankfurt, September 16th, 1810, he met Miss Caroline Brandt, who sang the principal part and with such success that the composer himself was loudly called for; on which occasion she had to drag the half-frightened youth before the curtain to receive the applause. How little did Weber dream that the hand which then clasped his was that of his future wife !

Six years after this the composer became Kapell-meister to the King of Saxony. 'Long,' he wrote to his intended, ' did I look on Count Vitzthum's letter, without daring to open it. Was it joy, was it sorrow? At length I took courage. It was joy ! So round I went to all my friends, who laughed, and made the new Kapellmeister a most reverential bow. . . . I ought to have an extra kiss from you for this good news.' They were now married, and, after a short trip, went to the 'comfortable sweet nest' which Weber had provided for his 'little birdie.' That he entered upon matrimony in a right spirit may be seen from an entry in his diary : 'May God bless our union, and grant me strength and power to make my beloved Lina as happy and contented as my inmost heart would desire! May His mercy lead me in all my doings !' This prayer was answered, for Weber made his wife and children happy, and worked hard for them until the 'machinery' of his frail body was quite 'shattered.'

The marriage of Mendelssohn, in 1837, with Cécile Jean Renaud was a very happy one. She was the beautiful daughter of a no less handsome mother who was the widow of a French Protestant pastor. So guarded was the composer in his approaches to the young lady that people at first thought his attentions were directed to the mother instead of to the daughter.

When Rossini was a bachelor and was living at Naples, his handsome person and musical talents were so much admired that his career on more than one occasion narrowly escaped an untimely close from the jealousy of lovers and husbands. Once a page came to him, gave him a note and hastily withdrew. It was a tender invitation to meet at a romantic spot outside the town. On arriving Rossini sang his 'Aria' for a signal, and from the gate of a park issued his unknown inamorata. On parting it was agreed that the same messenger should bring notice of the second appointment. Rossini, suspecting that the envoy was the lady in disguise, hastened after so fast that a change could not be made, and his guess was verified. The page was the wife of a wealthy Sicilian, widely known for her beauty. The next time Rossini attempted a visit, he had only just arrived at the gate of the park when a bullet passed his head and two masked assailants sprang towards him with drawn rapiers. The composer being unarmed, had no option but to take to his heels.

One reason, perhaps, why Rossini was so popular with the ladies is because he had a very high opinion of himself. He said to a beautiful woman who was standing between him and the Duke of Wellington : 'Madame, how happy should you be to find yourself placed between the two greatest men in Europe !'

Rossini married his favourite *prima donna*, Madame Colbraw, and about three years afterwards visited England for the first time. He was very indignant at the cold reception given here to his wife, to whom he was devotedly attached.

It is impossible even to imagine a more united couple than were Donizetti and his wife. 'They loved as a pair of lovers,' and when, after living together in Elysium for two years, cholera took away the wife, the husband lost all concern for himself or for what became of him.

There was a tender romance in the early life of Bellini. The father of the girl he loved, a Neapolitan judge, refused his suit on account of his inferior social position. When Bellini became famous the judge wished to change his mind, but Bellini's pride interfered. Soon after the young lady, who loved him unalterably, died, and it is said the composer never recovered from the shock.

Schumann had great trouble in getting for a wife Clara Wieck, but she was well worth it. She was the daughter of the master under whom he studied, and in whose house he lived. He saw her every day and heard her wonderful playing on the pianoforte. As a natural consequence they loved, but Wieck did not desire for a son-in-law a penniless musician, and forbade Schumann to see or write to his daughter. Then a bold idea came into the young man's head. He edited a musical journal, and printed in the paper 'Letters to Clara,' in which he poured forth rhapsodies of love side by side with essays on harmony and reports of concerts. Eventually the opposition of Wieck gave way, and Clara was married to the composer in 1840.

Schumann and his wife had the same tastes and perfectly understood one another. So much was this the case that he proposed to her on the pianoforte, without ever uttering a syllable of language to tell her what he meant. And after they were married eight or ten years, they would sit down to the piano side by side and perform piece after piece together, she playing the treble with her right hand, he the bass with his left. Often their disengaged arms were locked round one another's waists in an embrace of mutual affection. Schumann did his best to make a muddle of his life, but his wife, like some good angel, came after him wherever he went and put everything straight. When in the end he became quite mad, she supported him and their seven children.

For many years after her husband's death, Madame Schumann, who may be called the queen of pianists, interpreted her husband's music to the public as only she could. Before doing so she used to read over some of the old love-letters that he wrote her during the days of their courtship, so that, as she said, she might be 'better able to do justice to her interpretation of the spirit of his work.'

The saying that when 'poverty comes in at the door, love flies out at the window,' was sadly illustrated by the marriage of Wagner. When he was twenty-six years of age he fell in love with a beautiful opera singer, a girl not endowed with unusual artistic gifts, but appreciative of music and very sympathetic. Wagner had faith that his was the music of the future, but unfortunately it did not pay for firewood, or an overcoat, in the present, two things that just after his marriage, the composer told Liszt, he wanted. Indeed, if it had not been for the help of Liszt and for occasional engagements to conduct orchestras, the pair could never have got over the first twenty years of their married life. Wagner was excitable and irritable, and his wife, thinking that he was growing weary of her, took to opium. To do the composer justice, he did his best to wean her from the fatal habit; but the husband and wife had come to that condition that only two links were left to bind them to their childless hearth—their common love of a dog, which they had possessed for years, and of a canary. At length these two pets died, and just at the time when fortune turned, Wagner and his wife agreed to separate.

Among the composer's friends in Munich, where his operas were now being produced, was Hans von Bülow, who had married a daughter of Liszt. The man's irascible temper rendered his wife unhappy, but she was consoled by Wagner. Divorce was resorted to, Cosimar von Bülow became the wife of Richard Wagner, and the pair were happier than perhaps they deserved to be. The composer died at Venice in 1883. As a last token of love and admiration, his widow cut off her hair, which the deceased had so much admired, and placed it on a red cushion under his head in the coffin.

Verdi's parents were very poor Italian peasants, living near Busseto. Giuseppe's earliest recollection was the organ of the little village church, to which he listened with delight. When a boy he one day heard a skilful performance on a fine piano while passing by one of the better houses of Busseto. From that time a constant fascination drew him to the house. Its owner was Antonio Barezzi, a rich merchant and a cultivated man. It was his daughter whose playing gave young Verdi such pleasure. Signor Barezzi had often noticed the lingering and absorbed lad, so one day he asked him why he came so constantly and stayed so long doing nothing.

'I play the piano a little,' said the boy, 'and I like to come and listen to the fine playing in your house.'

'Oh ! if that is the case, come in with me that you

may enjoy it more at your ease, and hereafter you are welcome to do so, whenever you feel inclined.'

The delighted boy did not refuse the invitation, and the kind merchant soon came to regard the young musician with much affection. He helped him in many ways during the years that followed, and when Verdi was earning enough to marry upon, he gave him for a wife the girl whose music had so much charmed him.

The celebrated musical conductor, Sir Michael Costa, said after an unsuccessful wooing that he would 'never again be troubled with a woman, and he never did marry. He had, however, the following experience, which he imparted to a lady after a great musical festival :—

'Madame, the ladies of the chorus here are very exuberant! One of them, a pretty Yorkshire young woman, came up to me as I was entering my room, and said, "O Sir Michael, you conduct like an angel; I should so much like to kiss you."'

'Well, Sir Michael,' eagerly asked the lady, 'and did you kiss her?'

'Madame, madame,' he quickly replied, 'if you please that is my business.'

CHAPTER XII

LOVE OFF THE STAGE

ISAAC DISRAELI tells us that Molière, though so 'skilful in human life, married a girl from his own troupe who made him experience all those bitter disgusts and ridiculous embarrassments which he himself played off at the theatre.

David Garrick was once in love with Peg Woffington, who, from being a 'bricklayer's orphan and a pedlar of fruit and vegetables,' became a great actress. There was much more in her than Horace Walpole saw when he called her an 'impudent Irish-faced girl.' The connection between her and Garrick was stopped by her flirtations, which were many—or it may have been by the latter's economy. He complained that she made her 'tea as red as blood.'

In the year 1749 Garrick married Eva Maria Violetti, who was, according to one account, the daughter of the Earl of Burlington and a young Italian lady. Another story says that she was the daughter of a Viennese citizen, who sent her to England for reasons that seem incredible. When she first came over she was a dancer at the Haymarket Theatre, and was much admired by people of rank for 'her speaking face' and the 'poetry of her motion.' The Earl and Countess of Burlington are believed to have settled £6000 on her at her marriage.

'She was cheerfully grave, did not speak much, but was followed and addressed by everybody.'

'I like her exceedingly,' said Walpole; 'her behaviour is all sense and sweetness too.'

Much Ado About Nothing was revived the season after the marriage, and the passages in the part of Benedick applicable to Garrick's own case occasioned infinite mirth : 'Have you seen Benedick the married man?' 'When I said I would die a bachelor, I did not think I should live to be married.'

Never was marriage happier. During thirty years of wedded life they were not one day apart. 'He never was a husband to me,' she said, speaking in old age of Garrick to a friend; 'he was always my lover.' When he died she told his friends that death was now 'the most agreeable object' to her; but she was called upon to survive him 'who gladdened life' forty-three years.

Rumour was very busy about the marriage of John Philip Kemble before he entered into that state. It was said that he was engaged to a widow, the celebrated novelist, Mrs Inchbald. Others gave him to Miss Philips, afterwards the beautiful Mrs Crouch, with whom he sometimes acted. Probability was lent to this report by the fact that when on one occasion at Cork the young actress had been annoyed by the attentions of some Militia officers, Kemble had showed himself ready to risk his life for her. But the popular actor did not marry as the public thought he would and should. ' If he had much regarded either birth or fortune, both would have eagerly courted his acceptance.' He did not do so, but married in the year 1787 an actress, the widow of a young actor called Brereton who had died in a lunatic asylum. At the conclusion of the wedding ceremony one of the party, Mrs Bannister, an actress, asked Kemble and his wife where they intended dining. The former replied, ' At home, I suppose.' Mrs Bannister thereupon invited them to join their family dinner. After the meal Mrs Kemble went off to the theatre to act as if nothing had happened, and was brought back afterwards by her husband to the house which had been prepared for her reception. Next evening she played Lady Anne in *Richard III.*, but it was not her own husband who had to exclaim to her, ' With all my heart——I hate you.'

When Charles Mathews was twenty-one years of age he met Eliza Strong, the orphan of a physician, who had been left in penury. The story of her helpless youth and honourable struggles made such an impression upon him that though he had only twelve shillings a week as an actor and was remonstrated with by his father, who spoke of the young people starving together, he married her on the 19th day of September, 1797. Four years afterwards Mrs Mathews died. She pathetically deplored leaving her husband, for she feared that he might marry a woman who would less understand his valuable quali- ties of heart and mind than she had done. To prevent this, on her death-bed she took the hand of a young actress, Miss Jackson by name, who was visiting her and whom she greatly respected, kissed it, and placing it in the hand of her husband, called upon both in the most solemn manner to become man and wife after her death. They did so, and Mathews was as happy with his bequeathed wife as he had been with her predecessor.

Charles Mayne Young married Julia Grimani, a member of an illustrious Venetian family. She died in giving birth to a first child, and her husband, though he survived her fifty years, never forgot her or thought of marrying again. One of his dying utterances was to thank God that they would be at last reunited.

In 1808, when playing with Miss Chambers, an Irish girl, who was making her debut as an actress at Cheltenham, Edmund Kean forgot his part and spoiled hers. She asked the manager, 'Who is that shabby little man with the brilliant eyes?' Overhearing the question, Kean walked up to the manager and asked, 'Who the devil is she?' The next night the actress forgot her part, but Kean received her apologies with perfect good humour. Result—friendship, love, and marriage in July of the same year. The bridegroom was twenty-three years of age and the bride twenty-nine. She had not the money which Kean thought she possessed when he proposed to her, and he was so poor that the bridesmaid had to lend him half a sovereign to buy the wedding-ring. The landlady of the Dog Tavern good-naturedly gave them a breakfast.

A brilliant career was before the actor, and there was no presentiment for some time of the unhappy division that afterwards took place between him and his wife. It arose in this way. One night when Kean was playing Othello, a certain Mrs Cox fainted in a private box. She was removed to the green-room and there introduced to Othello. An intimacy sprang up. Mrs Cox was fascinating, and not being as good as Desdemona, made passionate overtures to Kean, who was not as noble as the Moor of Venice. In 1825 his appearance in the divorce suit of Cox v. Cox and Kean raised against him a violent storm of unpopularity, which expressed itself in a refusal to give him a hearing on the stage.

Towards the close of Kean's career a reconciliation took place with his son Charles, and then, pale and worn with illness, he wrote the following note to his wife: 'Dear Mary,—Let us be no longer fools. Come home; forget and forgive. If I have erred, it was my head, not my heart, and most severely have I suffered for it. My future life shall be employed in contributing to your happiness; and you, I trust, will return that feeling by a total obliteration of the past.' On receiving this she went at once to him and a reconciliation took place.

'A trifling occurrence at Glasgow,' writes Macready, 'to be remembered in after life, fell out on the night of my benefit. A pretty little girl, about nine years of age, was sent on at very short notice to act the part of one of the children in *The Hunter of the Alps*. She was imperfect in the words she had to speak, having had no time to learn them. Not being aware of this, I scolded her on coming off the stage for her neglect, which I was afterwards sorry for, as it cost her many tears.' Five years afterwards, the same girl, whose name was Catherine Atkins, and who had become the support of her family, again played with the great actor. In her unaffected pathos and sprightliness he saw the germ of rare talent, and did his best to develop it. Soon the friendship between pupil and teacher gave place to a warmer feeling, and when the girl lost her father and brother by the wreck of a Liverpool steamer, Macready took her under his protection by becoming her husband, on June 24th, 1824.

'It was,' said Samuel Phelps, 'while receiving the munificent stipend of eighteen shillings a week, that I took to myself a wife. It was a love match—we were boy and girl—but that is not a thing to be talked about.'

The following is told by John Coleman in his *Memoirs of Phelps*. Coleman and he were acting *Othello* at York, where Phelps had not been since his first-born saw the light there. Tired as he was, and dangerous as it was for him to go out in the night air, after so arduous a task—for he was then past sixty-five—when the play was over he insisted upon taking me round to Stonegate, where he pointed out, in the moonlight, the room in which his eldest child was born.

'Ah!' said he, 'many a time have I seen her standing there, looking down upon me when I came in in the morning, and when I went away at night. That was five-and-forty years ago! The season was over here, and we had to go to Leeds. I was obliged to leave her behind me, because she was near her time; it wouldn't run to coaching. I used, therefore, to start on "Shank's mare" over Leeds bridge every Saturday night as soon as the play was over, and get to York as the Minster bells were calling to church on Sunday morning, and as regularly as they tolled twelve on Sunday night I started off and walked back to Leeds, arriving just in time for Monday morning's rehearsal. Yet, amidst it all, how happy we were, we two, boy and girl together. I can see her now, in her plain white muslin dress, her eyes shining like stars, her face lighted up like the moon herself. Every night when I went away she used to stand there in the window yonder and look at me to the last. Ah! I was much happier then at five-and-twenty "bob" a week, with her to share it, than I am now, when I get half the house every night.'

With that he hurried home as if in a dream.

Charles James Mathews, son of Charles Mathews, had a long illness from which when recovering he paid a visit to the Olympic Theatre. At the end of the performance he was carried out, and a lady remarked in passing, 'Ah! poor young man! it's all over with him—he's not long for this world!' The lady's name was Madame Vestris, and little she knew when she spoke that she would be for eighteen years wife of the 'poor young man.'

Mathews married her on the 18th of July, 1838, and eighteen years afterwards wrote from Lancaster Castle, where he was imprisoned for debt, letters which prove

the constancy of his love for her.   Here is the first of
them :—

'Lancaster Castle.

'MY OWN DEAREST LOVE,—In spite of all my hard
struggles, I have the sad task to announce to you that I
have been arrested and brought here.   For God's sake,
do not let the news overwhelm you !   I know no other
mode of acquainting you with it, and think that a long
beginning is almost worse than the truth at once. . . .

'I leave you to conceive the agony of my despair.
But one thought rushed upon me—the thought of you,
my poor, suffering, beloved wife.   How were you to be
informed of it, and what would be the effect it would
have on you? . . . .

'God bless and give you strength to support this present misfortune, and preserve you to enjoy the happiness that I trust will follow.   A thousand, thousand
kisses, my own dearly beloved wife.

'I have your dear picture before my eyes all day.   It
has been a real comfort to me, and I speak to it and kiss
it every night.

'Once more, God bless you.

'Your affectionate husband,

'C. J. MATHEWS.'

The poor man had only returned to his wife a few days
when she died.   Some time after her death Mathews,
being again in financial difficulties, accepted an engagement to act in America.   He did not return with as
many dollars as he expected, but he brought back a
real treasure—'a prudent, economical, industrious
little helpmate.'   She was a widow and a 'delightful
actress' (on the stage is meant), and her name was Mrs
Davenport.   Mathews says that by two or three years
of good management she repaired his fortune, and did

for him what he had never been able to do for himself
—kept his expenditure within his income.

The once celebrated actors Thomas Betterton and
Charles Macklin had also wives who were literally for-
tunes to them. Not only did they earn much money by
playing with them, but they were equally good in the
rôle of wife. So much did Mrs Betterton love her husband that when he died she lost her reason.

Bancroft fell in love at first sight with his future wife,
Marie Wilton. She was 'the thinnest girl he had ever
seen,' but he stuck to her through thick and thin (there
was no thin) and they lived together very happily.

CHAPTER XIII

LOVE AND DIVINITY

SINCE the time when St Paul discussed the question of
the marriage of Christians, in the seventh chapter of his
first Epistle to the Corinthians and elsewhere, it has been
a matter of controversy whether the usefulness of a
minister of the Gospel is increased or diminished by
putting on what are sometimes called the bonds of
matrimony.

We can hardly realise the shock it must have been to
his contemporaries when Martin Luther married the nun,
Catherine de Bora; but it was a good thing for the world
in our opinion, and there can be no doubt that it made
the Reformer himself a much happier man. Catherine
was a pretty woman, but better still, she was a faithful
and affectionate wife. Her temper was not the sweetest,
and her tongue at times could scold, but Luther loved
her dearly. When she frowned, he smiled; when she
scolded, he bantered. With the gentlest soothing he
chided her anxiety, and with the most self-denying

devotion he sought to make her life happy. Nor did he allow her to forget her good fortune in getting such a husband. In one of his letters he wrote to her : 'The greatest favour of God is to have a good and pious husband, to whom you can trust your all, your person, and even your life, whose children and yours are the same. Catherine, you have a pious husband who loves you. You are an empress; thank God for it.' This, however, did not prevent him from teasing her a little on occasions, as when he used to say, 'If I were going to make love again, I would carve an obedient woman out of marble, in despair of finding one in any other way.'

The Doctor and his wife lived very happily together, and at times, when he relaxed a little, he was quite sportive in his mode of addressing her : 'My Eve, my Kit, my rib Kit, that most learned dame, Catherine Luther— ah Kit, thou shouldst never preach ! How much these same ribs have to answer for !'

When Luther resolved to marry the fair sister, he had a wedding-ring made after a design of his own. On the surface are engraved the Crucifixion and the implements connected with it. Inside there is the simple inscription—

D. Martino Luthero.
Catharina Boren.
13 Junii, 1525.

Thus did Catherine ever carry about her the emblems of the dying of the Lord Jesus, and by them both she and her husband were reminded that their united lives should be consecrated to Him and should be lives of self-sacrifice.

Though an apostle pronounces 'the forbidding to marry' 'a doctrine of devils,' yet, for a considerable time after marriage was permitted to the clergy, it was viewed without favour as a lower state than celibacy.

Thus, Bishop Hall, when describing how he got married, begins by a sort of apology for 'condescending' to matrimony. He says: 'The uncouth solitariness of my life, and the extreme incommodity of my single housekeeping, drew my thoughts to the necessity of the married state, which God, no less strangely, provided for me; for walking from the church on Monday in the Whitsun week with a grave and reverend minister, I saw a comely and modest gentlewoman standing at the door of that house where we were invited to a wedding dinner, and inquiring of that worthy friend whether he knew her, "Yes," quoth he, "I know her well, and have bespoken her for your wife."'

To have things taken in this way out of his hands naturally surprised the Bishop, until it was explained that he could not do better than marry the girl chosen. He did so, and enjoyed the company of that helpmeet for the space of forty-nine years. What condescension!

Another divine who was driven into marriage by the 'incommodity of simple housekeeping' was Bishop Newton. He found that 'the study of sacred and classic authors ill agreed with butcher's and baker's bills; and when the prospect of a bishopric opened on him, more servants, more entertainments, a better table, etc., it became necessary to look out for some clever, sensible woman to be his wife, who would lay out his money to the best advantage, and be careful and tender of his health, a friend and companion at all hours, and who would be happier in staying at home than be perpetually gadding abroad.'

Bishop Ken of Bath and Wells expressed his feeling about marriage when he wrote these lines :—

A virgin priest the altar best attends;
Our Lord that state commands not, but commends.

That may have been the starting-point of what was afterwards a matter of mild pleasantry among the

Bishop's friends, that he made a vow every morning as he rose 'that he wouldn't be married that day.'

If our readers are not weary of Episcopal benedicts we would mention one more. He was a Bishop of Salisbury, and he never spoke of condescension or of making vows, at least against marriage. Indeed, so kindly did he take to that 'harmless amusement,' that he married four times, the motto, or poesy, on the wedding-ring at his fourth marriage being—

> If I survive,
> I'll make it five.

The Bishop used to declare that the reason his wives did not live long was that he never contradicted them. 'Give them their own way and they become gross and lethargic for want of this exercise.'

The poet and divine, John Donne, who became Dean of St Paul's in 1621, had married a daughter of Sir George Moore without the consent of her parents, and in consequence was treated with great asperity; in fact, he was told by his father-in-law that he was not to expect any money from him. The Doctor went home and penned the pithy note, 'John Donne, Anne Donne, *undone*,' which he sent to the gentleman in question, and this had the effect of restoring them to favour. The couple were very poor at first, but things soon got brighter, and they lived most happily together until Mrs Donne, who had been married when only sixteen years of age, died sixteen years afterwards, at the birth of her twelfth child. 'She had been,' says Walton, 'the delight of his eyes and the companion of his youth, and a commensurable grief took as full a possession of him as joy had done.' He does not appear to have had the smallest inclination to replace her, and indeed he had promised her on her death-bed that he would never give a step-mother to her children. The first sermon he preached after her death was in the church of St Clement's Danes, where his lost love lay buried, and he took for his text the words, 'I am the man that hath seen affliction.'

Another poet and divine who was not undone by his marriage, but greatly helped and comforted, was George Herbert. He and his wife married on the third day after their first interview. Indeed, the match had been pre-arranged by friends who, Izaak Walton tells us, 'well understood the tempers and knew the estates of both parties, and the Eternal Lover of mankind made them happy in each other's mutual and equal affections and compliance. Indeed, so happy that there never was any opposition betwixt them, unless it were a contest which should most .incline to a compliance with the other's desires.' In his acts of charity—a grace to which he devotes a special chapter in his *Country·Parson*— Herbert found a hearty helper in his wife, whom he made his almoner, and paid to her regularly a tenth of all he received to give away.

Jeremy Taylor was qualified to write his book *The Wedding Ring* by experience, for he himself married twice. His second wife was said to have been the natural daughter of Charles I. She had a considerable estate.

In one respect amongst others Swift was wiser than the modern curate. He would not rush into matrimony before he could afford that luxury. He said in a letter: 'My ordinary observations have taught me experience enough not to think of marriage till I settle my fortune in the world.' It is a pity that he did not marry when his fortune was settled.

Thackeray said : 'The book of Swift's life opens at leaves kept by these blighted flowers—Varina, Stella, Vanessa. This great genius, but miserable man, was ordained in 1694 and given the small benefice of Kilroot, in the North of Ireland. Here for the first and last time in his life Swift proposed marriage. The lady, Miss

Waring (Varina), refused, and this may have been one
of the reasons why ever afterwards he spoke so bitterly
of matrimony. 'It has,' he used to say, 'many children : Repentance, Discord, Spleen, Loathing.'

Human nature has, perhaps, never before or since
presented the spectacle of a man of such transcendent
powers as Swift involved in such a pitiable labyrinth of
the affections. Who has not heard of Stella (Esther
Johnson), of Swift's 'little language,' of the 'only a
woman's hair' incident? Esther Johnson was the
daughter of a merchant who died young. Her mother
was known to the sister of Sir William Temple, and
this is how Mrs Johnson, in the capacity of housekeeper,
came to live with her daughter at Moor Park, Temple's
place. The girl was a little over eight when Swift first
came to Temple. She grew to be a beautiful, graceful, and
agreeable young woman. 'Her hair was blacker than a
raven, and every feature of her face in "perfection."'
Nor was her character less admirable, if we may trust
the tutor who taught her to write, guided her education,
and came to regard her with an affection which was at
once the happiness and the misery of his life.

Years passed, and another character enters the drama.
Abelard wins the affections of another Héloïse. Her
name was Hester, the daughter of a Mrs Vanhomrigh,
with whom Swift was on terms of such intimacy that
when he was in London he kept his best gown and
periwig' at her house, and frequently dined there, out
of mere listlessness,' as he wrote to Stella. A full
account of the relations between Miss Vanhomrigh and
Swift is given in the remarkable love-poem called
Cadenus (which means of course *Decanus*) *and Vanessa.*
Vanessa, Swift tells us, united masculine accomplishments to feminine grace. The fashionable fops who
tried to entertain her with the tattle of the day had no
charm for her. Swift behaved to Vanessa as a father
might behave to a daughter. He was flattered, however,
that a girl of eighteen, of beauty and accomplishments,

'sighed for a gown of forty-four,' and he did not stop to weigh the consequences.

The removal of Vanessa to Ireland, partly no doubt to be near Swift, as Stella had gone before—her irrepressible passion, which no coldness or neglect could extinguish—her life of deep seclusion, only relieved by the occasional visits of Swift, each of which she commemorated by planting with her own hands a laurel in the garden where they met—her agonising remonstrances, when all her devotion and her offerings had failed, are touching beyond expression.

It does not appear that Swift encouraged Vanessa. Indeed, her ardour was exceedingly inconvenient. He was grieved and perplexed that she should continue to write passionate letters to him. His letters imply embarrassment, and, for the most part, take a lighter tone; he suggests his universal panacea of exercise, tells her to read diverting books, and generally gives advice more judicious than comforting.

At last the collision between Swift's two slaves, which he greatly dreaded, came about in this way. Vanessa wrote, it is said, a letter to Stella, and asked whether she was his wife. Stella replied that she was, and forwarded Vanessa's letter to Swift. He instantly rode to the residence of the unhappy Vanessa; entered her room, 'silent, but awful in his looks'; threw down her letter on the table, and rode back to Dublin. He had struck Vanessa's death-blow. She died soon afterwards, her death no doubt being hastened by her hopes being disappointed, and by the unrestrained wrath of him for whose sake she had indulged them. The story of the last fatal interview has been denied, but, whatever be the facts, Swift had reason enough for bitter regret, if not for deep remorse.

Even Stella, though believed by her friends to have been ultimately united to Swift, died without any public recognition of the tie. They were married, it is said, at midnight in a little house at the bottom of the deanery

garden. He would not let her take his name; they never
lived in the same house; they were never alone together
from the day they were married.

A story is told (on slight evidence) that Delany went
to Archbishop King's library about the time of the
supposed marriage. As he entered, Swift rushed out
with distracted countenance. King was in tears, and
said to Delany: 'You have just met the most unhappy
man on earth; but on the subject of his wretchedness
you must never ask a question.' We, too, may refrain
from asking questions about the love affairs of one who
seems to have been constitutionally incapable of being
happy himself, or of making another happy; for not
one of the theories on the subject quite explains the
facts.

When death removed Stella from Swift, and he was left
alone to think of what he had lost, he described her as
'the truest, most virtuous, and valuable friend that I, or
perhaps any other person, was ever blessed with.' The
tenderness of which his attachment to Stella had been
the strongest symptom, deeply as it had struck its roots
into his nature, withered into cynicism. But a lock of
Stella's hair is said to have been found in Swift's desk
when his own fight was ended, and on the paper in
which it was wrapped were written words that have
become proverbial for the burden of pathos that
their forced brevity seems to hide—'Only a woman's
hair.' It is for each reader to read his own meaning
into them.

Because the Reverend Laurence Sterne, author of
Tristram Shandy and *A Sentimental Journey*, made
anxious preparations for his wife and daughter when
they were coming to meet him in France, and never
seems to have stinted them in money, his latest biographer concludes that 'Yorick' was a good and
thoughtful husband. This is as contrary to the received
opinion as it is, we think, to the truth. There was
certainly one marriage vow which Sterne did not keep.

He did not forsake all others and keep only unto his wife, for he was a gay Lothario, and had always, as he said himself, some Dulcinea in his head. There was his 'witty widow,' 'Lady P——,' the 'Toulouse' lady, and many others.

He married a Miss Lumley of Staffordshire, for whom he pretended the deepest devotion; but the devotion be-- fore very long was transferred to Catherine Formantel, or Fourmantelle, who died in a lunatic asylum, and whose memory is perpetuated in the Maria of the *Sentimental Journey*. To her 'Yorick' used to send sweetmeats and honey, with the message that neither of them was so sweet as herself. She was his 'Dear, dear Kitty,' for 'a squeeze' of whose hand 'he would have given a guinea.'

Mrs Sterne, who was drawn in Mrs Shandy, was disagreeably candid, and declared herself happier without Sterne; but the latter ought not to have told his 'dear Kitty' that there was 'but one obstacle,' *i.e.* his wife, to his happiness.

The next great amour after 'Kitty' was given up of this man whose head (he had no heart) 'was spoilt by the incense of the great, as his stomach was by their *ragoûts*,' was Eliza Draper, the wife of a Bombay lawyer, who was about to sail to India. To her he wrote : 'Talking of widows, pray Eliza, if ever you are such, do not think of giving yourself to some wealthy nabob, because I design to marry you myself. My wife cannot live long, and I know not the woman I should like for her substitute so well as yourself.'

How many have laughed over the love-letters which Sterne wrote when courting Miss Lumley—'My L'— which might have come from the pen of the lovelorn Werther ! Copies of these letters were taken due care of, put by for years, and destined to do double service. After making some suitable changes and variations, Sterne actually sent the same letters to the fair 'Bramine,' Mrs Draper, the divine Eliza. This cold-blooded second edition of love-letters for another person was made, either because the author was too indolent to compose new ones, or because he thought that they were in a more genuine strain than he could afterwards tune himself to. It reminds us of Lord Byron, who found writing love-letters very troublesome work, and copied his out of *Les Liaisons Dangereuses*. Whenever a fresh inamorata appeared on the scene, she unconsciously received facsimiles of previous epistles.

But to return to Sterne. What made his conduct especially abominable was the handsome way he was treated by Miss Lumley before and after her marriage. At one time her ill-health, which her relations feared might end in consumption, seemed likely to prevent her marrying. Accordingly, one evening when Sterne was sitting with her, she said: 'My dear Laurey, I can never be yours, for I verily believe I have not long to live; but I have left you every shilling of my fortune.' Becoming stronger, she did marry, and no matter how badly Sterne treated her, she never ceased to love him.

In the letter which Rev. Rowland Hill wrote to Miss Tudway proposing that she should marry 'a poor worm in the character of a minister of Christ,' he warned her that as an itinerant preacher he would have to be frequently away from home, and would be a 'despised pilgrim' for his once 'despised Master.' They enjoyed— yes, enjoyed—a union of nearly sixty years, and never in a single instance did Mrs Hill 'suffer personal convenience or inclination to impede such movements as her husband considered it his duty to make.' With peculiar tact she controlled his ardent nature without checking his usefulness or activity. Many stories told of Rowland Hill's humorous sayings and doings are untrue. They amused himself as much as any one, and he said, 'I wonder at people's invention'; but when told it had been reported that he had made some remarks in public on Mrs Hill's dress, he exclaimed with indignation:

'It is an abominable untruth—derogatory to my character as a Christian and a gentleman; they would make me out a bear.'

William Carey, 'the most extensive translator of the Bible and civiliser of India,' had a wife who was deficient in education, intellectually inferior, and out of harmony with his tastes. During the last twelve years of life she lost her reason, but never did reproach or complaint escape the missionary's lips. As a tender nurse or guardian, he watched over her many a time when 'he would fain have lingered at his desk, or sought the scanty sleep which his jealous devotion to his Master's business allowed him.' But if Carey's first marriage was unhappy, the second one with Charlotte Emelia, the only child of the Chevalier de Rhumohr, was just the reverse. She was especially talented in learning languages, and made herself acquainted with Bengali that she might be as a mother to the native Christian families. Of a cheerful mind, and full of resources for the employment of her time, she did not allow herself to fret at her enfeebled health. This, however, became worse and worse, and she died, after giving to her husband thirteen years of great domestic happiness.

CHAPTER XIV

MORE LOVE AND DIVINITY

THE only outlet Archbishop Whately allowed himself for his inmost feelings was his common-place book, and in it he remarked, in the year 1820, 'Happiness must, I conclude from conjecture, be a calm and serious feeling.' The following year he added in a note in Latin, 'I proved it, thank God ! July 18th'—his wedding day. His first living, Halesworth, in Suffolk, disagreed with his wife's health. Several times her life was in danger; and more than once Whately's medical knowledge, singular presence of mind, and promptness of action, were called into play, both in her case and in that of a sister, who had come to nurse her and been herself seized with typhus fever.

Mrs Whately was a most sympathetic companion to her husband. She lived, worked, and rested on the strength of the Lord Jesus Christ, and yet she was clever and able to converse on many subjects which some good people would have been afraid of, or would have considered too abstruse to be interesting.

The common sense with which Whately was well supplied was never so conspicuous as in his home life. He greatly objected, for instance, to teach his children to learn by rote what they did not understand; remarking that to teach thus mechanically, in the hope that the children would afterwards find out the meaning of what they had learned, was to make them 'swallow their food first and chew it afterwards.'

'When Mrs Whately and I first married,' he observed many years later, 'one of the first things we agreed upon was, that should Providence send us children, we should never teach them anything that they did not understand.'

'Not even their prayers, my lord?' asked the person addressed.

'No, not even their prayers,' he replied.

We are all more or less familiar with the description which Dean Stanley has given of Dr Arnold at home. We can almost hear his cheerful voice as he goes before breakfast through the headmaster's house, calling up the several members of his family. We know that he never worked so well or so happily as when surrounded by his children, or liked any recreation so much as a 'skirmish' with them over the country, except, perhaps, a quiet walk beside his wife's pony. It was what he called 'the rare, the unbroken, the almost awful happiness' of his domestic life that made him what he was, and enabled him to reform the system of public schools in England.

Anna Delicia was only eighteen years of age when Dean Hook married her, but 'beneath her girlish playfulness and sparkling vivacity of manner, there was a deep fund of sound practical wisdom and earnest piety.' In her husband's household she was 'a regulating, controlling principle; and without her it is probable he never would have become what he was, or have accomplished the things which he did.'

Another Dean who was very happy in married life was Alford. He married his cousin, who had grown up with him from childhood. When he was only fifteen years of age he wrote to her on the occasion of her confirmation, to explain the serious nature of the engagement she had entered into. When they were betrothed the young lady pointed out 'certain peculiarities of character' which she considered required alteration in Alford, and he thought her his 'best earthly friend' for doing so. Even in their love-letters the serious young people tried to learn and teach Biblical Greek. After marriage the bride came down every morning to the bridegroom's study 'with her bundle of books to be tutorised, with health and happiness on her rosy cheeks.'

Alford was a wonderfully kind father. A letter to his daughter Mary contains the following words: 'I feel and know that I am often hasty and wayward to dear Alice and you, and that my manner and words discourage and grieve you. This is very sinful in me; and when you see it, you see that your father on earth is not like your Father in heaven, on whose brow there is never a frown, who never is wayward or hasty.'

Dr Whewell, Master of Trinity College, Cambridge, lost his wife after fourteen years of wedded bliss; and we are told that for months after her death he 'used to be seen going alone to the cemetery to weep there.' But about three years later he married again, his second wife being Lady Affleck, the widow of Sir Gilbert Affleck. At her death, seven years later, the grief and despair of her husband are said to have been pitiable to see. Both wives were well suited for the graceful performance of the social and other duties of their position; and of the second, Whewell might also have said what he did say of the first: 'She shared our thoughts from hour to hour. And if I did anything good and right and wise, it was because I had goodness and right-mindedness and wisdom to prompt and direct me.'

The following is told of Whewell, but modifications of the story are saddled on other divines who were less good-looking than their wives. One day as the Professor and Mrs Whewell were getting into their carriage, he overheard some undergraduates remark, 'There go beauty and the beast.' He turned sharply round and said, 'Gentlemen, you may say what you like about me; but I won't have my wife called a beast.'

Pusey had not reached his eighteenth year when he met and fell in love with Miss Maria Catherine Barber, who was then seventeen. His parents disapproved, and he was thrown into a condition of despair, which made him fear for a time that he would lose his reason. It was not until after nine years that the course of true love began to run smoothly. Then, at Cheltenham, on the last day of September, 1827, the young theologian asked Miss Barber to marry him, and was accepted. To the last, the memory of this interview remained with Dr Pusey.

Not many years before his death the gift of a lemon-scented verbena plant from his daughter caused him to burst into tears. 'When I asked your mother to marry me,' he explained, 'I offered her a sprig of verbena, and I always associate it with her.'

Even a delicate wife may make an earthly paradise for her husband, as Keble, author of *The Christian Year*, discovered. She entered into all his hopes for the

Church, and greatly helped him in his work.   She was, he said, his conscience, his memory, and his common sense.

The Reverend Sydney Smith had no riches except his own fine character and great talent when he married Miss Pybus, who was equally impecunious, the school-friend of his sister.

One day before their marriage he ran into the room where his *fiancée* was, flung into her lap six small tea-spoons, which, 'from much wear, had become the ghosts of their former selves,' and said : 'There, Kate, you lucky girl, I give you all my fortune !'

Whether this was or was not done to symbolise that they were to be 'spoons' after marriage as well as before it, they certainly did love each other until death separated them.   Notwithstanding this, Sydney Smith was often attacked by low spirits, a malady to which brilliant humorists are especially liable.

A lady once congratulated Mrs Sydney on having such a merry companion as Mr Sydney Smith, to which she replied : 'Oh, if you knew Sydney as well as I do, you would not say that.'

It may interest lady readers to know that the money required to buy furniture and other things necessary for setting up house was procured by Mrs Sydney Smith. She sold for five hundred pounds a pearl necklace, almost the only piece of jewellery she possessed.   Two or three years afterwards she saw it for sale in a shop window and asked the price.   The answer was fifteen hundred pounds.

A present, not less interesting than Sydney Smith's six spoons, was made to the lady of his choice by Dr Wordsworth, Bishop of Lincoln, when he was Head-master of Harrow.   He sent to her the nine gold medals won by him at Winchester and Cambridge.   Their married life has been described as as near perfection as anything on this side of Eden could be.   Their union was so complete that the mutual understanding seemed like an instinct, and their children can never remember a day or even an hour when, even in surface matters, the perfect harmony was infringed upon.' Indeed, the Bishop used often laughingly to say of his wife that he wished it put on their tombstone that they were never reconciled.

Years before leaving the Church of England, Cardinal Manning married Caroline Sargent, sister of the wife of Wilberforce, Bishop of Winchester. After the death in four years' time of his beautiful wife, he was unable to dwell upon the past except in direct acts of devotion, and got relief only in full employment. On the second anniversary of his wife's death, her mother, who was staying with him, entered his study and found him 'in an agony of tears.' They went together to a service, as it was the eve of St James's day. 'As we were going into the church, Henry said, "My dear friend Gladstone is just now going to be married"; and upon my saying something of the strange differences in the lot of those we love, he said, in the most plaintive voice, "Yes, but it all leads to the same blessed end."'

Charles Kingsley met his future wife when he was only twenty years of age. He was at the time full of doubts about religion, and his face, with its unsatisfied, hungering look, bore witness to the state of his mind. He told her his doubts and she told him her faith, and the former were dispelled by the latter. Like many other eminent men, he attributed his success to the sympathy and influence of his wife, saying that but for her he never could have become a writer.

Writing to Mrs Kingsley from the seaside, where he had gone in search of health, he says: 'This place is perfect; but it seems a dream and imperfect without you. Absence quickens love into consciousness. I never before felt the loneliness of being without the beloved being whose every look and word and motion are the keynotes of my life. People talk of love ending at the altar. . . . Fools! I lay at the window all morning, thinking of nothing but home; how I long for it !'

Sickness and other crosses visited the home of Kingsley and his wife, but these crosses they took up together in the right spirit, and helped each other to bear them. Sympathising with a husband's anxiety, Kingsley once wrote to a friend : 'I believe one never understands the blessed mystery of marriage till one has nursed a sick wife, nor understands, either, what treasures women are.' A little before this good husband died his wife became very ill. On being told that her life was in great danger, he said : 'My own death-warrant was signed with those words.' He was warned that his recovery depended on the same temperature being kept up in his bedroom, and on his never leaving it; but one day he indiscreetly leapt out of bed, came into his wife's room for a few minutes, and taking her hand in his, said : 'This is heaven; don't speak.' But after a short time a severe fit of coughing came on; he could say nothing more, and they never met again. For a few days the sick husband and wife wrote to each other in pencil, but it became too painful, and the letters ceased. A few days after he died.

'God and woman are the rocks upon which most men split.' This saying of Robertson of Brighton was illustrated to some extent in his own case. After a too short acquaintaneeship he married a lady who was incapable of understanding either him or his work, or of making home happy.

A paradise on earth was lost by Wilberforce, Bishop of Winchester, when his wife died. Though he was a widower for thirty-two years, he never forgot her. At his own funeral might be seen the wreath of lilies which his hand had only a few weeks before hung over the cross that marks her grave. 'My happiest time,' he used to say, 'was when I was rector at Brighstone, with my dear wife and my children all about me.' Nothing in his biography is more touching than the references to his domestic affections. On his introduction to Court, his prevailing sentiment is that he had lost *her* to whom, on his return home, he might describe the scene. After her death, returning home from any place was always rather painful. When she was with him, 'if I went home to her, it was beyond all words. If I went home *with* her, I got apart to see her meet her children; and now—— !'

One day an uncle of Catharine, daughter of Archdeacon Spooner, said jokingly to her, 'I suppose you are making these slippers for Mr Tait.' This was a curious anticipation, as at the time Miss Spooner and Mr Tait had only casually met and had no thoughts of each other. They did not meet again for years, but then they did think of each other. The uncle married them, and at the wedding quietly remarked, 'So: Kitty, you were after all making those slippers for Mr Tait.'

Speaking of his wife when he was Dean of Carlisle, and before their loss of five children within five weeks, Archbishop Tait says : 'The chief happiness of her domestic life was in the children, who, one after another, were born to give brightness to the dingy old deanery. Each day while we were in residence she would sally forth in our open car with the whole body of them, when an interval came from the work of the day. In spring-time and in summer we would encamp some four or five miles beyond the smoke of the city, and wander with them, seeking wild flowers in the woods or loitering pleasantly by the riverside. And then, as the elder of them grew up, what pleasant hours she spent in reading with them and how wonderfully she was able to interest their growing intelligence in all the good works which she herself did for Christ's sake.'

In 1843 David Livingstone wrote to a friend: 'There's no outlet for me when I begin to think of marriage but that of sending home an advertisement to the *Evangelical Magazine*, and if I get very old, it must be for some decent sort of widow. In the meantime, I am too busy to think of anything of the kind.'

E

He had not, however, to marry by advertisement, for when he returned to England for a rest he met Mary Moffat, who was born in Africa, the daughter of an honoured missionary, herself familiar with missionary life, and gifted with the winning manner and the ready helping hand that were so peculiarly adapted for this work. They were married and went to Africa, and for eight years worked happily together. Then her health and his expeditions caused many sad separations. Mrs Livingstone, however, had the satisfaction of being with her husband when she died at Shupanga. The loss of such a wife was a heavy blow, for no one could have been better fitted to cheer up lonely, isolated work.

'In our intercourse,' wrote Livingstone after her death, 'in private there was more than would be thought by some a decorous amount of merriment and play. I said to her a few days before her fatal illness, "We old bodies ought now to be more sober, and not play so much." "Oh, no," said she, "you must always be as playful as you have always been; I would not like you to be as grave as some folks I have seen."'

Dean Stanley was wont to say that he had never really lived until his marriage. Going soon after this event to visit his friend, Hugh Pearson, at Sonning, he went on the box of the fly.

'I see you've got Lady Augusta Bruce inside,' said the driver. 'I remember her very well at Windsor.'

'Not Lady Augusta Bruce; she is Lady Augusta Stanley now. She is my wife.'

'Well, then, I do wish you joy; for your wife is just the best woman in England.'

Highly delighted was the Dean with this; and well he might be, for cabbies are generally shrewd judges of character.

Indeed there could not have been a more suitable marriage than that between Dean Stanley and Lady Augusta Stanley. It was said of her that she united

the warm heart of a woman to the instinct of a statesman.' When death parted the Dean from her

> Whose smile had made the dark world bright,
> Whose love had made all duty light,

he could find no fitter words in which to describe her
supporting love than that 'her character, though cast in
another mould, remained to him, with that of his
mother, the brightest and most sacred vision of his
earthly experience.'

Mrs Alexander, wife of the Archbishop of Armagh,
was known as the writer of hymns that are everywhere
sung by children. Her husband also wrote poetry,
which, however, he never thought worthy to be compared to that of his wife. Perhaps, however, the sympathetic matrimonial life they lived together was the
best poem either produced. Bishop Wilberforce, among
many others, considered them an ideal couple. They
were real chums, if it be not audacious to speak in this
way of an archbishop and his wife.

CHAPTER XV

THE LOVE AFFAIRS OF FOUR GREAT PREACHERS

THE wooing of George Whitefield was scarcely human. He wrote to the parents of the girl he preferred, when he found, 'upon many accounts,' that it was his 'duty to marry': 'This comes like Abraham's servant to Rebekah's relations to know whether you think your daughter, Miss E., is a proper person to engage in such an undertaking? If so, whether you will be pleased to give me leave to propose marriage unto her? You need not be afraid of sending me a refusal; for, I bless God, if I know anything of my own heart, I am free from that foolish passion which the world calls love. I write only because I believe it is the will of God that I should alter my state; but your denial will fully convince me that your daughter is not the person appointed by God for me.'

In a letter to the young lady herself this tepid lover asked her if she could trust in Him who feeds the ravens, and whether, having a husband, she could be in all respects as though she had none. 'I make no great profession to you, because I believe you think me sincere. The passionate expressions which carnal courtiers use, I think, ought to be avoided by those that would marry in the Lord. I can only promise, by the help of God, to keep my matrimonial vow, and to do what I can towards helping you forward in the great work of your salvation. If you think marriage will be in any way prejudicial to your better part, be so kind as to send me a denial.' The reply which he received informed him that the lady was in a seeking state only, and surely, he said, that would not do : he must have one that was

full of faith and the Holy Ghost. Such an one he
thought he had found in a widow at Abergavenny, by
name James, who was between thirty and forty, and
neither rich nor beautiful, but a despised follower of the
Lamb.

On the day before his wedding, writing to Lord
Levin, Whitefield remarked : 'God calls me to retirement, being to enter the marriage state to-morrow.
I am persuaded your Lordship will not fail to pray,
that we may, like Zacharias and Elizabeth, walk in
all the ordinances and commandments of the Lord
blameless.'

Notwithstanding this good beginning, the marriage
was not a happy one, and the death of his wife set
Whitefield's mind 'much at liberty.' Four days after
the event he preached a funeral sermon, the text of
which was : 'For the creature was made subject to
vanity.'

When he married, the evangelist had said that his wife
was a true child of God, and one who would not attempt
to hinder his work for the world, and this character was
nothing more than she deserved. Never did she give
Whitefield occasion to say, 'I have married a wife, and
therefore I cannot come,' though it was hard to be left
alone before the honeymoon was over. As long as she
had strength to do so she accompanied him on his
preaching journeys, and on more than one occasion
seemed to be the better man of the two, so to speak.
One of these occasions occurred when they were on a
voyage to Georgia. The ship was threatened by an
enemy. Guns were mounted and chains put about the
masts. The wildest confusion prevailed, and Whitefield
was forced to acknowledge that he was 'naturally a
coward'; but his wife 'set about making cartridges,'
and did her utmost in having all things ready for the
'fire and smoke.' On another occasion, when her husband was surrounded by a mob, and began to show
symptoms of alarm as the stones flew in all directions

she, standing by his side, cried with true heroism, 'Now, George, play the man for God.'

'My brother,' said Charles Wesley, 'was, I think, born for the benefit of knaves.' The story of some of John Wesley's love affairs supports this opinion. His first love was a Miss Betty Kirkman, about whom he speaks with fervour : 'On this spot she sat,' 'Along this path she walked,' 'Here she showed that lovely instance of condescension which gave new beauty to the charming arbour and meadows.'

About five years afterwards Wesley formed another attachment, this time with a Miss Sophia Causton. 'Miss Sophy,' as he called her, made herself very agreeable, even laying aside all gaudy attire, which he disliked, and dressing in white. But though the revivalist thought that he liked 'Sophy,' he was so little in love that he laid the matter before the elders of the Moravian Church. They replied : 'We advise you to proceed no further in this business,' and Wesley said : 'The will of the Lord be done.' Sophia did not break her heart, but very soon married a friend of her late lover, an event which Wesley thus entered in his diary : 'Saturday, March 12. God being very merciful to me, my friend performed what I could not.'

Grace Murray, a sailor's widow, was thirty years old when she nursed John Wesley, as she used to do the other preachers when sick, through an illness that overtook him at Newcastle. She managed the Orphan House, and had a hundred members in her class. Wesley made her an offer of marriage, to which she replied : 'This is too great a blessing for me; I can't tell how to believe it. This is all I could have wished for under heaven.' She travelled with him through a good part of England and Ireland, and was useful beyond description. 'She examined all the women in the smaller Societies, settled the female bands, visited the sick, and prayed with the penitent. She anticipated all Wesley's wants, acted as his monitor when she thought she saw anything amiss in his behaviour,' etc., etc.

All this time the poor lady was distracted by the attentions of another lover, a preacher of Wesley's, concerning whom she said to the chief : 'I love you a thousand times better than ever I loved John Bennet in my life, but I am afraid if I don't marry him he'll run mad.'

Still, she would have married Wesley, and risked Bennet's madness, but for the interference of Charles Wesley. This meddling marplot, having himself married a Welsh squire's daughter, could not allow his brother to marry one who had been a servant. He said that if such a misalliance took place, their preachers would leave and the Societies would be scattered. John Wesley refused to be dismayed, whereupon Charles rode to Newcastle and visited this dangerously attractive woman. 'Grace Murray,' he exclaimed, 'you have broken my heart !' Explanations followed, and Grace Murray, thinking that if she married Wesley, Bennet would go mad, the Wesley family would be broken up, and the Methodist Societies ruined, married Bennet within a week.   John Wesley was furious. For ten years it seemed as if God had been preparing a fellow-labourer for him, and now she was taken from him. He said : 'I fasted and prayed and strove all I could, but the sons of Zeruiah were too hard for me. The whole world fought against me, but, above all, my own familiar friend.' This brotherly action deprived John Wesley of one who might have been to Methodism what Mrs Booth was to the Salvation Army, and condemned him to twenty years' matrimonial misery with a termagant.

The termagant was a widow, by name Vizelle, with four children and an independent fortune; but Wesley had this settled upon herself, and refused to have any command over it. It was agreed also, before their marriage, that he should not preach one sermon nor travel one mile the less on that account. 'If I thought

I should,' said he, 'as well as I love you, I would never see your face more.'

Instead of being a ministering angel and an inspiring genius, sharing all her husband's aspirations and efforts, Mrs Wesley allowed the meanest jealousies to occupy her attention. She would drive a hundred miles to ascertain what he was doing, and who was with him when he entered a town. She opened his letters, and listened at the door of his study when any one called upon business. She made him feel that his house was *not* his castle, and that when he went abroad he was only a prisoner at large. She even occasionally relieved her feelings by acts of personal violence. ' John Hampson,' writes Mr Telford, 'one of Wesley's preachers, told his son that he once went into a room in the North of Ireland, where he found Mrs Wesley foaming with rage. Her husband was on the floor. She had been dragging him about by his hair, and still held in her hand some of the locks that she had pulled out of his head. Hampson found it hard to constrain himself when he saw this pitiable sight. More than once she laid violent hands upon him, and tore those venerable locks which had suffered sufficiently from the ravages of Time.'

If any one wishes to see the pathetic picture of a hen-pecked saint, he should turn to a letter of John Wesley given by his biographers, in which, after ten years of matrimonial misery, the methodical man sets forth with the precision of a Puritan sermon the various points of her conduct that ought to be changed 'in the fear of God, and in tender love to her soul.'

It is too long to quote with its ten statements of griev-ance, but here are one or two of them : 'I dislike,' writes the tormented one, 'not having the command of my own house, not being at liberty to invite even my nearest relations so much as to drink a dish of tea with-out disobeying *you*. . . I dislike your talking against me behind my back, and that every day, and almost

every hour of the day, making my faults (real or supposed) the standing topic of your conversation.'

Even a worm, however, will turn, and in one letter
Wesley, who was a man and no worm, soundly rebuked
his wife and endeavoured to cultivate in her the grace of
humility. 'Know me,' he wrote, 'and know yourself.
Suspect me no more, asperse me no more, provoke me
no more : do not any longer contend for mastery, for
power, money, or praise : be content to be a private,
insignificant person, known and loved by God and me.
Attempt no more to abridge me of my liberty, which I
claim by the laws of God and men : leave me to be
governed by God and my own conscience; then shall I
govern you with gentle sway, even as Christ the Church.'
He reminded her that she had laid to his charge things
that he knew not, under the pretence of vindicating her
own character; 'whereas,' said he, 'of what importance
is your character to mankind? If you were buried just
now, or if you had never lived, what loss would it be
to the cause of God?'

Still, as one of the hymns of the Revival says, 'The
bitter is sweet, and the medicine is food.' Wesley
repeatedly told a friend that he believed God overruled
this prolonged sorrow for his good, and that if Mrs
Wesley had been a better wife he might have been
unfaithful to his great work, and might have sought
too much to please her.

Something ought also to be said from Mrs Wesley's point
of view. It was not an easy thing to live with such a tire-
less enthusiast as John Wesley, especially when he was a
second husband and the marriage was barren of children.

Then Wesley's habit of corresponding with miscel-
laneous women would have displeased wives with dispositions less jealous than that of his own wife. True, the
letters were written in perfect innocency, and to benefit
the recipients, but none the less we can understand Mrs
Wesley's resentment as described in the following letter
to Sarah Ryan, who was at one time housekeeper at the

school at Kingswood: 'Last Friday, after many severe words, my wife left me, vowing she would see me no more. As I had wrote to you the same morning, I began to reason with myself till I almost doubted whether I had done well in writing, or whether I ought to write to you at all. After prayer, that doubt was taken away; yet I was almost sorry that I had written that morning. In the evening, while I was preaching at the chapel, she came into the chamber where I had left my clothes, searched my pockets, and found the letter there which I had finished, but had not sealed. While she read it, God broke her heart; and I afterwards found her in such a temper as I have not seen her in for several years. She has continued in the same ever since. So I think God has given a sufficient answer with regard to our writing to each other.' But he says to the same person, eight years afterwards: 'It has frequently been said, and with some *appearance* of truth, that you endeavour to *monopolise* the affections of all that fall into your hands; that you destroy the nearest and dearest connection they had before, and make them quite cool and indifferent to their most intimate friends. I do not at all speak on my own account; I set myself out of the question : but if there be anything of the kind with regard to other people, I should be sorry both for them and you.'

The fact is, men who, like Whitefield and Wesley, are almost always away from home ought not to marry, for prolonged absence may cause indifference on both sides. Wesley seems to have had no real affection for his wife. This is shown by two entries in his journal. One was when Mrs Wesley left his house and went to her own people. On that occasion he simply wrote, *Non eam reliqui non demisi, non revocabo*—'I have not left her, I have not sent her away, I will not call her back.' When he heard of her death, he wrote : 'I came to London, and was informed that my wife died on Monday. This evening she was buried, though I was not informed of it till a day later.'

Wesley wrote a book called *Thoughts on a Single Life*, in which he advised some 'to remain single for the kingdom of heaven's sake'; 'but the precept,' he adds, 'is not for the many.' It is a pity that he joined 'the many' himself.

It is a relief to turn from the rather wretched love affairs just mentioned to the more human one of a great preacher of our own day. Soon after he reached his twenty-first year, Charles Haddon Spurgeon married 'Susie,' daughter of a friend in Falcon Square, E.C., on January 8th, 1856. Two thousand applicants failed to obtain admission, after the New Park Street Chapel was packed for the ceremony.

That the bridegroom had a high ideal may be seen from the following words which he spoke at the wedding of a friend: 'Marriage is the only thing that has come down to us out of Paradise, and that has something of the paradisiacal state clinging to it. . . . Jesus wrought His first miracle at a wedding, and it was a very significant miracle, turning water into wine, as if to show that life, after marriage, becomes more full, more rich, more exhilarating than it was before. And the golden Book of Revelation closes with a wedding, the marriage of the Lamb ! Just as many a story of fiction winds up, " they were married, and lived happily ever afterwards," so God's great story of fact, the old, old story of Jesus and His love, winds up with a wedding. . . You cannot love your wife too much. I have never yet heard of a man who loved his wife too ardently; I have heard of wives who had been said to be too attentive to their husbands, but I have not met with any such.'

The vexed question of conjugal obedience was by him settled in this characteristic way. Addressing the bride as to her future lord, he said : 'Let him be the head, and do you be the neck, and turn him which way you please.'

What Spurgeon was as a husband may be seen from the following strange but true story told by his wife, who was, for several years after her marriage, a great invalid. Here it is in Mrs Spurgeon's own words :—

'One ever-recurring question, when my dear husband had to leave me in those times of illness, was, "What can I bring you, wifey?" I seldom answered by a *request*, for I had all things richly to enjoy except *health*. But one day, when he put the usual query, I said playfully— for the pain had not taken *all* the fun out of me—"*I should like an opal ring and a piping bullfinch.*" He looked surprised and rather amused, but simply replied : "Ah ! you know I cannot get those for you."

'Two or three days we made merry over my singular choice of desirable articles; but one Thursday evening, on his return from the service at the Tabernacle, he came into my room with such a beaming face and such love-lighted eyes that I knew something had delighted him very much. In his hand he held a tiny box, and I am sure his pleasure exceeded mine as he took from it a beautiful little ring and placed it on my finger. "There is your opal ring, my darling," he said; and then told me of the strange way in which it had come. An old lady, whom he had once seen when she was ill, sent a note to the Tabernacle to say she desired to give Mrs Spurgeon a small present, and could some one be sent to receive it. Mr Spurgeon's private secretary went, and brought the little parcel, which, when opened, was found to contain the opal ring !

'Not long after that I was moved to Brighton, there to pass through a crisis in my life, the result of which would be a restoration to better health—or death. One evening, when my dear husband came from London, he brought a large package with him, and, uncovering it, disclosed a cage containing a lovely piping bullfinch ! . .

'He had been to see a friend of ours, whose husband was sick. She said : ''I want you to take my pet bird to Mrs Spurgeon. His songs are too much for my poor husband in his weak state, and I know that 'Bully' will interest and amuse Mrs Spurgeon in her loneliness,

while you are so much away from her. I would give
him to none but her." . . . With that cage beside him,
the journey to Brighton seemed a very short one; and
when "Bully" piped his pretty song, and took a hemp-
seed as a reward from the lips of his new mistress, there
were eyes with joyful tears in them, and hearts overflowing with praise to God in the little room by the sea
that night.'

The chronic illness of Spurgeon's wife did not prevent
his home from being very happy. 'It was,' says an
intimate friend, 'the abode of perfect peace and tender
affection.' Into his home were born twin sons, and the
observation of their growth was a source of continual
pleasure to the parents. The twins were photographed
at birth and every year afterwards until they came of
age. Included in one frame the twenty-one photo-
graphs were hung up on a wall of his dining-room, and
the great preacher used to say, 'If we could only grow
in grace like that !'

From personal experience the evangelist Dwight L.
Moody has strong opinions about the value of wives, and
thinks that they alone can understand their husbands.
He once said to a man who called himself a 'perfection-
ist,' and professed to have got rid of sin, 'I won't believe
a word of it until I hear it from your wife.'

On the 28th of August, 1862, Mr Moody married Miss
Emma C. Revell, a most helpful assistant in his meet-
ings, and a girl of noble character. A daughter and a
son came to gladden their simple cottage, and there was
no happier home in Chicago. One morning he said to
his wife: 'I have no money, and the house is without
supplies. It looks as if the Lord had had enough of me
in this mission work, and is going to send me back again
to sell boots and shoes.' But very soon two cheques
came, one of ten pounds for himself, and another for his
school.

Six years after his marriage his friends gave him the
lease of a pleasant furnished house. This home had a

welcome for all who sought the true way to live. One day a gentleman called at the office, bringing a young man who had recently come out of prison. The latter shrunk from going into the office, but Mr Moody said, 'Bring him in.' He took him by the hand, told him he was glad to see him, and invited him to his house. When the young man called, Mr Moody introduced him as his friend. When his little daughter came into the room, he said, 'Emma, this is papa's friend.' She went up and kissed him, and the man sobbed aloud.

When she left the room, Mr Moody said, 'What is the matter?'

'Oh, sir,' was the reply, 'I have not had a kiss for years. The last kiss I had was from my mother, and she was dying. I thought I would never have another kiss.'

CHAPTER XVI

LOVE AND LAW

LOVE and Law are often contrasted, and legal studies are generally supposed to be of an unromantic nature. Then we sometimes read speeches in which barristers dissect the passion of love, and ridicule love-letters in a cold-blooded way that makes us fancy that they are not flesh-and-blood mortals. And yet lawyers can fall in love.

Sir Thomas More, when a young man, wrote some beautiful Latin poetry in praise of the bright eyes, snowy neck, and flowing locks of a certain *Cara Eliza-betha*. Then the hideous thought came into his mind that the highest and holiest of human affections was no more than a carnal appetite which was strenuously to be resisted. When at length he had determined, by the advice and direction of his 'ghostly father,' to be a married man, he chose his wife for compassion rather than from love. Mr John Colt, of New Hall, Essex, who happened to meet the young barrister, was so delighted with his company that he invited him to his house, and gave him the choice of any of his daughters, who were 'young gentlewomen of very good carriage, good complexions, and very religiously inclined.' Although he liked the second, or prettiest, best, More married the eldest 'out of a kind compassion, when he thought that it would be a grief and some blemish to the eldest to have a younger sister preferred before her.' Whether or not this conduct was a little too considerate, there is no doubt that the good man did his duty by Jane Colt, as a conscientious tutor might, but something more than this is required in a husband. Still, the marriage was not an unhappy one, but its duration was short. After giving birth to four children, one of whom was that dutiful daughter and noble woman, Margaret Roper, Jane died, leaving the young husband, who had instructed her sedulously, to mourn her sincerely.

More's second choice of a wife was a widow named Alice Middleton, who was attractive neither in appearance nor in manners. Erasmus says that 'though verging on old age, and not of a yielding temper,' she was prevailed upon by More 'to take lessons on the lute, the cithara, the viol, the monochord, and the flute, which she daily practised to him.' No wonder that as a relief from all this effort to 'make herself a lady,' the poor thing should once have gone 'on the rampage' for a week!

If Mrs More was ambitious her ambition was of a low kind. When her husband, by continuing his opposition to Henry VIII., lost the Chancellorship, she taunted him as follows: 'Tilly vally, what will you do, Mr More? will you sit and make goslings in the ashes? My mother hath often said unto me, "It is better to rule than to be ruled."' To which familiar expostulation More's usual reply, muttered in the mildest of humorous voices, was: 'Now, in truth, that is truly said, good wife; for I never found you yet willing to be ruled.'

It must be confessed that More, though a martyr to duty, was sometimes aggravating. Other women besides his wife would have failed to see a joke in the way he announced his resignation of the Chancellorship. The day after he went with his family to Chelsea Church. It had been the custom on these occasions for one of the Chancellor's attendants to go when the service concluded to his wife's pew and say to her, 'Madam, my lord is gone.' On this occasion he went himself to his wife's pew, and making her a low bow, said, 'Madam, my lord is gone.' To divert the ill-humour she displayed at the loss of this dignity, More began to find fault with her dress. She scolded her daughters for not noticing what was wrong; but they affirmed that there was no fault in the dress. More then said, 'Don't you perceive that your mother's nose is somewhat awry?' which caused that lady to retire from him in a passion.

There is recorded a *bon mot* of Sir Thomas on the birth of his son. He had three daughters; his wife was impatient for a son; at last they had one, but not much above an idiot. 'Thou hast wearied God with prayers for a man-child,' said More, 'and He has given thee one who will be always a child.'

This was not as worthy of the good man as the reply he made to his wife when she urged him in the Tower to yield up his scruples of conscience, and, as a consequence, to leave the 'close, filthy prison with rats and mice.'

Having heard her out, More replied with a cheerful countenance, 'I pray thee, good Mistress Alice, tell me one thing.'

'What is it?' she said.

'Is not this house as near Heaven as my own?'

Sir Thomas More was looking toward 'a house not made with hands, eternal in the Heavens.' Mistress Alice had her eye upon their 'right fair house' at Chelsea, as she called it.

One of the favourite maxims of Sir Thomas More was, that every one ought to be as agreeable towards others as possible, and he himself, however wearied he was, upon his return from his professional duties or State cares always found time to interest himself in his home life.

Even in affliction he was merry. When the house at Chelsea, already mentioned, with its offices and granaries, had been almost destroyed by fire, he writes to his wife to be of good cheer and to take all the household with her to church, and there thank God for what He had given and what He had left. If poor persons had lost anything by the fire she was to recompense them, and not discharge any servant until he had found another place, and lastly, she and her children were to be 'merry in God.'

Two great judges of Elizabeth's reign, Bacon and Coke, were not greater rivals in law and politics than they were in love. Sir William Hatton's widow, who was a cousin of Bacon, rejected his suit in favour of Coke, though against the latter there were 'seven objections—his six children and himself.' She made Coke as miserable as his first 'most beloved and most excellent' wife had made him happy, refusing even to take his name, separating from him, doing everything to vex and annoy him, and teaching his child to rebel against him.

It is said that to this fact the law world owes the celebrated commentary on Littleton. The lady's bad temper made Coke glad to escape to his chambers and devote his time to writing. At least two other lawyers—Chief Justice Holt, who lived in the following century, and Jeffrey Gilbert, Baron of the Exchequer, who died in 1726—are reputed to have laid the foundation of their success in hours of banishment from hearths made miserable by scolding wives.

One of the reasons Bacon gave in a letter to Secretary Cecil for asking that knighthood might be conferred upon him was 'because I have found out an alderman's daughter, a handsome maiden to my liking.'

In his essay on Love 'the wisest, brightest, meanest of mankind' says: 'You may observe that amongst all the great and worthy persons whereof the memory remaineth, either ancient or recent, there is not one that hath been transported to the mad degree of love— which shows that great spirits and great business do keep out this weak passion. There was never proud man thought so absurdly well of himself as the lover doth of the person loved; and therefore it is well said that it is impossible to love and to be wise.'

In reference to the alderman's daughter, Alice Barnham, Bacon did not at all depart from his notions of what was becoming in 'a great and worthy person ; for instead of offering incense to Venus, he was only considering a scheme to make his pot boil. In spite of his economical habits, he had contracted some debts which were troublesome to him; and it was uncertain whether there might be an opening for him in the office of Solicitor-General during the life of the Queen, who was now labouring under the infirmities of age. He therefore made an attempt to restore his position by matrimony.

Miss Barnham had a moderate fortune, but this was counterbalanced by a troublesome father and mother, whose lawsuits vexed the later years of their son-in-law. Otherwise his domestic life, entered on with the calmness and business precision of a man almost perfectly passionless, seems to have been a smooth one. The marriage was celebrated with characteristic pomp on the 10th of May, 1606. On the morning after, Dudley Carleton wrote of the bridegroom : 'He was clad from top to toe in purple, and hath made himself and his wife such store of fine raiment of cloth of silver and gold that it draws deep into her portion.'

Jeffreys, the infamous judge of the Bloody Circuit, was declared by women to be irresistible. Tall, well-shaped, and endowed by nature with a pleasant countenance and agreeable manners, he was one of the most fascinating men of his time. He was still poor, unknown, and struggling with difficulties when he induced an heiress to accept his suit. The union was forbidden by the lady's father, and she herself when it came to the point would not elope. Jeffreys consoled himself by marrying her confidential friend and paid companion, who had been discharged by the enraged father of the heiress for having acted as the confidante of the clandestine lovers. The second wife of Jeffreys was much inferior to his first.

William Cowper, the first earl of his line, was reclaimed from dissipation and a disreputable connection by an early marriage which he contracted a year before

his call to the Bar. Having lived happily with his good
wife for twenty years, he married, in 1706, the year
after her death, which occurred just before his elevation
to the Woolsack, the beautiful Mary Clavering, lady of
the bed-chamber to the Princess of Wales. Her diary
and their published letters show the loving terms on
which they lived. Here is one entry in the diary :
'After dinner we went to Sir Godfrey Kneller's to see
a picture of my lord, which he is drawing, and is the
best that was ever done for him; it is for my drawing-
room, and in the same posture that he watched me so
many weeks in my great illness.'

Simon Harcourt may be said to have owed his elevation to the Woolsack to an early marriage, which at the
time seemed to his friends to be little short of madness.

Judging from the quantity of rhyme written by Henry
Erskine, afterwards Lord Advocate of Scotland, in
pressing his suit with Christina Fullerton, whose
'glances were as gentle as the music of her lute,' his
engagement must have been unusually long, and was
apparently beset with repeated obstacles. When at
last the young couple did marry they were very happy,
for there was perfect confidence between them. This
confidence sometimes caused interruptions which many
men less busy than Erskine would have resented as
inopportune. As the learned lawyer sat late into the
night, working at his cases and marshalling the arguments which should extinguish his adversaries on the
morrow, often his wife would enter his study and pro-
pound deep questions of domestic management. Once
she actually awoke her husband in the dead of night
with the question, 'Harry, lovey, where's your white
waistcoat?' And yet the lady was not a fool, but
exceedingly clever. After the loss of more than one
child she fell into bad health, and, though ever kind and
gentle, ultimately became a confirmed invalid.

The parents of the young lady to whom Lord Mans-
field—then simply William Murray—was attached,

wished her to marry a certain squire of broad acres, and she, 'blind to wit and worth,' did unite herself to the 'rich dullness' of this 'son of earth.' For a long time the young barrister seemed broken-hearted. At length briefs began to come in, owing to his success in a sensational lawsuit, and he obtained the hand of Lady Elizabeth Finch, a daughter of the Earl of Winchelsea. From the 20th of November, 1738, the day on which he married this lady, his passion for his former love was only remembered by him to illustrate the maxim which he inculcated, that a first love may be succeeded by a second as pure and as ardent.

In the year 1774 the witty Irish lawyer, John Philpot Curran, married, and the year afterwards was called to the Bar. He thus describes his domestic circumstances when his first considerable brief came to him: 'My wife and children were the chief furniture of my apartments, and as to my rent, it stood pretty much the same chance of its liquidation with the national debt. Mrs Curran, however, was a barrister's lady, and what she wanted in wealth she was well determined should be supplied by dignity. The landlady, on the other hand, had no other idea of any gradation except that of pounds, shillings, and pence. I walked out one morning to avoid the perpetual altercations on the subject; with my mind you may imagine in no very enviable temperament, I fell into the gloom to which, from my infancy, I had been occasionally subject. I had a family for whom I had no dinner, and a landlady for whom I had no rent. I had gone abroad in despondence—I returned home almost in desperation. When I opened the door of my study—where Lavater alone could have found a library —the first object which presented itself was an immense folio of a brief, twenty golden guineas wrapped up beside it, and the name of old Bob Lyons marked upon the back of it.'

Curran was extremely sensitive, and domestic misfortunes rendered his home unhappy. He had a favourite little daughter, who was a sort of musical prodigy.   She died at the age of twelve, and was buried in the midst of a small grove just adjoining his garden.   A little rustic memorial was laid over her, and often has the father been seen, ' the tears chasing each other down his cheeks,' to point to his daughter's monument and wish to be 'with her at rest.'

Curran used to say that when he addressed a court for the first time, if he had not felt his wife and children tugging at his gown, he would have thrown up his brief and relinquished the profession of a lawyer.

CHAPTER XVII

MORE LOVE AND LAW

CONSIDERING the ungainly figure and awkward address of the young barrister afterwards Lord Ellenborough, it showed a good deal of assurance for him to aspire to the hand of Miss Towry, who had a great many suitors and had refused several good offers. He asked her father, who was a Commissioner in the Navy, for permission to pay his addresses to the fashionable beauty. Consent was given, but the young lady was not so easily won. Though her admirer was the most rising lawyer in Westminster Hall, she three times refused to marry him.

At last, however, the charm of his conversation and the persuasion of her relations induced her to change her mind and accept him. They were married on the 17th of October, 1789.

Such admiration did the young wife's beauty arouse that she was followed even by the princes of the blood to balls and assemblies, and strangers used to collect in Bloomsbury Square to gaze at her as she watered the flowers in her balcony. In spite of all this flattery she continued to be tenderly attached to her husband, and never gave him the slightest cause for jealousy.

In his domestic life Lord Ellenborough was very amiable, although on rare occasions a little hasty. When his wife by trying to smuggle some lace caused the family coach to be seized, all he said was, 'We have only to pay the penalty.' There was one thing, however, that he could not tolerate in his carriage—a band-box. On one occasion, when Lady Ellenborough accompanied him on Circuit, the Chancellor, stretching out his legs under the seat of the carriage in front of him, kicked against one of the flimsy receptacles he had frequently prohibited. Down went the window with a bang and out went the band-box into a ditch. The startled coachman commenced to pull up, but was ordered to drive on and let the thing lie where it was. They reached the assize town in due course, and his lordship proceeded to robe for Court.

'And now, where's my wig?—where's my wig?' he demanded, when everything else had been donned.

'Your wig, my lord,' replied the servant, tremulously, 'was in that band-box your lordship threw out of the window as we came along.'

Lord Chancellor Campbell did manage to get married, though, as he said, he had no time 'to run after any woman.' And the courtship was troubled as well as short. Miss Scarlett, who afterwards became his wife, at first refused him. When, however, the lady changed her mind, she brought to Campbell an amount of happiness that fully repaid him for the pain he had suffered.

When Charles Abbott, afterwards Lord Tenterden, told John Lamotte that he wished to marry his daughter, he was asked for 'a sight of his rent-roll,' to which the rising young lawyer replied, 'Behold my books and my pupils.' Before long the lovers were married and lived harmoniously together, although of very different dispositions. He was simple in his tastes, but she was fond of finery and the brilliancy of her complexion was evidently not natural. Once her husband made a sly allusion to this last fact. When talking of some chambers to Lord Campbell, he said: 'Now, if my wife had these chambers, she would immediately *paint* them, and I should like them the better for it.'

In the correspondence of Daniel O'Connell, lately published, we find letter after letter of the most exquisite tenderness addressed through thirty-three years (1802-1835) to his wife. Here is a specimen : 'My own and only love, it was Kate' [his daughter] 'wrote the letter I got this morning, and I do most tenderly, tenderly love

Kate. Yet, sweetest Mary, I could have wished to see one line also in that handwriting which gives me recollections of the happiest hours of my life, and still blesses one with inexpressible sweetness and comfort when we, darling, are separate. All the romance of my life *envelopes* you, and I am as romantic in my love this day as I was twenty-three years ago, when you dropped your not unwilling hand into mine. Darling, will you smile at the *love-letters* of your *old* husband? Oh no— my Mary—my own Mary will remember that she has had the fond and faithful affections of my youth, and that if years have rolled over they have given us no cause to respect or love each other less than we did in early life.'

In another letter he writes : 'My own sweet darling Mary—Need I tell you that I was delighted to get a letter all in your own handwriting? but I was a little uneasy at its being so long, lest you should thereby have inconvenienced yourself, and yet, sweet Mary, I *do* like to get a long letter from you. Now, saucy little woman, let me scold you for getting this attack. I will lay a pound to a penny that I know how you got it. The hot weather made you dress lighter, and so, in this climate, it not being capable of being done with impunity, you caught cold. Do not deny it, sweetest, like a little *fibbing* old woman, as you are. For my own part, I continue to wear my winter dress, except my cloak, and even that I put on after nine in the evening if I go out. But I never, thank God, enjoyed better health. There is all the buoyancy of youthful spirits about me now that you are well, and all the racy triumphs at the success of agitation which an agitator by profession can alone enjoy. Indeed, darling, as you are better I am happy. The Beresfords are determined to die hard. They will continue the poll to-morrow, and probably Tuesday, but I think they must be exhausted by Tuesday at the latest. The moment the election is over I will fly to you.'

The great agitator had hard fighting out-of-doors, but there was no agitation in his home.

Sir William Scott saw his future wife for the first time in the Old Bailey, when he was trying the Marquis of Sligo for luring into his yacht two of the king's seamen. Either under the influence of sincere admiration for the judge, or impelled by desire for vengeance on the man who had presumed to lecture her son in a court of justice, the Marchioness wrote a few hasty words of thanks to Sir William Scott for his salutary exhortation to her boy. She even went so far as to say that she wished the erring Marquis could always have so wise a counsellor by his side. The communication was made on a slip of paper, which the writer sent to the judge by an usher of the court. Sir William read the note as he sat on the bench, and having looked toward the fair scribe, he received from her a glance and a smile that were fruitful of much misery to him. Within four months the judge was tied to a beautiful, shrill, voluble termagant, who exercised marvellous ingenuity in rendering him wretched and contemptible. Reared in a stately school of old-world politeness, the unhappy man was a model of decorum and urbanity. He prided himself on the perfection of his tone and manner, and the Marchioness —whose malice did not lack cleverness—was never more happy than when she was gravely expostulating with him, in the presence of numerous auditors, on his lamentable want of style, tact, and gentleman-like bearing.

Simon Harcourt and Lord Eldon also owed their professional advancement to marriages which at the time were thought by friends to be imprudent. When the last mentioned had received the Great Seal from the King, and was about to retire, he was addressed by his Majesty with the words, 'Give my remembrance to Lady Eldon.' The Chancellor, in acknowledging the condescension, intimated his ignorance of Lady Eldon's claim to such notice. 'Yes, yes,' the King answered;

'I know how much I owe to Lady Eldon. I know that you would have been yourself a country curate, and that she has made you my Lord Chancellor.'

Who has not heard of the elopement of handsome Jack Scott (Lord Eldon's name before his elevation) with the lovely Bessie Surtees? The lady's family refused consent, and wished their Bessie to marry an aged suitor, Sir William Blackett, so there was nothing for her to do but descend from her window into Scott's arms and run away with him to the matrimonial altar. Eldon used to describe the pitiable plight of himself and Bessie on the third morning after their union. 'Our funds were exhausted; we had not a home to go to, and we knew not whether our friends would ever speak to us again.' The fathers of the bride and bridegroom, however, soon met and came to terms, and the young couple settled in New Inn Hall, Oxford, where Scott acted as substitute for Sir Robert Chambers, Professor of Law. This easy-going professor, while holding his Oxford appointment, was a judge in India, and sent lectures to be read by his deputy. 'The first lecture which I read,' says Eldon, 'and which I began without knowing a single word that was in it, was upon the statute of young men running away with maidens. Fancy me reading, with about a hundred and forty boys and young men all giggling at the professor.'

It was probably the scanty means of their early married life which caused the parsimony that was apparent in Lady Eldon's management, even after she became well to do. The Chancellor was fond of shooting, and usually went into the country for a few weeks towards the end of the season, where he was in the habit of riding a Welsh pony, for which he had given fifty shillings. One morning his lordship ordered 'Bob,' the pony, to be saddled. Lady Eldon told him he could not have it, but, company being in the room, gave no reason. In a few minutes, however, the servant opened the door and announced that Bob was ready.

'Why, bless me,' exclaimed her ladyship, 'you can't ride him, Lord Eldon; he has got no shoes on.'

'Oh yes, my lady,' said the servant; 'he was shod last week.'

'Shameful!' exclaimed her ladyship. 'How dare you, sir, or anybody have that pony shod without orders?—John,' continued she, addressing her husband, 'you know you only rode him out shooting four times last year, so I had his shoes taken off and have kept them ever since in my bureau. They are as good as new, and these people have had him shod again. We shall be ruined at this rate.'

However much at times Lord Eldon might have regretted his wife's peculiarities, he never allowed her to see it; and to those who told him that she should go more into society, he would reply: 'When she was young and beautiful, she gave up everything for me. What she is I have made her, and I cannot now bring myself to compel her inclinations. Our marriage prevented her mixing in society when it afforded her pleasure; it appears to give pain now, and why should I interpose?'

In numerous little thoughtful ways he proved that his early deep devotion to his wife had never changed, and even after her death several anecdotes are told of his affection for her. On one occasion he visited his estate in Durham, but could not summon courage to cross the Tyne bridge and look at the house from which he took her in all the spring-tide bloom and tenderness of her girlhood. When invited to visit Newcastle, he replied: 'I know my fellow-townsmen complain of my not coming to see them; but *how can I pass that bridge?*' Then, after a pause, he added: 'Poor Bessie! if ever there was an angel on earth she was one. The only reparation which one man can make to another for running away with his daughter is to be exemplary in his conduct towards her.'

The marriage of Lord Eldon, which his friends thought must certainly ruin him, turned out far more happily than did the alliance of Serjeant Hill with an heiress, Miss Medlycott, of Cottingham, Northampton-shire. Forgetting all about his wedding-day, the eccentric serjeant received his clients as usual, until a band of friends forcibly brought him to church, where his bride had been waiting for him more than an hour. After the ceremony he hastened back to his chambers to be present at a consultation. Notwithstanding her sincere affection for him, the lady proved but an in-different wife. Empowered by Act of Parliament to retain her maiden name after marriage, she caused her husband constant annoyance by availing herself of the privilege. He used to say, 'My name is Hill, madam; my father's name was Hill, madam; all the Hills have been named Hill, madam; Hill is a good name, and, madam, you *shall* use it.'

On other matters the serjeant was more compliant, humoring her old-maidish fancies in a most conciliatory manner. Mrs Medlycott took great pride in the fault-lessness of her domestic arrangements. To maintain the whiteness of the pipe-clayed steps before the front door of her Bedford Square mansion was a chief object of her existence, and, to gratify her in this particular, Serjeant Hill used daily to leave his premises by the kitchen steps.

Having outlived the lady, Hill observed to a friend who was condoling with him on his recent bereavement: 'Ah, my poor wife is gone ! She was a good sort of woman—in *her* way, a *very* good sort of woman. I do honestly declare my belief that in *her* way she had no equal. But—but—I'll tell you something in confidence: if I ever marry again *I won't marry merely for money!*'

CHAPTER XVIII

LOVE AND MEDICINE

IN his celebrated work *Religio Medici*, Sir Thomas Browne wished that 'we might procreate like trees,' and declared that 'the whole world was made for man, but only the twelfth part of man for woman,' and that man 'is the whole world, but woman only the rib, or crooked part of man.' And yet Sir Thomas took to himself the 'twelfth part of man' in the shape of Mrs Mileham, a lady of good family and 'of such symmetrical proportion to her worthy husband, that they seemed to come together by a kind of natural magnetism.' The good physician lived happily with his rib for forty-one years, and was a kind father to his ten children. He proved that marriage was not what before experience he said it was, 'the foolishest act a wise man commits in all his life.'

Alluding to the fact that rich men when sick are willing to give almost anything to their physicians, a successful and honourable practitioner said with a laugh to a friend, 'I wonder at my moderation.' Considering the opportunities medical men have for pressing a suit in love, the moderation which as a rule they have shown in refusing to take an unfair advantage of them is much to be admired.

Dr Cadogan, of the time of Charles the Second, married a rich woman, but old, and one who did not bring him a fortune in her temper. After spending a few months in alternate fits of jealous hate and jealous fondness, the poor creature began to fancy that her husband was bent on destroying her with poison. One day when surrounded by her friends, and in the presence of her husband, she fell on her back in hysterics, exclaiming :

'Ah ! he has killed me at last. I am poisoned !'

'Poisoned !' cried the lady friends, turning up the whites of their eyes. 'Oh ! gracious goodness !—you have done it, Doctor !'

'What do you accuse me of?' asked the doctor, with surprise.

'I accuse you—of—killing me—ee,' responded the wife, doing her best to imitate a death struggle.

'Ladies,' answered the doctor, with admirable nonchalance, bowing to Mrs Cadogan's associates, 'it is perfectly false. You are quite welcome to open her at once, and then you'll discover the calumny.'

The famous John Hunter was married to a woman who caused her husband no little vexation by her fondness for society. She was in the habit of giving enormous routs, at which authors and artists used to assemble. Hunter, who grudged every moment that took him from his museum and laboratory, returned one day from visiting patients, hoping to have a quiet evening at home for study. He found all the hubbub and confusion of a grand party. Walking straight into the middle of the principal reception-room, he faced round and surveyed his unwelcome guests, who were not a little surprised to see him dusty, toilworn, and grim, so unlike what the man of the house' ought to be on such an occasion. 'I knew nothing,' was his brief address to the astonished crowd, 'I knew nothing of this kick-up, and I ought to have been informed of it beforehand; but, as I have now returned home to study, I hope the present company will retire.'

A little more than a century ago Dr Thomas Dawson was much admired by the inhabitants of Hackney as a pulpit orator and a physician. Amongst the doctor's circle of acquaintances Miss Corbett, of Hackney, was the richest, the most devout, and the most afflicted in bodily health. Ministering to her body and soul, Dr

Dawson had frequent occasions for visiting her. One day he found her alone, sitting with the large family Bible before her. The doctor read the words to which her forefinger pointed—the words of Nathan to David, 'Thou art the man.' He took the hint, and on the 29th of May, 1758, married the pious lady.

Just before marrying Mary Howard, of Lichfield, a girl of eighteen, Erasmus Darwin wrote to her a long letter of advice. He says that matrimony 'is a serious affair if anything be such,' and warns her against confidants, the best of whom 'could as easily hold a burning cinder in their mouth as anything the least ridiculous about a new married couple.' Then he sends the following recipe for making love, which, he says, he found in an old book : 'Take of sweet-william and of rosemary as much as is sufficient. To the former of these, add of honesty and herb-of-grace; and to the latter of eyebright and mother-wort, of each a large handful; mix them separately, and then, chopping them altogether, add one plum, two sprigs of heart's ease, and a little thyme. And it makes a most excellent dish.' He was going to add from the same book a recipe 'To make a Good Wife,' but he broke off thus : 'Pshaw ! an acquaintance of mine, a young lady of Lichfield, knows how to make this dish better than any other person in the world, and she has promised to treat me with it sometime.'

Mrs Darwin was remarkable for strong understanding and refined taste, but her health failed when she became a mother. However, by his great care and skill, her husband was enabled to prolong her life for thirteen years.

Darwin's second matrimonial venture was in 1781 with Mrs Pole, a widow, and the marriage was a complete success. Perhaps we ought not to have spoken of this enterprise as a 'venture,' because the wily physician had taken great pains to discover the intellectual and moral qualities of the widow before proposing to her.

· MEN OF LETTERS ·

Thomas Carlyle.

Lord Tennyson.

Nathaniel Hawthorne.

Robert Browning.

L. A.

F

In March, 1788, Jenner, who did so much to save us from the smallpox scourge, married Miss Catherine Kingscote, whose manners were elegant and whose understanding was vigorous. In her counsel and sympathy he found support when jealousy and bigotry assailed him. He had implicit confidence in her judgment. On one occasion, when discussing with a friend the evils connected with man's structure, our crimes, our capacity for suffering, and other problems of life, he observed, 'Mrs. Jenner can explain all these things; they cause no difficulty to her.' She had obtained peace and comfort from the Source of Strength herself, and extended them to all around her. For years before she died she was unable to leave her room, and during all the time the attachment and kindness of Jenner were unfailing.

The house of the famous surgeon and botanist, Haller, 'resembled a temple consecrated to science and the arts.' The votaries were his wife and the other members of his family. He inspired them with a taste for his various pursuits. They transcribed manuscripts, consulted authors, botanised, drew and painted specimens, and generally made themselves useful to the head of the house.

The wife and children of the once celebrated British physician Matthew Baillie, were not less good. He appreciated the blessing, and was careful that nothing on his part should spoil the harmony of his home. His health, however, was delicate, and this, together with the fact that he worked for long hours—sometimes sixteen out of the twenty-four—made him inclined to be irritable. To prevent this, his natural kindness of heart suggested the following little expedient. When he came to his dinner-table after a day of fatigue, he would hold up his hands to the family circle, eager to welcome him home, and say, 'Don't speak to me.' Then, after he was a little rested and had eaten a few mouthfuls, he would look round and say with a smile of affection, 'You may speak to me now.'

The marriage of Abernethy was a happy one, though it is said that when he proposed to Miss Anna Threlfall, his future wife, he had only seen her once. Then he wrote, saying that he would like to marry her, but as he was too busy to 'make love,' she must entertain his proposal without further preliminaries, and let him know her decision by the end of the week.

It is told of a professor of mathematics, that one day he informed his pupils that he should have to miss the next lecture, because he was going away on a matter of business (his marriage) not likely to occur again ! It is characteristic of Abernethy that he did not allow this matter of business' to interfere with his lecture at the hospital. He gave it as usual a few hours after the wedding.

Sir Astley Cooper was also so conscientious, or so un-romantic, that on the evening of his marriage-day he delivered his surgical lecture, his pupils not having the slightest suspicion of what had occurred. The wedding was a curious stealthy affair. In consequence of the death of the lady's father, it had to take place very quietly. So the couple joined a christening party on its way to church, got married, and then retired as if they had been merely witnesses of the christening ceremony. The wedding was on January 9th, 1800, but the honeymoon was postponed till the following June.

The famous physician, Robert Gooch, had very domestic tastes. When some time after the death of his first wife, his friend Southey advised him to marry again, he wrote to him as follows : 'There is no fear but I shall again become a husband, nor will a second attachment become less likely from being deferred another year or two. I am too friendly to marriage in general, too sick of a solitary fireside, too indisposed to relish even the innocent pursuits which single men depend upon for amusement, too thoroughly convinced that gaiety, as it is commonly called, is incapable of affording me pleasure, too disposed to the pursuits of knowledge, and too well aware that the endearments of affection are necessary for my happiness in this world.'

In 1814 Gooch announced to Southey his approaching nuptials thus : ' Lost time is lost happiness; the years of man are three-score and ten, the months therefore 840, about 360 of my share are already gone, how many have I to spare? On the 1st of February, God permitting, I bring home my wife '

The mention of Southey reminds us that the poet had a brother who was very popular as a family physician. The ladies were all in love with him, and hence he got the name of 'Thalaba the Destroyer,' from his brother's poem. He had four wives, so he made as many women happy as was in his power. He married early and as often as necessary, for he was a man who could not do without a home and a loving wife to greet him after his day's work.

In 1840 Sir James Y. Simpson became Professor of Obstetric Medicine in the University of Edinburgh. A few weeks before he had removed what had been considered a disqualification for the Chair, by his marriage to Miss Jessie Grindlay, the daughter of a Liverpool shipowner. He had thus written to Mr Grindlay :—

'In asking your daughter's hand, I ask it, not with any *certainty* of being elected, and thus having a future at once at my feet—I ask it for better or for worse, whether I succeed, or what is more probable, do not succeed.'

There was no honeymoon. The canvass absorbed every hour almost night and day.

After the election, he wrote this characteristic letter to his Liverpool relatives :—

'MY DEAR MOTHER,—Jessie's honeymoon and mine is to begin to-morrow. I was elected Professor to-day by a majority of *one*. Hurrah ! Your ever affectionate son,

'J. Y. SIMPSON.'

CHAPTER XIX

ARMS AND THE WOMAN

'Out of the strong came forth sweetness' might be said of many famous soldiers. An eye like Mars to threaten and command, but also a smile that betokened a loving disposition. Brave men are tender-hearted and chivalrous, and the sweetest domestic affections have not seldom been shown by those who were towers of strength against the enemies of their country.

In a register of St Giles Cripplegate there is an entry, 'August 22, 1620. Oliver Cromwell to Elizabeth Bourcher.' It was to the house at Huntingdon where his mother and sisters were living that the bridegroom, who was only twenty-one years and four months old, brought his bride, the daughter of a knight and wealthy London merchant. The gentle disposition of Elizabeth seems to have enabled her to agree with her mother and sisters-in-law. At any rate it was not until eleven years had passed that Oliver removed to a house of his own at St. Ives, where he farmed 'boggy lands fringed with willows.' Mrs Cromwell may not have had much character, but her husband never ceased to love her, and thirty years after their marriage he writes to her (the day after Dunbar) : 'Truly, if I love you not too well, I think I err not on the other hand much. Thou art dearer to me than any creature ; let that suffice.' And she writes to him : 'Truly, my life is but half a life in your absence.' They had nine children, and three times the Protector's heart bled at the loss of a beloved child. Robert, the eldest son, died in his eighteenth year. Nineteen years afterwards, fresh from his daughter's death-bed, almost on his own death-bed, the broken-hearted father recurred again to this his first great loss. He had read to him those verses in St Paul's Epistle to the Philippians which end, 'I can do all things through Christ, which strengtheneth me'; and then he said: 'This Scripture did once save my life, when my eldest son died, which went as a dagger to my heart; indeed it did.' His second son died of smallpox. The third great loss, that of his favourite daughter, undoubtedly has-tened his death. For the thirty-eight years of his married life Cromwell was all that a loving husband and father could be : overflowing with affection, even on the battlefield and in the stress of affairs; indulgent, but not weak; considerate, provident, just, counselling, reproving, exhorting; yearning to lead his children to feel his own intense sense of God's presence.

Colonel Hutchinson and Lucy his wife were as attached to each other as they were to what they be-lieved to be true. He was a Puritan, and on the acces-sion of Charles II. he was imprisoned in Sandown Castle. His wife took a little lodging near, that she might see and comfort him. He was offered freedom and life if he would abjure his faith, but was too brave to do so. He languished and died in prison, but from that prison has come down to us a scrap or two from his diary, showing the love he bore his wife and children, and the longing he had to be free with them once more. Before this good husband died he charged his wife as she was far above other women in goodness and constancy, so to be also far above them in bearing her sorrow. She was not to give way to grief for him, or mourn unrestrain-edly; other duties lay before her, and she must learn to rule herself. Very great was the sorrow of her heart, but she bore herself nobly under it, as his last words had directed. She had her children to educate and her husband's memory to preserve by writing his bio-graphy, and she lived a long life of devotion to these aims. 'So as his shadow she waited upon him,' she writes of herself and her husband, 'till he was taken into that region of light which admits of none, and then she vanished into nothing.'

The portraits of John Churchill, afterwards Duke of Marlborough, represent him as being, when a young soldier, strikingly handsome, and his manners were irresistible either to man or woman. So it came to pass that Barbara, Duchess of Cleveland, a mistress of Charles II., fell in love with the young guardsman. Becoming aware of this fact, the Duke of Buckingham, who had quarrelled with the lady, bribed her servant, and so contrived that the King found Churchill in her bedroom and banished him for some time from Court. It would be unjust, however, to judge the great soldier from this very early indiscretion, for from his twenty-fifth year, when he first met Sarah Jennings, his future wife, he was a pattern of domestic virtue. Sarah's beauty, though of a scornful style, was very great, and over those with whom she talked she exercised a charm that held them enthralled as much by her graceful wit as by her seductive beauty. Her education had been neglected, but she had acquired not a little practical knowledge ; and as for the temper and disposition concealed by the lovely exterior of this celebrated woman, they were those of a tiger.

The stories of the violence of Sarah, Duchess of Marlborough (insanity was in her family), are numerous. Here is one. During an altercation with the Duke, being the more provoked by his imperturbable calmness, she determined to make him feel where she knew he could be most easily wounded. He, with every one else, admired her long and beautiful tresses of hair. So she cut them off and placed them where he must see them. After the Duke's death this woman, whose temper overpowered her vanity, found the tresses locked up in a cabinet amongst her husband's most cherished treasures.

Sarah, Duchess of Marlborough, lived at Court

from the age of twelve, at a time when it was said that if men had gone into mourning for the immorality of their wives, sisters, and daughters, half the Court would have been continually in black. Yet her virtue was above suspicion; not because of religion, of which she had none, but because she loved her husband with a fierce exclusive earnestness all her own. True, but not tender, she lived for forty-four years with the Duke as happily as her domineering nature would have allowed her to live with any one.

When left a widow Sarah was still handsome, and the 'proud Duke of Somerset' asked her to marry him. 'Were I only thirty,' said she, 'I would not permit even the Emperor of the world to succeed in that heart which has been devoted to John, Duke of Marlborough.' She destroyed most of her own letters to her husband, preserving only those from him; but when examining the Blenheim Palace papers Lord Wolseley found the following scrap in her handwriting : 'Wherever you are, whilst I have life my soul shall follow you, my ever dear Lord Marlborough; and wherever I am, I shall only kill the time (until) night that I may sleep, and hope the next day to hear from you.' In her later years, this good wife, if not good woman, was ever on the watch to guard her husband's reputation, and she evinced the keenest anxiety that he should be handed down to posterity as the greatest man of his age.

And Marlborough's love for his wife was deep, pure, and unselfish. From a worldly point of view he might have done better had he married Catherine Sedley, a kinswoman whom his parents designed for him, as her large fortune would have been of great assistance to the rising young officer. The lady, however, squinted and was anything but good-looking, and John Churchill was not in the matrimonial market. His love-letters to Sarah breathe the most fervent devotion, as when he writes: 'I do love and adore you with all my heart and soul—so much, that by all that is good I do and will ever be better pleased with your happiness than my own; but oh my soul, if we might be both happy what inexpressible joy that would be !—I will not dare to expect more favour than you shall think fit to give me, but could you love me, I think the happiness would be so great that it would make me immortal.' It is characteristic of the man, too, that he continued to write in the same strain even when he was married, and in a letter written after the birth of his second child, he says to his absent wife : 'I am impatient to have you with me : do not lose a moment in coming to him who adores you above his own soul.' It is curious to find the great Marlborough, the terror of Europe, writing to his young wife about their child in these terms : 'I hope all the red spots of our child will be gone against I see her, and her nose straight, so that I may fancy it to be like the mother, for she has your coloured hair. I would have her to be like you in all things else.'

Sarah went to Margate to see him off when he was starting for Holland, and at the end of his voyage he wrote : 'It is impossible to express with what a heavy heart I parted with you when I was at the waterside. I could have given my life to come back, though I knew my own weakness so much that I durst not, for I should have exposed myself to the company. I did for a great while with a perspective glass look upon the cliffs, in hopes I might have had one sight of you.' When Marlborough wrote this letter he had been married nearly a quarter of a century.

It is pleasing to observe him at his busiest moments fondly reverting to his favourite retreat of Sandridge, near St Albans. Thus he says to Lady Marlborough at the opening of his first important campaign : 'We have now very hot weather, which I hope will ripen the fruit at St Albans. When you are there pray think how happy I should be walking alone with you.' **No** ambition, he assures her, can make him indifferent to being separated from her, and the grand scenery on the Rhine in the midst of which he was when he wrote, is to him far less beautiful than St Albans, though that place was never celebrated for its scenery.

Marlborough values his titles chiefly because he hoped to transmit them to his only son. The young man died of smallpox at Cambridge, and the grief of his parents was intense. Marlborough longed for another son, and on one occasion when his wife complained about her health, he rejoined : ' Pray let me have in every one of your letters an account how you do. If it should prove such a sickness as that I might pity you, but not be sorry for it, it might yet make me have ambition.' He had, however, little time to indulge in sorrow, and was soon busy preparing for the next campaign. 'The greatest ease I now have,' he writes to the Duchess, 'is sometimes sitting for an hour in my chair alone, and thinking of the happiness I may yet have of living quietly with you, which is the greatest I propose to myself in this world.'

The love affairs of General Wolfe were as disappointing as they were romantic. His first love was a Miss Lawson, one of the maids of honour to the Princess of Wales. There was a Miss Hoskins, of Croydon, with a fortune of £30,000, whom his parents wished him to try and marry, but these prudent people could not dissuade their son from his 'senseless passion.' At length the girl herself rejected his suit.

After some time another lady engaged Wolfe's affections. With her his courtship was as rapid and successful as his first love affair had been tedious and unavailing. The hero of Quebec wore the portrait of Miss Lowther (that was her name) next his heart until the eve of the engagement, when, having a presentiment that he would be killed, he gave it to an officer, and requested him to return it to the lady should the foreboding be fulfilled. He was killed, as we know, in the moment of victory, on September 13th, 1759, and the portrait was sent to Wolfe's mother, who had it set in diamonds and restored to Miss Lowther.

On the 14th of July, 1768, Charles, first Marquis of Cornwallis, married Jemima Tullikens Jones. Though she was the daughter of a colonel she was not suited to be an officer's wife. When her husband was given a command in America, she so dreaded his absence that she made interest with the King to allow him to relinquish the appointment, which, however, Cornwallis would not do. After being away nearly two years the General returned to England, but had to leave it again in four months' time. Grief so preyed upon his wife's mind as eventually to bring on a kind of jaundice, of which she died on February 14th, 1779. She requested that no stone should be erected over her remains, but that a thorn-tree should be planted above the vault where she was to be buried, as nearly as possible over her heart—significant of the sorrow which destroyed her life.

On the other hand, it was a wife who was the indirect cause of the military reputation obtained by Thomas Graham. He and his wife lived happily together for eighteen years, and then she died, leaving him inconsolable. To forget his sorrow—and, as some thought, to get rid of the weariness of life without her—Graham, at the age of forty-three, joined Lord Hood as a volunteer, and distinguished himself by his bravery at the siege of Toulon. He served all through the Peninsular War and rose to be second in command. He was commonly known as the 'hero of Barossa,' because of his famous victory at that place. He was raised to the peerage as Lord Lynedock and lived to a very advanced age, but to the last he tenderly cherished the memory of his dead wife.

It is said of Washington that he always liked fine women, and he began to do so early, for when he was only fourteen he fell in love with a Mary Bland, of

Westmoreland, whom he called his 'Lowland Beauty.' His next love affair was with a Miss Sarah Carey, concerning whom the following is told : She was returning, belated and overtaken by dusk, into Williamsburg, when the town was under military rule, accompanied only by her negro maid-servant, and much taken aback when challenged by a sentry demanding the password for the day. Blushing, yet imperious, she stamped her little foot and said, 'But I am Miss Sallie Carey.' 'Pass,' said the sentry, and the young lady was made thus aware of the gallantry of the officer who had selected her name as a password for the protection of the garrison. Washington proposed to Miss Carey, but the lady was obdurate and we hear no more of love affairs until much later.

Riding with despatches, Washington stopped at a friend's house to dine, and there he met the widow of Daniel Parke Custis. She was young, pretty, intelligent, and rich, and she attracted the soldier. The afternoon wore away, the horses were brought to the door, and after being walked about for a long time were returned to the stable. The sun went down, but still Colonel Washington lingered. The next morning he rode away with his despatches, but stopped at the home of Mrs Custis and then and there engaged himself to the charming widow. They were married a few months afterwards.

The only letter known to be in existence that Washington wrote to Mrs Custis during their engagement is the following :—

'*Fort Cumberland, 20th July*, 1758.

'We have begun our march to the Ohio. A courier is starting for Williamsburg, and I embrace the opportunity to send a few words to one whose life is now inseparable from mine. Since that happy hour when we made our pledges to each other, my thoughts have been continually going to you as to another self. That all-powerful Providence may keep us both in safety is the prayer of your faithful and ever-affectionate friend,

'G. WASHINGTON.'

The great general was very kind to his step-children, and always affectionate to his wife. After his death, her portrait, which he had worn round his neck for forty years, was found upon his breast. No shadow rested on their married life, and when he died she only said, 'All is over now. I shall soon follow him.'

CHAPTER XX

OTHER LOVING SOLDIERS

A LADY once said to the Duke of Wellington, 'I sup-pose, Duke, during your life, you have inspired a great deal of admiration and enthusiasm among women, both abroad and at home.' The Duke replied, 'Oh, yes, plenty of that! plenty of that! but no woman ever loved me: never in my whole life.'

Of course the Duke knew best, but it does seem as if Lady Catherine Packenham, third daughter of the Earl of Langford, did love Captain Wellesley, as Wellington then was, when she first met him. He proposed to her, but Lord Langford refused his consent because there was not enough money. However, the lady gave him the assurance that she would always consider herself betrothed to him, and he left for India with his regiment.

The beauty of Lady Catherine, which had been cele-brated at the Dublin viceregal Court, was destroyed by smallpox not long after Wellesley's departure. On his return she offered to release him from his engagement, but Colonel Sir Arthur Wellesley, like a true knight, thought that it would be dishonourable to avail himself of her generosity and married her. When she was presented to Queen Charlotte, her Majesty said in allusion to the nine years that had elapsed between the departure and return of the betrothed officer :—

'I am happy to see you at my Court, so bright an ex-ample of constancy. If anybody in this world deserves to be happy, you do.' Then her Majesty inquired, 'But did you really never write one letter to Sir Arthur Wellesley during his long absence?'

'No, never, madam.'

'And did you never think of him?'

'Yes, madam ; very often.'

About nine years after this Maria Edgeworth, whose family was very intimate with the Langfords, wrote a letter to one of them, of which the following is an extract : 'How happy Lady Wellington must be at this glorious victory ! Had you in your paper an account of her running as fast as she could to Lord Bury at Lord Bathurst's when he alighted to learn the first news of her husband? *Vive l'enthusiasme !'*

The Duke's home, however, was not happy, and in moments of despondency he was wont to say, 'There is nothing in this world worth living for.' Perhaps the turn of his mind, and the constant dedication of his energies to the public service, in some degree unfitted him for the quiet enjoyment of domestic life. For years before the death of the Duchess, which took place on the 22nd of April, 1831, the Duke had seen little of her. There was no natural congeniality between them in tastes, habits, or pursuits, and the Duke's confidence was much more largely given out of the domestic circle than within it. Notwithstanding this, in his wife's last illness he was indefatigable in his attentions to her.

There was in Wellington a mixture of playfulness and irritability. The members of his family used to speak of his explosions of anger as letting off steam, but they knew that they would be followed, especially if they were unreasonable, by a greater amount than usual of urbanity and kindness. Lord Charles Wellesley, the Duke's second son, was sent from Malta with despatches of importance; he reached London a fortnight later than he was expected. The Duke, who thought that he had loitered amid the amusements of Paris, reprimanded him, and for some days would not speak to him. Then hearing accidentally that Lord Charles had been delayed at Marseilles for the lost time by quarantine, he went up to him, after breakfast, and in the gentlest manner, pressing him to his breast, said,—

'Charles, you would like to hunt this winter, would you not?'

'I have no horses, sir.'

'I have sent a thousand pounds to your bankers, you can buy some.'

A lady friend once ventured to ask General Gordon why he never married. For some seconds the General remained in silence, and then, speaking slowly, answered: 'I never yet have met a woman who, for my sake, and perhaps at a moment's notice, would be prepared to sacrifice the comforts of home and the sweet society of loved ones, and accompany me whithersoever the demand of duty might lead—accompany me to the ends of the earth, perhaps : who would stand by me in times of danger and difficulty, and sustain me in times of hardship and perplexity. Such a woman I have never met, and such an one alone could be my wife !'

This ideal of what a soldier's wife should be was realised by the wife of Sir Henry Lawrence. Soon after his marriage he had to survey a dense jungle at the foot of the Nepaul Mountains. The dews and fogs were so heavy that no tent could keep them out. Fires had to be lighted constantly to keep off tigers and wild elephants. It was in such a place that the assistant of Sir Henry Lawrence found Lady Lawrence. 'She was seated on the bank of a nullah, her feet overhanging the den of some wild animal. While she, with a portfolio in her lap, was writing overland letters, her husband, at no great distance, was laying his theodolite.' A woman of a highly gifted mind, as well as of a most cheerful disposition, she helped her husband in his reports and other literary compositions even when undergoing roughings like those described. While easily falling into her husband's ways of boundless hospitality, she cared nothing herself for luxury. She would be quite content with a tent some ten feet square, a suspended shawl separating her bedroom and dressing-room from the hospitable breakfast-table.

That the scarcely less celebrated Lord John Lawrence also enjoyed an earthly paradise in his home may be seen by the following anecdote. His lordship was sitting in his drawing-room at Southgate, with his sister and others of the family; all were reading. Looking up from the book in which he had been engrossed Lawrence discovered that his wife had left the room.

'Where's mother?' said he to one of his daughters.

'She's upstairs,' replied the girl.

He returned to his book, and looking up again, a few minutes later, put the same question to his daughter, and received the same answer. Once more he returned to his reading; once more he looked up, with the same question on his lips. His sister broke in,—

'Why, really, John, it would seem as if you could not get on five minutes without your wife.'

'That's why I married her,' he replied.

This admirable woman was the daughter of an Irish clergyman, and it was to her that Lawrence whispered, with his dying breath, 'To the last gasp, my darling!'

'A child, particularly a young one, seemed often able to calm John Lawrence when he was most ruffled, and to cheer him when he was most wearied with the anxieties and the vexations of his daily work.' He is only known to have wept on two occasions. One of them was when one of his little ones was suddenly cut off by death. Then 'he was seen weeping like a child as he followed the body to the grave.' Another time was when, many years afterwards, he was setting out to undertake his charge as Governor-General of India. In that great

moment of his life, thoughts of the dignity and respon-
sibility to which he had been advanced, and which fitly
crowned his career, were for the moment lost in the
bitterness of the farewell which he had to take of his
beloved family.   And when he said good-bye to the
youngest, a bright little boy of two years, whom he
had loved to carry on his shoulder and whose baby-
talk had been sweetest music to him, the feeling of
his heart burst forth in overflowing tears and in
the cry of irrepressible tenderness, 'I shall never see
Bertie any more.'   He meant that, when he returned,
the child would have grown out of the babyhood that
had been so sweet and winning to the heart of the
strong man.

In his domestic relations, Lord Clive was singularly
happy.   He married a lady of great beauty and accomplishments.   To her constant care much of the comfort
of his life was due.

Love at first sight is easy enough; what a girl wants is
a man who can love her when he sees her every day.
This sort of a man the wife of Garibaldi did find.   The
great liberator fell in love with his future wife at first
sight, and, what is more, at sight of her only through a
telescope.   The story is told in his 'Autobiography':
'I had need of some human being who would love me.
Without such an one near me, existence was becoming
insupportable.   Although not old, I knew men well
enough to know how difficult it is to find a real friend.
But a woman !   Yes, a woman; for I had always considered them the most perfect of beings; and whatever
men may say, it is infinitely easier to find a really loving
heart among them.   I was walking on the quarter-deck
of the *Itaparica*, wrapped in my sad thoughts, and
having reasoned the matter in all ways, I finally concluded to seek a wife for myself, who would draw me out
of this depressing and insupportable state of things.
My glance fell by chance upon the houses of the Barra,
a little hill thus called at the entrance of the Laguna

(of St Catherine, in Brazil), on which are some simple but picturesque dwellings. With the aid of my glass, which I habitually held in my hand when on the quarter-deck, I saw a young girl. I ordered the men to row me ashore in that direction, and disembarked, and made for the house which contained the object of my voyage, but could not find it, when I encountered a person of the place whom I had known on my first arrival. He invited me to take coffee at his house. We entered, and the first person on whom my gaze fell was the one who had caused my coming on shore. It was Anita, the mother of my children : the companion of my life in good and evil fortune : the woman whose courage I have so often desired ! We both remained in an ecstatic silence, gazing at each other, like two persons who do not meet for the first time, and who seek in each other's lineaments something which shall revive remembrance. At last I saluted her, and I said, 'You must be mine !' I spoke but little Portuguese, and I spoke these audacious words in Italian. However, I seemed to have some magnetic power in my insolence. I had tied a knot which death alone could break.'

Anita was the ideal wife for a soldier. She stood beside him in battle, waving her sword over her head to encourage the men to their utmost. When a soldier fell dead at her feet, she seized his carbine, and kept up a constant fire. When urged by her husband in a ship engagement to go below, because almost frantic with fear for her safety, she replied, 'If I do, it will be but to drive out those cowards who have sought concealment there, and then return to the fight.' In one of the land battles she was surrounded by twenty or more of the enemy; but she put spurs to her horse, and dashed through their midst. At first they seemed dazed, as though she were something unearthly; then they fired, killing her animal, and she was made a prisoner. Obtaining permission to search among the dead for her husband, and

not finding him, she determined to make her escape.
That night she seized a horse, plunged into the forests,
and for four days lived without food. On the last night
—a stormy one—closely pursued by several of the
enemy, she urged her horse into a swollen river, five
hundred yards broad, and seizing hold of his tail, the
noble creature swam across, dragging her with him.
After eight days she reached her agonised husband, and
their joy was complete.

At the time of the birth of their first child, Garibaldi
says : 'The poverty of our army was at that time so
great that I could contribute nothing for my dear wife
and the baby but one pocket-handkerchief. . . . Twelve
days afterwards she had to fly from the enemy with
her baby before her on the saddle.

In 1842 Count Von Moltke married Miss Burt, who
was half English, and lived most happily with her until
her death, which took place on Christmas Eve, 1868.
Very touching was his devotion to her memory. Upon
his estate at Kreisan he built a mausoleum, situated on
an eminence, embowered in foliage. In front of the
altar in this little chapel was placed the simple oak
coffin, always covered with leaves, in which the remains
of his wife reposed. Sculptured in the apse was a finely
carved figure of our Lord in an attitude of blessing.
Above were inscribed the words, 'Love is the fulfilment
of the law.'

At the time of the general's bereavement, Mr George
Bancroft, the distinguished historian, then United
States Minister at Berlin, met, when riding, Moltke,
also on horseback. 'My first impulse,' said Mr Bancroft,
 was to trot into another lane. On second thought,
however, I turned my horse alongside his, remembering
that it was for him to talk or be silent. To my surprise,
he forthwith began a lively conversation, describing the
happiness with which his wife had blessed her husband,
and expatiating upon her manifold virtues. Then of a
sudden he became silent, as if a new current of thought

had carried him away. "Do you know," he said, when his lips were again opened, "it has just been brought home to me that, after all, perhaps it was better that this happened now than at another time. You see, I am convinced that a French invasion is impending; it will burst upon us sooner or later, whatever the plea may eventually be. Now, think, if the fortune of war was to be adverse to our arms ! Why, her grief over the country's adversities must have cut her life short. No, no; that would have been worse ! " '

The great American general, 'Stonewall' Jackson, was as steadfast in love as he was in war. His first wife, the daughter of a college president, only lived fourteen months, and he was so prostrated by the loss that he had to travel to Europe for a change. Three years afterwards, he married the daughter of a Presbyterian minister of North Carolina. She was the sunshine of his home, and his home was a perpetual sunshine to him. If he had professional or other perplexities he dismissed them on reaching his own door. Within all was love ; his sternest rebuke when he saw anything unseemly being, 'Ah ! that's not the way to be happy.'

Jackson's letters to his wife run over with affection. He addresses her as his 'pet,' his 'darling,' his 'sunshine,' and his 'little somebody,' as if he would wrap her in a veil of mystery. His freedom from egotism was shown by his never writing even *our* house, *our* garden, but *your* house, as though he had no possession in it. Even the pay he drew he called '*your* salary.' Something had occurred to depress Mrs Jackson, and being absent from her at the time, he thus wrote : 'Try to look up and be cheerful. Trust your kind Heavenly Father, and by the eye of faith see that all things with you are right and for your best interests.' Equally encouraging was he even when dying of his wounds. When his wife came to see him and he remarked the look of dismay that crossed her countenance as she saw the terrible alteration of his features, he said, with a smile of love and peace : 'Cheer up, Anna, you know I love a bright face in a sick-room.' And then, alluding to his increasing deafness: 'Speak distinctly; I want to hear every word you say.'

It was, no doubt, from feeling his helping hand in her daily life that the wife of Sir Bartle Frere thus described her husband. She had driven to meet him at a railway station, and had told the footman to go and find the General. The servant, who was a new one, and had been engaged in his master's absence, asked :

'But how shall I know him?'

'Oh,' replied Lady Frere, 'look for a tall gentleman helping somebody.'

The description was sufficient. The servant went, and found the General helping an old lady out of a railway carriage.

Few people realise what it is to be the wife of a successful soldier. Since her marriage, which occurred some twenty-four years ago, Lady Wolseley has seen her husband go through five campaigns. If, however, the face of this devoted wife bears traces of the anxiety she has had so often to endure, she has also upon her, on full-dress occasions, the rewards of victory. We allude to her specially fine diamonds, which came off the sword presented to Lord Wolseley by the people of Cairo. Another trophy of war which is greatly prized by Lady Wolseley is in a little gilt frame, and hangs in her boudoir. It is the autograph copy of the words spoken by the Queen when she proposed the health of the Commander-in-chief at Balmoral shortly after his return from Egypt.

Lord Roberts dedicates his book *Forty-one Years in India* 'To my wife, without whose loving help my forty-one years in India could not be the happy retrospect it is.' Readers of the work cannot fail to see how well deserved is this tribute. Lady Roberts is the true metal for a soldier's wife. She was always willing that 'Bobs' should go on active service regardless of her own feelings and convenience, and in spite of ill-health she accompanied him in his tours of inspection, visits to cholera camps, and indeed to every place possible where he went. She was always ready too with her sympathy and help when any scheme was suggested that might improve the condition and lessen the temptations of soldiers and their families.

CHAPTER XXI

FAMOUS SAILORS IN LOVE

SIR FRANCIS DRAKE married Mary Newman, and after her death Elizabeth, daughter and sole heiress of Sir George Sydenham, of Combe-Sydenham, in the county of Devon. It was generally believed that the great seaman had the power of working miracles, which shows how strongly the romantic character of his exploits, and the extraordinary celebrity which he obtained, impressed the imagination of his countrymen. The following is a Devonshire tradition about the 'old warrior,' as they call him, and his wife : When Sir Francis left home for one of his voyages, he told his wife that if he did not return within seven years, according to some versions, ten according to others, she might conclude that he was dead and consider herself at liberty to marry again. During those years Madame Drake, though assailed by many suitors, remained true as Penelope to her absent lord; but after the term had expired she accepted an offer. One of Drake's ministering spirits, whose charge it was to convey to him any intelligence in which he was nearly concerned, brought him the tidings. Immediately he loaded a cannon, and fired it down through the globe on one side and up on the other, with so true an aim that it made its way into the church, between the two parties most concerned, just as the marriage service was beginning. 'It comes from Drake !' cried the wife to the expectant bridegroom; 'he is alive ! and there must be neither troth nor ring between thee and me.'

On his return in 1582 from putting down a rebellion

in Munster, Sir Walter Raleigh was warmly welcomed at Court. His graces and accomplishments pleased 'the maiden queen,' and by one adroit act of gallantry he established himself in her favour. Meeting the Queen near a marshy spot, and observing her Majesty hesitating to proceed, Raleigh instantly spread his rich cloak on the ground for a footcloth to his royal mistress. Having ventured to write upon a window, which the Queen could not fail to pass, this line, 'Fain would I climb, but that I fear to fall,' Elizabeth is said, upon observing it, to have written beneath it, 'If thy heart fail thee, do not climb at all.'

Raleigh married Elizabeth Throgmorton, one of the Queen's maids of honour, though not very honourable in another sense, her fair name having suffered on his account. The Queen was highly incensed, for it was one of her foibles that the admiration of her courtiers should be concentrated upon herself. Raleigh and his wife were committed to the Tower, and were not liberated until the former had recourse to a stratagem that caused the Queen to relent because it appealed to her vanity.

Sometimes we may believe even a monument, and when we know how keenly Admiral Lord Hawke felt the death of 'Kitty,' his wife, we may credit what is said on the monument of the happy couple, that 'the beauty of her person was excelled only by the accomplished elegance of her mind,' and that 'in their conjugal duties they were equalled by few, excelled by none.'

In 1753 Admiral Sir George Rodney married the sister of the Earl of Northampton, but his happiness was of short duration, as the lady died in a little more than three years. By his second wife he had seven children, and he took the keenest interest in their education.

Another admiral, who in the midst of dangerous and difficult work thought much about the bringing up of

his daughters, was Lord Collingwood. It is pleasing
to find one of the heroes of Trafalgar writing a note like
the following : 'My darlings, little Sarah and Mary, I
was delighted with your last letters, my blessings; and
desire you to write to me very often, and tell me all the
news of the city of Newcastle' (Lady Collingwood was
a daughter of an alderman of Newcastle). 'I hope we
shall have many happy days and many a good laugh
together yet.' In other letters he gives to his girls
advice about the management of temper, letter-writing,
and other practical matters.

Writing to his wife, Collingwood says about his daughters : 'I beseech you, dearest Sarah, I beseech you keep
them constantly employed; make them read to you, not
trifles, but history, in the manner we used to do in the
evenings : blessed evenings indeed ! The human mind
will improve itself if it be kept in action; but grows dull
and torpid when left to slumber. I believe even stupid-
ity itself may be cultivated.'

And in another letter : 'How would it enlarge their
minds if they could acquire sufficient knowledge of mathematics and astronomy to give them an idea of the
beauties and wonders of the creation ! I am persuaded
that the generality of people, and particularly fine
ladies, only adore God because they are told it is proper
and the fashion to go to church; but I would have my
girls gain such knowledge of the works of the creation
that they may have a fixed idea of the nature of that
Being who could be the author of such a world. Whenever they have that, nothing on this side the moon will
give them much uneasiness of mind.'

No day passed in which Lady Collingwood had not
her husband's blessing and his prayers for her happiness,
nor was he unmindful of such anniversaries as her
birthday or their wedding-day. Thus in a letter with
the address 'Ocean' and the date June 16th, 1806, he
writes : 'This day, my love, is the anniversary of our
marriage, and I wish for many returns of it. If ever

we have peace, I hope to spend my latter days amid my family, which is the only sort of happiness I enjoy.'

As he had no son, Collingwood tried to get the peerage that had been granted to him made hereditary in female succession, but the favour was refused notwithstanding the length and hardship of his service—fifty years, of which forty-four were passed in active service abroad.

When Nelson commanded the *Albemarle* he had a very narrow escape of matrimony. The ship was about to leave Quebec, and had gone down the river to the place of anchorage. Next morning as Alexander Davison, a friend of Nelson, was walking on the beach, to his surprise he saw that officer landing from his boat. Upon inquiring the cause of his reappearance, Nelson took his arm to walk towards the town, and told him he found it utterly impossible to leave Quebec without again seeing the woman whose society had contributed so much to his happiness there, and offering her his hand.

'If you do,' said his friend, 'your utter ruin must inevitably follow.'

'Then let it follow,' cried Nelson, 'for I am resolved to do it.'

'And I,' replied Davison, 'am resolved you shall not.'

Nelson, however, upon this occasion was less resolute than his friend, and allowed himself to be led back to the boat.

The second attachment which Nelson formed was with Miss Andrews, the daughter of an English clergyman, when he was on half-pay and staying at St Omer. It was less ardent than the first, and he got over it when he left France. Getting another ship called the *Boreas* he sailed to the West Indies. At Antigua the woman's sympathy and adulation which were almost a necessity to Nelson were supplied by a Mrs Montray. 'If it were not for her,' he wrote, 'I should almost hang myself in this infernal hole.'

Mrs Montray left for England, and the gallant sailor consoled himself with Mrs Nisbet, the young widow of a physician. She was staying with her uncle, the president of Nevis. Nelson called upon the president, who, hastening half dressed to receive him, exclaimed, on returning to his dressing-room, 'Good God! if I did not find that great little man, of whom everybody is so afraid, playing in the next room, under the dining-table, with Mrs Nisbet's child!' A few days afterwards Mrs Nisbet herself was introduced to him, and thanked him for his kindness to her little boy. Her manners were mild and winning, and she and Nelson were married on March 11, 1787. Before long the bridegroom had to leave the bride, but his letters to her were very loving. In one he wrote: 'Have you not often heard that salt water and absence always wash away love? Now, I am such a heretic as not to believe in that article; for behold, every morning I have had six pails of salt water poured upon my head, and instead of finding what seamen say to be true, it goes on so contrary to the prescription, that you must, perhaps, see me before the fixed time.'

This is how Nelson wrote to his wife eleven years after they were married: 'Rest assured of my most perfect love, affection, and esteem for your person and character, which the more I see of the world the more I admire. The imperious call of honour to serve my country is the only thing which keeps me a moment from you, and a hope that by staying a little longer it may enable you to enjoy those little luxuries which you so highly merit. I pray God it may soon be peace, and that we may get into the cottage.' Like all sailors, Nelson was always dreaming and talking of life and love in a cottage.

Before attacking Teneriffe he tried to dissuade Josiah Nisbet, his step-son, from accompanying him, saying,

'Should we both fall, what will become of your poor mother?' And after he lost an arm at that engagement he wrote : 'My dearest Fanny, I am so confident of your affection that I feel the pleasure you will receive will be equal, whether my letter is wrote by my right hand or left. It was the chance of war, and I had great reason to be thankful : and I know that it will add much to your pleasure in finding that Josiah, under God's providence, was principally instrumental in saving my life. . . . I shall not be surprised to be neglected and forgot, as probably I shall no longer be considered as useful. However, I shall feel rich if I continue to enjoy your affection. The cottage is now more necessary than ever.'

In another letter he wrote : 'Absent from you I feel no pleasure : it is you who are everything to me. Without you, I care not for this world; for I have found, lately, nothing in it but vexation and trouble. These are my present sentiments. God Almighty grant they may never change ! Nor do I think they will. Indeed there is, as far as human knowledge can judge, a moral certainty that they cannot.'

We know, alas ! that these sentiments *did* change when Nelson was introduced at Naples to Lady Hamilton. This was done by her husband, who told her that he was about to 'introduce a little man to her, who could not boast of being very handsome; but such a man as, he believed, would one day astonish the world.'

Lady Hamilton was once Amy Lyon, a servant-girl, residing at Hawarden. Taking to evil ways she at last became the mistress of Charles Greville, who handed her over to Sir William Hamilton. When Nelson met the 'bewitching siren' she was 'lithe and lissom with chestnut hair and a waist none too small for health and classic grace.' She was a sweet singer, played the harp agreeably, and was an excellent actress.

For a dozen or so years Lady Nelson was rendered

uneasy by rumours about Lady Hamilton, and by remarks which Nelson himself made in letters to his wife and on the rare occasions when he was at home with her. The crisis came in the winter of 1801. Lord and Lady Nelson were at breakfast one morning and the former incidentally referred to something which had been said or done by 'dear Lady Hamilton.' Lady Nelson at once rose and exclaimed with some heat : 'I am sick of hearing of *dear* Lady Hamilton, and am resolved that you shall give up either her or me.' Nelson calmly answered: 'Take care, Fanny, what you say. I love you sincerely, but I cannot forget my obligations to Lady Hamilton, or speak of her otherwise than with affection and admiration.' Muttering something about her 'mind being made up,' Lady Nelson left the room, and shortly after drove from the house.

Only once again did Nelson see his wife, and then he is reported to have said, 'I call God to witness, there is nothing in you or your conduct that I wish otherwise.' It is a pity, however, that she remained in England, and allowed Nelson after being wounded to be nursed at Naples by a fascinating and unscrupulous woman. It was unfortunate, too, that Lady Nelson should have regarded her husband's relations as the natural enemies of her son, and treated them with an incivility that caused much uneasiness between herself and Nelson.

Lady Nelson was not of her husband's heroic mould. When he wrote to her after the battle of St Vincent, that he had taken, by boarding, two of the largest of the enemy's ships, she thus replied: 'What can I attempt to say to you about boarding? You have been most wonderfully protected. Now may I—indeed I do—beg of you never to board again. *Leave* it for *captains.*'

It was not the fault of the forsaken wife that she had not enough cleverness and ambition to know how to deal with her husband, and our sympathies are at once given to her when we read the following, which is recorded by Nelson's latest and most exhaustive biographer : 'Her eldest grandchild, a girl, was eight or ten years old at the time of her death. She remembers the great sweetness of her grandmother's temper, and tells that she often saw her take from a casket a miniature of Nelson, look at it affectionately, kiss it, and then replace it gently; after which she would turn to her and say, "When you are a little older, little Fan, you may know what it is to have a broken heart."' This trifling incident, transpiring as it does now for the first time after nearly seventy years, from the intimate privacies of family life, bears its mute evidence to the truth of the witnesses which Captain Mahan has adduced to prove that Lady Nelson 'neither reproached her husband nor was towards him unforgiving.'

Thus sadly ended an attachment which for many years satisfied Nelson's heart. Shortly after the battle of the Nile, when a friend said to him that no doubt he considered the day of that victory as the happiest in his life, he answered : 'No, the happiest was that on which I married Lady Nelson.'

The great seaman had been for some time off his element; that is to say, had been living on shore without work. One day as he was pacing a walk in his garden, which he used to call the quarter-deck, Lady Hamilton came up to him, and told him she saw he was uneasy. He smiled, and said : 'No, he was as happy as possible; he was surrounded by his family, his health was better since he had been on shore, and he would not give sixpence to call the king his uncle.' She replied, that she did not believe him, that she knew he was longing to get at the combined fleets, that he considered them as his own property, that he would be miserable if any man but himself did the business ; and that he ought to have them, as the price and reward of his two years' long watching, and his hard chase.

'Nelson,' said she, 'however we may lament your

absence, offer your services; they will be accepted, and you will gain a quiet heart by it; you will have a glorious victory, and then you may return here, and be happy.'

He looked at her with tears in his eyes : ' Brave Emma ! Good Emma ! If there were more Emmas there would be more Nelsons.'

If this story told by Lady Hamilton be true, it may only prove that Nelson deceived himself into thinking that she encouraged him in the path of hardship and self-denial. What seems to be true is that Nelson's services were requested by the Government and the whole country in the expedition that ended with Trafalgar. Indeed we are disposed to agree with Captain Mahan, that at first the influence of Lady Hamilton was altogether bad. Wife of the British Minister, bosom friend and confidante of the Queen of Naples—who was a daughter of Maria Theresa, a sister of Marie Antoinette—Lady Hamilton was a potent factor in all the combinations that centred round Naples; and Naples, at the moment, in its turn, was one of the centres of the great European drama on which France through Napoleon, and England through Nelson, were fighting the war of giants for national supremacy. This was, then, the network into which Nelson's passion took him ; and it is impossible to defend many of the acts into which he was thus drawn—an obscured judgment as to his duty to his country; something like a judicial murder; a hot partisanship for sovereigns, either worthless or useless to his own cause. This, undoubtedly, is the tragedy of Nelson's life, and it was not the least part of the tragedy that it prevented 'the darling hero' of England from coming down to us as much without reproach as he was without fear.

It is not every woman who has newly-discovered countries called after her name by an exploring lover, but this is an honour which Sir John Franklin conferred upon the two girls who became successively his wives. He called a group of islands, discovered by him in the Arctic Sea, the Porden Islands after Miss Eleanor Porden, and gave the name of Point Griffin to a promontory on the American coast after Miss Jane Griffin.

The gallant sailor's first wife was a beautiful and accomplished woman, but she died of pulmonary disease within a year after the marriage. It was a tragic situation. The day of the starting of Franklin's second expedition was fixed and the day and hour were fast approaching when his beloved wife was herself to begin 'a happier voyage, toward no earthly Pole.' It was plainly as much a question of days with one event as with the other; and in this grim race between Death and Duty the unhappy husband found himself almost wishing for the victory of the former in order that he might be with his wife to the end. It was not to be. The news of the death of her whose sympathy and self-forgetfulness had done so much for the expedition, reached Franklin at New York, on the way out.

The explorer, after three years of bereavement, married a Miss Jane Griffin, a lady whose sweetness of nature, bright intelligence, and playful humour were as conspicuous then as were afterwards her courage and perseverance when as wife or widow, she knew not which, she originated and continued the search for Franklin.

The home life of Nansen, the navigator, who has gone farthest north, is a very happy one. Frü Nansen is a great singer, but she thinks far more of her husband's explorations than of her own art. Brought up with tender care, indulged, made much of, in a home possessing all the simple luxuries of life, she accepts without a murmur his extreme asceticism, teaches herself to endure cold in the 'dog hutch,' eats his unpalatable messes —'mysost' (goat's milk cheese) and pemmican, which

STATESMEN

John Bright.

Lord Beaconsfield.

W. E. Gladstone.

Lord Salisbury.

he is testing for the polar expedition—or refrains from eating them, and goes hungry for days at a time when she is out with him on small expeditions.

Dr Nansen showed that he understood how much his wife suffered from anxiety when he was away in the *Fram* by dedicating *Farthest North*—'To her who christened the ship and had the courage to wait.'

CHAPTER XXII

LOVE AND SCIENCE

THE contemplation of Nature's calm and orderly working exercises a soothing influence upon her students, and
perhaps this is why there have been so many good husbands among celebrated scientists. They seem also to
have made in most instances a natural selection in reference to their wives.

Galvani was especially happy in his wife. She was the
daughter of Professor Galeazzi; and it is said to have
been through her quick observation of the leg of a frog,
placed near an electrical machine, becoming convulsed
when touched by a knife, that her husband was first led
to investigate the science which has since become identified with his name.

What we know about the queen bee and the other bees
was found out by a man living in Geneva called Hüber;
and yet he was blind, and only saw through the eyes of
Aimée, his wife. She observed the bees and told him
about them. Her friends said to her, 'Do not marry
Francis Hüber; he has become blind,' but she replied,
'He therefore needs me more than ever now.' No wonder that Hüber thus spoke of her in his old age : 'Aimée
will never be old to me. To me she is still the fair young
girl I saw when I had eyes to see, and who afterwards, in
her gentleness, gave the blind student her life and her
love.'

Equally fortunate was Sir Charles Lyell in his married
life. Miss Horner, whom he married in 1832, possessed
considerable personal attraction and a winning charm of
manner. When the weakness of his eyes interfered, as
often was the case, with his scientific inquiries, she acted

for him as a most intelligent observer. She was his constant companion and assiduous helpmate during forty years. When she passed away he remarked : 'At my age of nearly seventy-six the separation cannot be very long.'

When Miss Barnard showed to her father the letter which Faraday wrote proposing marriage to her, papa was uncomplimentary enough to remark that love made philosophers fools. She hesitated about accepting him, and went to the seaside to consider it; but the ardent lover followed, determined to learn the worst if need be. They walked on the cliffs overhanging the ocean, and Faraday wrote in his journal as the day drew near its close : 'My thoughts saddened and fell, from the fear I should never enjoy such happiness again. I could not master my feelings, or prevent them from sinking, and I actually at last shamed myself by moist eyes.' He blamed himself because he did not know 'the best means to secure the heart he wished to gain.' He knew how to fathom the depths of chemical combinations, but he could not fathom the depths of Sarah Barnard's heart.

At last the hour of her decision came, and both were made supremely happy by it. A week later he wrote her : 'Every moment offers me fresh proof of the power you have over me. I could not at one time have thought it possible that I, that any man, could have been under the dominion of feelings so undivided and so intense : now I think that no other man can have felt or feel as I do.' A year later they were married very quietly, he desiring their wedding-day to be 'just like any other day.' Twenty-eight years later he wrote among the important dates and discoveries of his life : 'June 12, 1821. I married,—an event which, more than any other, contributed to my earthly happiness and healthful state of mind.' The union has nowise changed, except in the depth and strength of its character. For forty-seven years 'his dear Sarah' made life a joy to him. He rarely left home; but if so, as at the great gathering of British scientists at Birmingham, he wrote back: 'After all, there is no pleasure like the tranquil pleasure of home; and here, even here, the moment I leave the table, I wish I were with you IN QUIET. Oh, what happiness is ours! My runs into the world in this way only serve to make me esteem that happiness the more.'

George Stephenson, the founder of the railway system, though a very busy man, managed to get himself married three times. To be sure he began early, for he was only twenty years old when he fell in love with Elizabeth Hindmarsh, a farmer's daughter. He used to meet her secretly in her father's orchard until his visits were discovered and prevented. After some time Ann Henderson, another farmer's daughter, won his affections. Observing one day that her shoes wanted mending, he obtained her consent to repair them; and when finished, proudly exhibited the precious objects to his friends. His mortification can be imagined when, on returning them to their owner, he was quietly informed by her that 'he wooed where he could never win.' The lady's sister Fanny was older and wiser, and when Stephenson turned to her for consolation, she was not unwilling to step into Ann's shoes. They were married, but within four years Mrs Stephenson died of consumption. For the next thirteen years George Stephenson worked with untiring energy, and saved money. Then meeting Elizabeth Hindmarsh, his early love, who had vowed never to have another man for her husband, he proposed and was accepted. On her death he married again, but only survived this event by seven months.

In 1829 the great engineer, Robert, son of George Stephenson, married Miss Fanny Sanderson. She was not beautiful though she had very expressive black eyes, but she was clever and to the last her will was law with her husband. This was probably because she never seemed to care about having her way. The expenditure of the young housekeeper was prudently adapted to their means, which were small. They even debated whether they should buy a drawing - room sofa. Stephenson opposed the outlay as unnecessary; but, 'reason or no reason,' he wrote to a friend in Newcastle, 'Fanny will have a sofa *à la mode* in the drawing room. I shall see you soon, when we will talk this over.' As might be expected, the 'talking over' resulted in a sofa being bought.

By her tact and amiability Mrs Stephenson made her husband popular amongst his professional brethren and in other ways helped him. So much had the renowned engineer to travel about that his presence at his own home was almost a surprise to its inmates, but whenever he was there it was always merrier.

After two years of acute suffering, most patiently borne, Mrs Stephenson died of cancer. Her husband recorded the event thus in his diary : 'My dear Fanny died this morning at five o'clock. God grant that I may close my life as she has done, in the true faith, and in charity with all men. Her last moments were perfect calmness.'

The death of his wife took away from Stephenson 'half his power of enjoying success.' When he was created a knight of the Order of Leopold, she was past caring for earthly honours, but she made a pathetic pretence of doing so for his sake. On her death-bed she urged him to marry again, but this was the only wish of hers with which he did not comply.

The famous engineer, James Brindley, fell in love with the daughter of a friend when she was a girl at school, and when he went to see her father he was accustomed to take a store of gingerbread for the daughter in his pocket. Shortly after she left school, at the age of only nineteen, Brindley, who was in his fiftieth year, proposed to her and was accepted. Nearly all his correspondence subsequent to his marriage was conducted by his wife, who, notwithstanding her youth, proved a most clever, useful, and affectionate partner.

Before Hugh Miller, the famous geologist, fell in love with Miss Lydia Fraser, he intended building a little house in his mother's garden and making himself content in it, 'with a table, a chair, and a pot, with a little fire and a little meal to cook on it.' This philosophy was spoiled by Miss Fraser's pretty face and sympathetic appreciation. 'I am not now,' he writes to her, 'indifferent to wealth or power or place in the world's eye. I would fain be rich, that I might render you comfortable; powerful, that I might raise you to those high places of society which you are so fitted to adorn; celebrated, that the world might justify your choice. I never think now of building the little house or of being happiest in solitude.' After a long courtship they were married on January 7th, 1837.

James Nasmyth, the inventor of the steam-hammer, speaking of his wife, said : 'Forty-two years of married life finds us the same devoted "cronies" that we were at the beginning.'

Considering how weak the health of Charles Darwin was, he would probably never have been able to make his fruitful discoveries, if he had not had a wife and children who saved him from trouble, and gave to him the leisure of a very happy home.

The wives of scientists have sometimes a good deal to put up with. The wife of the late Professor Agassiz was one morning putting on her stockings and boots. A little scream attracted the Professor's attention. Not having risen he leaned forward anxiously on his elbow and inquired what was the matter.

'Why, a little snake has just crawled out of my boot !' cried she.

'Only one, my dear?' interrogated the Professor, calmly lying down again. 'There should have been three.'

He had put them there to keep them warm.

Not every wife is as tolerant of a husband's ruling passion, or enters into his pursuits in the way that Mrs

Owen did. Here are one or two extracts from her diary :—

'Richard spent the evening in examining some of the minute worms found in the muscles of a man. I looked at one or two through the microscope and saw one cut open. I could not get over the smell of the decaying piece of muscle for hours. R. only laughed, and assured me that in comparison to what surgeons had often to meddle with, it was quite sweet !' . . .

'Last night a kangaroo (dead) came to R. from the Zoo. This morning he dissected some entozoa from the kangaroo. By ingeniously opening these thread-like worms, he has succeeded in making some beautiful preparations, showing their almost invisible insides.' . . .

'To-day, Richard cut up the giraffe which died at the Zoological Gardens.'

Despite the strange odours of dissected penguin, defunct elephant, and other interesting 'subjects,' she merrily drew for him wombats' brains and sharks' teeth, corrected 'Hunterian proofs,' read from Cuvier or translated from the German. After nearly forty years of companionship she died in 1873.

There was something of romance in the first meeting of the well-known geologist, Dean Buckland, with Mary Morland, of whom he had heard from mutual friends as a lady of scientific culture and artistic genius. Buckland was travelling by coach in the west of England, and was reading a new book by Cuvier, which he had just received from the publisher. A lady was also on the coach, and she was reading this identical book, which Cuvier had himself sent to her. They got into conversation, the drift of which was so peculiar that Buckland at last exclaimed, 'You must be Miss Morland, to whom I am about to deliver a letter of introduction.' He was right, and the lady soon became Mrs Buckland.

What a helper she was to her husband is thus described by her son, in the preface to one of his father's works which he edited. 'During the long period that

Dr Buckland was engaged in writing the book which I now have the honour of editing, my mother sat up night after night, for weeks and months consecutively, writing to my father's dictation; and this often till the sun's rays, shining through the shutters at early morn, warned the husband to cease from thinking, and the wife to rest her weary hand. Not only with her pen did she render material assistance, but her natural talent in the use of her pencil enabled her to give accurate illustrations and finished drawings, many of which are perpetuated in Dr Buckland's works. She was also particularly clever and neat in mending broken fossils.' And with all this devotion to her husband's pursuits, Mrs Buckland kept her home in perfect order and carefully instructed her children.

Tyndall married a daughter of Lord Claude Hamilton. Her family did not like the match, but it was a very happy one, and the Professor wrote thus of his wife : 'She has raised my ideal of the possibilities of human nature.' The tragedy that ended the union is well known. Tyndall was suffering from insomnia, and his wife by mistake gave him too large a dose of chloral, thinking it was magnesia. Discovering it he said, 'You have killed your John !'

Dr Buzzard, who was the pupil, the friend, and the physician of Tyndall, said, in answer to a question at the coroner's inquest : 'The relationship between Professor Tyndall and Mrs Tyndall was one of remarkable affection and devotion; I think, in the course of a very long experience, I have never seen the devotion which Mrs Tyndall showed to her husband surpassed.'

The late George John Romanes, so celebrated as a man of science, was happily married. When he had to leave home, he said that the letters from his wife were so 'jolly' that he felt disposed to follow the example of the 'distinguished man who lived apart from his wife because he so much enjoyed her letters.'

The idea of the great electrician, Edison, marrying,

was first suggested by an intimate friend, who told him that his large house and numerous servants ought to have a mistress. Although a very shy man, he seemed pleased with the proposition, and timidly inquired whom he should marry. The friend, annoyed at his apparent want of sentiment, somewhat testily replied, 'Any one.' But Edison was not devoid of sentiment when the time came. One day as he stood behind the chair of a Miss Stillwell, a telegraph operator in his employ, he was not a little surprised when she suddenly turned round and said, 'Mr Edison, I can always tell when you are behind me or near me.' It was now Miss Stillwell's turn to be surprised, for, with characteristic bluntness and ardour, Edison confronted the young lady, and, looking her full in the face, said, 'I've been thinking considerably about you of late, and if you are willing to marry me, I would like to marry you.' The young lady said she would consider the matter and talk it over with her mother. The result was that they were married a month later, and the union proved a very happy one.

Lord Kelvin has been most fortunate in marriage. Miss Crum, of Thornliebank, who became his wife, was a charming companion, and her early death was a terrible blow to his affectionate heart. The present Lady Kelvin, formerly Miss Blandy, seems to have been made for him, strong both in head and heart, of wide sympathies, and most engaging kindness. Nothing can be more delightful than their married life, as she, while herself forming a centre of attraction, enters into all his interests, and by her wise and loving care secures for him a restfulness that makes for health as well as study.

CHAPTER XXIII

LOVE AND POLITICS

ONE who knew Edmund Burke said : 'In the House of Commons only the fiercer peculiarities of his character were seen; while at home he seemed the mildest and kindest, as well as one of the best and greatest of human beings. He poured forth the rich treasures of his mind with the most prodigal bounty. At breakfast and dinner his gaiety, wit, and pleasantry enlivened the board, and diffused cheerfulness and happiness all round.' Indeed Burke frequently declared that every care vanished the moment he entered under his own roof. His wife, who was the daughter of Dr Nugent, his medical attendant, managed so well his private affairs, that his mind was kept free for public duties. One morning, on the anniversary of his marriage, he wrote and presented to Mrs Burke a paper entitled, 'The Idea of a Wife, the Character of ——,' leaving her to fill up the blank.

His description of his wife is too long to quote, but we must give an epitome of it. Of her beauty he said that it did not arise from features, from complexion, or from shape; 'she has all three in a high degree, but it is not by these that she touches the heart; it is all that sweetness of temper, benevolence, innocence, and sensibility which a face can express, that forms her beauty. Her eyes have a mild light, but they awe you when she pleases; they command, like a good man out of office, not by authority, but by virtue. Her stature is not tall; she is not made to be the admiration of everybody, but the happiness of one. She has all the firmness that does not exclude delicacy; she has all the softness that does not imply weakness. Her voice is low, soft music, not formed to rule in public assemblies, but to charm those who can distinguish a company from a crowd; it has this advantage, you must come close to her to hear it. To describe her body describes her mind; one is the transcript of the other. She discovers the right and wrong of things, not by reasoning, but by sagacity. No person of so few years can know the world better; no person was ever less corrupted by that knowledge. She has a true generosity of temper; the most extravagant cannot be more unbounded in their liberality, the most covetous not more cautious in their distribution. Her politeness seems to flow rather from a natural disposition to oblige, than from any rules on that subject. It is long before she chooses, but then it is fixed for ever; and the first hours of romantic friendship are not warmer than hers after the lapse of years. As she never disgraces her good nature by severe reflections on anybody, so she never degrades her judgment by immoderate or ill-placed praises : for everything violent is contrary to her gentleness of disposition and the evenness of her virtue.'

Burke had an only son upon whom he built great hopes. Just when he had obtained for him a seat in Parliament, the family consumption appeared, but the doomed man did his best to conceal from his parents his extreme weakness. On the day of his death, hearing sounds of weeping, he caused himself to be carried to their room, and, summoning up his little remaining strength, he walked twice or thrice across it, repeating those lines from Milton which the stormy weather without suggested :—

> His praise, ye winds, that from four quarters blow,
> Breathe soft or loud; and wave your tops, ye pines,
> With every plant, in sign of worship wave——

But the effort was too great; he fell insensible into his father's arms, and shortly breathed his last.

Burke never recovered this blow. It is said that thenceforward he could never bear so much as to look towards the church at Beaconsfield, where his hopes lay buried.

'One day, while he was walking in his park, the feeble old horse of his son came close up to him and laid its head upon his bosom; which so affected him that his firmness was totally overpowered, and, throwing his arms over its neck, he wept long and loudly.'

William Cobbett, who worked himself up from a private soldier to be a great reforming force in Parliament and out of it, saw his future wife, Ann Reid, in Canada, in 1787. She was the daughter of an artilleryman, and then only about thirteen. She was working at a washtub, and Tommy Atkins, as the future terror of abuses then was, exclaimed : 'That's the girl for me !'

On returning to England and leaving the army, Cobbett sent the industrious girl all his savings, which she kept untouched until she came to Woolwich to be married in 1792. She was in every way a helpmate. When her husband was imprisoned two years, and had to pay £1000 fine, for an article he wrote on military flogging, she bore it as thus described by Cobbett : 'I found Mrs Cobbett very well, and quite prepared for what had happened. She bears the thing with her usual fortitude, and takes hourly occasion to assure me that she thinks I have done what I ought to do. In this she is excellent. She is the only wife that I ever saw, who in such circumstances did not express *sorrow*, at least, for what her husband had done; and, in such cases, sorrow is only another word for *blame*.'

The famous Wilkes was the best-mannered but ugliest man of his day. 'I am,' he said, 'the ugliest man in the three kingdoms; but if you give me a quarter of an hour's start I will gain the love of any woman before the handsomest.'

He tells us that, to please an indulgent father, he

married a woman half as old again as himself because she had a large fortune. 'It was a sacrifice to Plutus, not to Venus. . . . I stumbled at the very threshold of the temple of Hymen.'

George Canning also married money, but with a very different result. The lady, Miss Joan Scott, had £100,000, and this little *dot* was very useful in developing and strengthening Canning's parliamentary interests. Nor was Venus slighted, for, besides her fortune, Mrs Canning gave to her husband a love as deep as it was unselfish. When he died the physician declared it necessary for her life or reason that she should obtain the relief of tears, for she had not wept once, either before or after his death, and this relief came to her when she saw her son.

According to the biographer of Charles James Fox, his chief aim was 'to treat women as beings who stood on the same intellectual table-land as himself; to give them the very best of his thought and his knowledge as well as of his humour and his eloquence; to invite and weigh their advice in seasons of difficulty; and, if ever they urged him to steps which his judgment or his conscience disapproved, not to elude them with half-contemptuous banter, but to convince them by plain-spoken and serious remonstrance.' It is strange that this chivalrous regard for women did not tempt him to acknowledge as his wife, until after ten years, the widow, Elizabeth Armstead, with whom he lived. She so well understood him that she could anticipate his thoughts, and frequently when he returned home, fretted 'by injustice and worn by turmoil,' she would take down a volume of *Don Quixote* or *Gil Blas* and read to him. No wonder that with such a home 'the world outside, with its pleasures and ambitions, became to him an object of indifference, and at last of repugnance.' And Fox was equally good and sunshiny. 'No man ever devoted such powers of pleasing to the single end of making a woman happy.'

William Lamb, afterwards Lord Melbourne, neither was nor deserved to be successful in matrimony. Lady Caroline, daughter of the Earl of Beesborough, whom he married, had some ugly ways, but she had others that were very pretty. After one of their serious quarrels, for instance, when everything was arranged for a separation, and he had gone away until the formal documents could be prepared, she followed him, and lay down like a faithful dog at the door of his room, so that he could not come out without treading on her. The following morning when the lawyers arrived they found her sitting on his knee, feeding him with bread and butter.

At a dinner party in Paris she asked one of the guests whom she considered the most distinguished man she ever knew in 'mind and person, refinement, cultivation, sensibility and thought.'

The guest replied, 'Lord Byron.'

'No,' was the answer; 'my own husband.'

Unfortunately Lady Caroline became acquainted with Byron and was infatuated by him. The story of her stabbing herself with scissors, or a metal dagger-shaped paper-knife, is confirmed by a document preserved among the Byron relics. Her attentions, however, bored him. One day, visiting his lodgings when he was out, she wrote under his name in a book that was on the table, 'Remember me !' to which he added these uncomplimentary lines—

> Remember thee ! remember thee !
>   Till Lethe quench life's burning stream,
> Remorse and shame shall cling to thee,
>   And haunt thee like a feverish dream.

> Remember thee ! ay, doubt it not,
>   Thy husband too shall think of thee :
> But neither shalt thou be forgot,
>   Thou *false* to him, thou *fiend* to me.

Compare with this the following letter :—

'LADY CAROLINE LAMB,—

'I am no longer your lover; and since you oblige me to confess it by this truly unfeminine persecution, learn that I am attached to another, whose name it would of course be dishonest to mention. I shall ever remember with gratitude the many instances I have received of the predilection you have shown in my favour. I shall ever continue your friend, if your ladyship will permit me so to style myself. And as proof of my regard, I offer you this advice, correct your vanity which is ridiculous; exert your absurd caprices on others, and leave me in peace.

'Your obedient servant,
'BYRON.'

Lady Caroline laid the blame upon her husband. She said: 'He cares nothing for my morals. I may flirt and go about with what men I please. He was privy to my affair with Lord Byron, and laughed at it. His indolence renders him insensible to everything. When I ride, play, and amuse him, he loves me. In sickness and suffering he deserts me. His violence is as bad as my own.'

This last was saying a good deal, for one day Lady Caroline threw a ball at the head of her page. 'It hit him,' she says, 'and he bled. He cried out, "Oh, my lady, you have killed me !" Out of my senses, I flew into the hall and screamed, "O God, I have murdered the page !" The servants and people in the streets caught the sound, and it was soon spread about.'

On another occasion, not liking the way the dinner-table was being decorated, she leaped upon it, and behaved so wildly that the butler ran for her husband. When Melbourne saw her, he only said in the gentlest tone of expostulation, 'Caroline, Caroline !' then took her in his arms and carried her out of doors into the sunshine.

Not long after this the illness from which she died took hold of her. Seeing her prostrate condition Melbourne's old love revived, especially when he heard how she had valued and treasured his letters. After her death, he used to speak of her with tears, and ask moodily, 'Shall we meet in another world?'

Robert Lowe, afterwards Lord Sherbrooke, married Georgiana, daughter of Mr George Orred, of Traumere, Cheshire. If we may credit a story that is told, the young people had not much money. One day it is said Lowe was criticising the Marriage Service, and especially the saying of the man—'With all my worldly goods I thee endow.'

'When I married,' he remarked, 'I had nothing to give my bride.'

'Oh, yes, Robert, you had your magnificent intellect,' suggested Mrs Lowe.

'My dear, I did not endow you with that.'

Notwithstanding this jesting reply Lowe used to speak with pride of the admirable qualities of his wife, and of the courage which enabled her to triumph over the many difficulties and anxious experiences they passed through.

On December 11th, 1839, Lord Palmerston married the widow of Earl Cowper. She surrounded his political existence with social charm, enthralling his friends and softening his opponents. Meeting Earl Beaconsfield— then Mr Disraeli—at the House one day, a very celebrated foreign diplomatist remarked to him : 'What a wonderful system of society you have in England ! I have not been on speaking terms with Lord Palmerston for three weeks, and yet here I am; but, you see, I am paying a visit to Lady Palmerston.'

Cobden married a pretty Welsh girl, Catherine Anne Williams. 'Whether,' writes Mr Morley, 'this union was preceded by much deliberation we do not know; perhaps experience shows that the profoundest deliberation in choosing a wife is little better than the cleverness of people who boast of a scientific secret of winning in a lottery.' Be this as it may, Cobden had no cause to regret his choice in after years, although his wife often sighed at his enforced absences from home, which were almost continual. In spite of good work done, fame and great position, she used sometimes to say to Cobden—and he agreed with her—that it would have been better for them both if, after they were married, they had gone to settle in the backwoods of Canada.

Then came money embarrassments and the loss of an only son to darken the Cobden home. This boy, the 'healthiest and strongest in his school,' was seized by scarlet fever, and died in three days. On hearing the news, a strange torpor seized Mrs Cobden and held her for a long time. She became 'as helpless as one of her young children, and required as much forbearance and kindness.' Both were forthcoming in abundance from her husband, who thought that he never could sufficiently repay her for the way she had always made the comfort of her domestic life subservient to his political engagements.

It was when John Bright was in the depth of grief, and almost of despair, at the loss of his first wife, that Cobden called upon him and suggested a joint crusade against the Corn Laws. After words of condolence, he said :—

'There are thousands of homes in England this moment where wives, mothers, and children are dying of hunger. Now when the first paroxysm of your grief is past, I would advise you to come with me, and we will never rest until the Corn Law is repealed.'

Mrs Bright was a careful and domestic woman. When he married her she said to him: 'John, attend to thy business and thy public affairs, and I will provide for the house and relieve thee from all cares at home.'

CHAPTER XXIV

LOVE AND POLITICS CONTINUED

MOST people know how Mrs Fawcett became eyes to the blind Postmaster-General. If any proof were required of Henry Fawcett's devotion to his wife, we could not quote a more touching incident than one which happened during the election contest at Brighton in February, 1871. Mrs Fawcett was starting for a ride with her husband, when her horse fell, and she was thrown with great force and rendered unconscious. Eye-witnesses have described the terrible agony he felt on this occasion, and the bitter tears he shed when he thought that her unconsciousness was only another name for death. Happily her accident was not so serious as he anticipated; and on the following day, when he addressed a large meeting and referred to his anxiety, he added that one reason why he had overcome obstacles was that he had had 'a helpmate whose political judgment was much less frequently at fault than his own.'

The picture that is given by his biographer of the home life of the Right Honourable William Edward Forster is a very beautiful one. He was never weary of acknowledging his indebtedness to his wife, whom he cherished with a chivalrous reverence not too common in the present age. She was the daughter of Dr Arnold, and the admission into a family of such distinction insensibly widened his sympathies, and brought his mind into contact with ideas of which he had known comparatively little before. He did his work in the same room with his family—he reading and writing at one table, his wife at another. The library was the scene of their joint life and companionship.

The graceful and interesting personality of his beautiful American wife contributed in no small degree to the popularity of the late Lord Randolph Churchill. 'The dusky one,' as she was early nicknamed by her more intimate friends, began life as Miss Jenny Jerome, the eldest of three lovely sisters, daughters of an American millionaire. Lord Randolph first met his future wife at a small dinner-party in Paris. Though the young statesman was little given to ladies' society, his attention was attracted to the lovely young American through the fluency and brilliant wit by which she carried on the conversation in French. When the evening was over, he said to a friend, 'That is the brightest girl I have ever met.'

In her husband's opinion Lady Randolph was a perfect electioneering agent. Once when he happened to be away just as his seat fell vacant at Woodstock, she proved the truth of his words by personally canvassing every elector in the district.

The biographer of the late Right Honourable W. H. Smith thus writes : 'Love-letters have often been penned amid strange environment—from dungeons and garrets, and from Arctic wastes and torrid African sands; but surely none were ever more tender or more true than those written by Smith to his wife from the Treasury Bench, amid the din of debate or the langour of obstructive talk.'

Here is an extract from one such letter written in 1887 : 'I had a very nice letter from the Queen, which I will show you to-morrow evening if, as I hope, I am able to get down to you. And this must come to you as my first greeting on the anniversary of that happy day when we became one. God has blessed us, and we do owe very much to Him, for all our trials have brought us closer to each other and to Him; and every day I realise more and more of the strength and guidance which you ask and help me to gain. The debate is going on in a dull way, and Childers is now speaking; but our Irish Attorney-General, Mr Holmes, made a very good speech indeed in opening.'

Compare with this a letter which Sir Stafford Northcote, afterwards Lord Iddesleigh, wrote to his wife after the settlement of the Alabama claims. He had been married then nearly thirty years :—

'*Washington, May 8th*, 1871.

'My Own C——,—The first and only use I make of this pen after signing the Treaty with it is to send you a notification of the fact.—Your devoted
'STAFFORD H. NORTHCOTE.'

Marriage was not a failure in the case of Lord Beaconsfield, Prince Bismarck, or Mr Gladstone, whom we take to have been the three greatest statesmen of our day.

Lord Beaconsfield married the widow of his friend, Mr Wyndham Lewis. She was not beautiful, but she had an income of several thousands a year. She was fifteen years older than Disraeli, and he said he would never marry for love. Indeed, he used to tell her that he married for money, and she would reply, 'That may be so, but if you were to marry me again you would do it for love.' Certainly there was an affection which stood the trials of thirty years, and deepened as they both declined into age. She was his helpmate, his confidante, his adviser; and the hours spent with her in retirement were the happiest that he knew. In defeat or victory he hurried home from the House of Commons to share his vexation or triumph with his companion, who never believed that he could fail. The moment in his whole life which perhaps gave him the greatest pleasure was that at which he was able to decorate her with a peerage.

To her he dedicated *Sybil*, 'I,' he says, 'would inscribe this work to one whose noble spirit and gentle nature ever prompt her to sympathise with the suffering, to one whose sweet voice has often encouraged, and whose taste and judgment have ever guided, its pages—the most severe of critics, but a "perfect wife."'

A party of young men once ventured a foolish jest at Mrs Disraeli's age and appearance, and rallied him on the motives of his marriage. 'Gentlemen,' said Disraeli, as he rose and left the room, 'do none of you know what gratitude means?'

A friend of Lord Beaconsfield, speaking of the time he was only Mr Disraeli, writes : 'We were congratulating him upon the result of an election. He had been returned by an enormous majority. One thing he said, I particularly remarked : "My wife will be very pleased."'

Another occasion when Lady Beaconsfield was very pleased was on April 12th, 1867, when her husband defeated Mr Gladstone's amendment to the Reform Bill. The younger members of the party extemporised a supper at the Carlton Club, and begged him to join them, but Lady Beaconsfield was never tired of repeating : 'Dizz came home to me'; and she would add how he ate half the pie she had prepared in anticipation of his triumph.

On the 3rd of April, 1872, this sympathetic wife hastened back from listening to a great speech in order to receive the orator. When she heard his carriage she hurried from the drawing-room to the hall, rushed into his arms, embraced him rapturously, and exclaimed : 'Oh, Dizzy ! Dizzy ! this is the greatest night of all ! This pays for all !'

After another oratorical triumph, this time at Edinburgh, the sympathetic couple danced about like children when they had retired to their bedroom. Indeed, so congenial a companion was this charming woman

that Lord Beaconsfield said of her when she was dying :
'For thirty-three years she has never given me a dull
moment.'

It must be admitted, however, that the admiration of
Lady Beaconsfield for her husband did sometimes in her
old age take ridiculous forms. She used to wear on her
left breast what looked like a large decoration. This
was 'Dizzy's' portrait in an oval frame. She was one
evening in the company of some ladies when the conversation wandered into a talk about fine figures : 'Mr A's,
Mr B's, Captain C's.' The old lady let them run on, and
then said pityingly : 'Ah ! You should see my Dizzy in
his bath !'

Mrs Gladstone is certainly one of the cleverest women
living. Her existence has been a semi-public one for
half a century. During that period she has been brought
into contact with the most distinguished people, and a
silly woman—any woman, indeed, but a remarkably
clever one—must have perpetrated under these circumstances a host of blunders.

Mrs Gladstone has steered clear of them all, and has
exhibited a not inferior dexterity in her management of
Mr Gladstone himself. She understands precisely how
to humour him and diet him, what friend to encourage,
whom to protect him against. Mr Gladstone has pub-
licly announced that every morsel of animal food which
he puts into his eloquent mouth requires, for the purposes of digestion, thirty-three—or is it thirty-two?—
distinct bites. Mrs Gladstone, therefore, takes care
that he should always eat slowly.

Mrs Gladstone is the daughter of Sir Stephen Glynne,
of Hawarden. She and her sisters were known as 'the
handsome Miss Glynnes.' That which first attracted
Miss Glynne's attention to Mr Gladstone was a remark
made by a Cabinet Minister, who sat beside her at a
dinner-party at which Mr Gladstone also was present.
'Mark that young man,' said he ; 'he will yet be Prime
Minister of England !'

Miss Glynne scrutinised the handsome and expressive features of the young M.P. who sat opposite to her; but it was not until the subsequent winter that she made his acquaintance in Italy. They were married in 1839, and at the golden wedding of the grand old couple, Mr Gladstone said that words failed him (fancy words failing Mr Gladstone !) to express the debt he owed his wife in relation to all the offices that she had discharged during 'the long and the happy period of our conjugal union.'

The one great drawback to Mrs Gladstone's happiness before her husband retired from active politics, was that she had not enough of his society. She has been known to remark that when Mr Gladstone was in office and in London during the season, it was quite a treat to her to be invited to a friend's house to dinner with him. She always then tried to get seated next him, 'when,' she said, 'it is at least possible for me to have some conversation with my husband : otherwise I see nothing of him.'

In many respects Princess Bismarck filled a place similar to that which was occupied with so much grace and distinction by Mrs Gladstone.

Very characteristic was the wooing of the 'Iron Chancellor.' Meeting and falling in love with Fräulein von Puttkammer at a wedding, young Bismarck wrote bluntly to her parents, demanding their daughter. This, from a wild young fellow whose pranks were the talk of the country, was rather alarming.

'It was,' said the father, 'as if some one had struck me on the head with a heavy axe !'

As, however, the lady's heart had evidently been stolen, there was nothing for it but to invite the robber to pay a visit for personal inspection. When the time came for him to arrive the parents put on an air of solemnity, and the young lady stood with her eyes modestly bent upon the ground. Bismarck rode up, and, alighting, threw his arms around his sweetheart's neck, and embraced her vigorously before any one had time to remonstrate. The result was a betrothal. Bismarck is fond of telling this tale, and he generally finishes with the reflection : 'She it is who has made me what I am.'

No home into which bores enter can be called a paradise; and, if it were for no other reason, Princess Bismarck deserved the undying gratitude of her husband because of her success in keeping at a distance these enemies of peace. An ambassador of one of the great Powers called on Bismarck, and in the course of a rather long conversation asked the Prince how he managed to get rid of troublesome visitors. 'Oh, that is very simple,' replied the Chancellor. 'When my wife thinks any one is staying too long, she merely sends for me, and thus the interview ends.' At that very moment a servant entered, and, bowing low, begged his master to favour the Princess with his presence for a few minutes. The ambassador blushed, as much as any diplomatist *can* blush, and at once withdrew as gracefully as possible in the trying circumstances.

The Marchioness of Salisbury is the daughter of Baron Alderson, who was one of the ablest judges of his time, and she is niece to Mrs Opie, whose writings were once very popular. The late Lord Salisbury, however, tried to prevent the match; but as his son, then Lord Robert Cecil, persisted, he so far relented as to make terms. These were that Lord Robert should undertake not to see or communicate with Miss Alderson for a year. The young lover stood the test, and, at the close of the year, he obtained his father's consent; but the Marquis, while continuing his allowance of £600 a year, declined to increase it. Still, he obtained a wife who has made his domestic life as happy as that of any public man of our time.

Lady Robert Cecil threw herself heart and soul into her husband's career, although she never allowed her social duties to interfere with her care of the many children which came to brighten her home. Following her husband's example, she found time to become a frequent contributor to the leading magazines and weeklies, and she is popularly supposed to have written some of the best articles which have ever appeared in *The Saturday Review*. This, however, did not prevent her from developing what the French call 'a genius for the comfortable' in the management of her several homes.

The American Statesman, Benjamin Franklin, began his career by arriving at Philadelphia, to seek for work, with only a Dutch dollar in his pocket. Weary and hungry, he bought three great rolls of bread. Walking out of the baker's shop, with a roll under each arm and eating the third, he passed the house of a Mr Read, whose daughter stood at the door, thinking the young man made a ridiculous appearance and little guessing that she was one day to be his wife. Some time afterwards the stranger was introduced to Miss Read, and she found him by no means as ridiculous as he had at first appeared to her. A mutual attachment was the result, and then Franklin went to London, where he remained several years. During the separation he neglected the young lady in a manner which he himself afterwards condemned. On his return, he found that she had married and become a widow. Franklin's early love revived, and he asked her forgiveness and a renewal of her affections, which were readily granted. Of their union, which continued nearly forty years, the husband remarks : 'We prospered together, and it was our mutual study to render each other happy. Thus I corrected, as well as I could, the error of my youth.'

A caricature has no value, except when founded upon reality, and therefore a picture which appeared in a celebrated comic paper when Mr Cleveland was re-elected President of the United States, shows what the nation thought of his wife. The caricature represented Mrs

Cleveland bringing back her husband on her shoulders to the White House.

A very beautiful girl of only twenty-two when she married, she filled the position of President's wife in a way that won praise from every one. Send a President home to his own fireside is a thing the Americans do, with few exceptions, every four years; but send away from the White House a woman like Mrs Cleveland— the Americans are gallant and would not do that.

CHAPTER XXV

THE LOVE AFFAIRS OF SHERIDAN

WHEN the Sheridans lived at Bath, there was another family there, called 'a nest of nightingales'—the family of Linley, the composer, who had been for years at the head of musical enterprise in the district. The voice of Elizabeth, the eldest daughter, was as lovely as her face, and she was the *prima donna* of her father's concerts. The young men were all at her feet, and not only the young men, as was natural, but the elder and less inno- cent members of society. Among these last was a Captain Matthews, who, though a married man, tor- mented the young lady with his attentions.

Richard Brinsley Sheridan becoming known to Miss Linley through his sister, who was her devoted friend, assumed the position of the young lady's secret guar- dian. He made friends with Matthews, and discovered the villainous designs which he entertained. At length the poor girl was so persecuted that she tried to take poison—searching for, and finding in Miss Sheridan's room, a small phial of laudanum, which fortunately was too small to do any great harm. After this evidence of her miserable state, Sheridan disclosed the full turpitude of Matthew's intentions, and showed her a letter in which the villain announced that he had determined to carry her off by force. What was to be done? The poor girl seems to have had no confidence in her father's power of protecting her, and probably knew the exped- iency of embroiling him with his patrons. Sheridan proposed that she should fly with him to France and take refuge there till the danger would be over. The persecuted fair one agreed to do so, and set off for Calais with her deliverer. Here the latter, in order to prevent scandal, persuaded her to consent to an informal marriage. Ignorant of this, Mr Linley proceeded to France, and after promising Sheridan that he might one day allow his daughter to marry him, took her back to England. ·Then Captain Matthews published a letter in which he called Sheridan a liar and a scoundrel. The result was a duel, which ended in a violent scuffle. Sheridan was brought home wounded, but the affair was kept secret from Miss Linley as long as possible. When at length she did hear of Sheridan's wounded condition, she almost betrayed their secret, which even now nobody suspected, by a cry of 'My husband! my husband!' which startled all who were present, but was set down to her excitement and distress, and presently forgotten.

And here we must quote part of a letter written by 'The Maid of Bath' to Sheridan at the period when, not daring to avow their informal marriage in France, they were necessarily living separated from each other. There is more love in it than grammar, but grammar and orthography were not common acquirements of ladies in those days.

'Twelve o'clock. You unconscionable creature to make me sit up this time of the night to scribble nonsense to you, when you will not let me hear one word from you for this week to come. Oh, my dear, you are the Tyrant indeed. You do not fancy I would do this if it was not equally agreeable to myself. Indeed, my dearest love, I am never happy except when I am with you, or writing to you. Why did you run away so soon to-night? Tho' I could not enjoy your conversation freely, yet it was a consolation to me that you was so near me. I gave up my cards the moment you left me, as I could not play with any patience. . . .

'My mother and me called on Miss Roscoe this evening, when we talked a great deal about you. Miss R. said she was sure you and I would make a match of it.

Nay, she said the whole world was of the opinion that we should be married in less than a month. Only think of this, bright Hevn's! God bless you, my dear, dear love. I am so weary I must go to bed. There is but one thing that could keep me awake and that is your company. Once more adieu. . . .

'Upon my knees, half naked, once more I am going to tire you with my nonsense. I could not bear to see this little blank without filling it up. Tho' I do not know with what, as I have almost exhausted the budget of news which I had collected since our long absence.'

A letter written by the young lady during a misunderstanding between the lovers brought about by a mysterious 'Miss C.' and a Mrs Lyster, the mischief-making wife of a medical man at Waltham Abbey, is curious from the evidence it supplies that Miss Linley did not regard the irregular marriage 'by a priest in a village not far from Calais' as precluding her from marrying another man if so disposed.

Here is the jealous missive of this much-courted beauty and popular vocalist :—

'You are sensible,' she says, 'when I left Bath [for France] I had not an idea of you but as a friend. It was not your person that gained my affection. No, S——n, it was that delicacy, that tender compassion, that interest which you seemed to take in my welfare, that were the motives which induced me to love you. . . . . There are insurmountable obstacles to prevent our ever being united, even supposing I could be induced again to believe you. I did not think to have told you of a great one, but I must, or you will not be convinced that I am in earnest. Know then, that before I left Bath, after I had refused Sir Thomas Clarges and other gentlemen of fortune, on your account, who I found had given up all thought of me, in the anguish of my soul which was torn with all the agonies of remorse and rage, I vowed in the most solemn manner upon my knees, before my parents, that I never would be yours by my own consent, let what would be the consequence. My father took advantage of my distress, and my upbraidings, mixed with persuasions, prevailed upon me to promise that I would marry the first man (whose character was unexceptionable) that offered. I repented that I had made this promise afterwards, for though I resolved never to be yours I had not the least intention to be another's. I comforted myself with thinking I should not be solicited, but I was deceived.

'My father, before we left Bath, received proposals for me from a gentleman in London, which he insisted on my accepting. I endeavoured to evade his earnest request, but he urged my promise in such a manner that I could not refuse to see him at least. He has visited me two or three times since we have been here. He is not a young man, but I believe a worthy one. When I found my father so resolute I resolved to acquaint the gentleman with every circumstance of my life. I did, and instead of inducing him to give me up he is now more earnest than ever.'

In the following Lent, Miss Linley came to London to sing in the oratorios, and it is said that young Sheridan resorted to the most romantic expedients to see her. He disguised himself as a hackney coachman, and drove her home on several occasions. But love conquered in the long run, and about a year from the time of Miss Linley's journey to Calais she was married to her gallant escort. And a devoted wife she made, forming for the nineteen years of her married life no small item in the success, as well as in the happiness, of her brilliant husband. Moore says of her : 'There has seldom perhaps existed a finer combination of all those qualities that attract both eye and heart than this accomplished and lovely person exhibited. To judge by what we hear, it was impossible to see her without adoration, or know her without love.' And Sheridan's latest biographer speaks of her as 'a thoroughly practical lady, which a great beauty seldom is, being an excellent housekeeper and a most sensible mother.' Then how enduring was her love for her husband in spite of his follies ! In a letter to her sister she writes : 'As you know, poor Dick and I have always been struggling against the stream, and shall probably continue to do so to the end of our lives. Yet we would not change sentiments or sensations with —— for all his estate.'

When Sheridan was preparing his matchless speech for the impeachment of Warren Hastings, Mrs Sheridan copied documents and arranged them, and her loving interest was such that when she heard the speech delivered, the pleasure became really painful from its intensity. When the orator had finished, Lady Lucan turned to his wife and said : 'You should consider yourself a very happy woman, Mrs Sheridan, to please that man who can please everybody.'

And Sheridan could appreciate and love in return this 'connecting link between woman and angel,' though he may sometimes have given her cause for jealousy. During her last painful illness he never left her one moment that could be avoided, and the doctor who attended said that his tenderness and affection was quite 'the devotedness of a lover.' A friend of his said that, happening a little after her death to sleep in the room next to him, he could plainly hear him sobbing. 'I have seen him,' says Kelly, 'night after night sit and cry like a child, while I sang to him at his desire a pathetic little song of mine— ''They bore her to a grassy grave.'' I have never beheld more poignant grief than Sheridan felt for the loss of his beloved wife.'

Such grief, however, could not last, and three years after, that is in 1795, the bereaved husband married Ester Jane Ogle, eldest daughter of the Dean of Winchester. He was forty-two and she was twenty years of age. Unauthenticated gossip says that the first time Miss Ogle met Sheridan, which was at Devonshire House, she called out 'Keep away, you fright, you terrible creature !' Being piqued, Sheridan exercised his powers of fascination, with the result that Miss Ogle gladly consented to marry him.   She had a dowry of £5000 and Sheridan settled £15,000 upon her.   She wanted it all, for she was careless and self-indulgent, repeatedly demanding another house or another horse.   Her husband's patience was almost inexhaustible even when she was writing to him contemptuous letters in reference to the way he managed his money matters.   One of his replies to her covered twenty-four closely-written pages of quarto paper, and is a most able and minute defence of his conduct.

Sheridan and his second wife had few tastes in common except fondness for their son, Charles Brinsley, and also for Tom, her step-son.   Yet her admiration for Sheridan was very great.   'As to my husband's talents,' she wrote, 'I will not say anything about them, but I *will* say that he is the handsomest and honestest man in all England.'

Sheridan's pet name for his second wife was Hecca, and he began letters to her in terms such as these : 'My dear, dear Hecca'; 'My sweet beloved'; 'My only delight in life'; 'My own Gypsy'; 'My soul's beloved'; 'My darling wench'; 'My pretty wench'; 'My own dear bit of brown Holland.'

The endings of his letters are not less uncommon : 'Bless your bones'; 'Bless your low forehead and your round elbows and your flowing tresses'; 'Bless your eyelids, my beloved'; 'Bless your knees and elbows'; 'Bless you ever and ever and all over.'

Her eyes, which he called green, he admired, and when she had been complaining of her sight, he wrote to reassure her: 'As for your emeralds, I will guarantee them'; 'Now you are fast asleep, your green eyes closed, and your arm round one of your rosy cheeks'; 'I will kiss your green beads on Saturday.'

He expected her to write to him every day, and when one day the letter did not arrive, he wrote : 'Gracious God! not a single line!   If a voice from Heaven had told me that any human being should have treated me thus, I should not have believed it.'

Her difficulty is candidly set forth. She tells him on one occasion that her letter is sent to prevent him feeling annoyed, though she has literally nothing to say now that her cold is better, adding : 'Pray, dear S., write, for I like of all things to hear from you, and when you write I feel as if I had something to say.' 'Oh ! Sheridan, if you were but here Hecca would be quite happy. . . . Sheridan, how much better you are than anything on earth, and how well I love you. I will hate everything you hate, and love everything you love, so God bless you.'

Moore describes the immediate result of the new marriage as the renewal of Sheridan's youth. To reclaim him, however, was beyond the young wife's power, as it was beyond his own. She had to endure the same troubles and anxieties as her predecessor, for Sheridan continued to be harassed by money difficulties, which drove him to all manner of shifts to raise the necessary supplies. But however careless about his own debts, Sheridan was anxious that his son Tom should be free from pecuniary embarrassments by marrying a certain lady with a large fortune. Tom preferred a Miss Callander. When his father found that his arguments were unavailing, he threatened that if he married Miss Callander, he would cut him off with a shilling.'

'Then, sir, you must borrow it,' retorted Tom.

CHAPTER XXVI

SOME OTHER FAMOUS MEN AND THEIR LOVES

SAMUEL PEPYS, who was Secretary to the Admiralty, and whose diary, extending from January, 1659-60, to May, 1669, is well known, married, when he was twenty-three, Elizabeth St Michel, a beautiful girl belonging to a good family, but only fifteen years of age.

Their early married life was a great struggle with poverty, but they gradually emerged into more prosperous circumstances, and in the end became rich. Pepys was unlike that husband of whom his wife said that she wished he had a tail to wag when he was pleased. The following is a tender wag of Pepys's tail :—

'Talking with pleasure with my poor wife, how she used to make coal-fires, and wash my foul clothes with her own hands for me, poor wretch ! in our little room at my Lord Sandwich's; for which I ought for ever to love and admire her, and do : and persuade myself she would do the same thing again, if God should reduce us to it.'

After this we can forgive him for his pride in his carriage.

'Abroad with my wife, the first time that ever I rode in my own coach, which do make my heart rejoice and praise God, and pray Him to bless it to me, and continue it.'

He and Mrs Pepys, however, had their quarrels like other couples, and these are recorded as honestly as other matters. An entry on 12th July, 1667, tells us that he 'did give her a pull by the nose and some ill words,' and the consequence was that when he 'went to the office to avoid further anger, she followed me in a devilish manner thither.'

Mrs Pepys was somewhat wilful, especially in matters pertaining to 'the fashions,' which at the time of the diary were frequently extravagant in the extreme. It had become the mode for ladies to wear fair hair, as is often to be seen in a certain type of stage ladies in our own day. Her husband was very wroth with her for what he considered was a disfiguring of her own beautiful hair; but Mrs Pepys persisted in following the fashion, and this 'scene' was the result : 'May 11, 1667. My wife being dressed this day in fair hair, did make me so mad that I spoke not one word to her, though I was ready to burst with anger. In my way home I discovered my trouble to my wife for her white locks, swearing several times, which I pray God forgive me for, and bending my fist that I would not endure it. She, poor wretch, was surprised with it, and made me no answer all the way home; but there we parted, and I to the office late, and then home, and without supper to bed, vexed.'

Possibly it was a suspicion on the part of Mrs Pepys of her husband's susceptibility that led to the following domestic 'scene,' in which her maid Mercer figured : 'To sing with my wife and Mercer in the garden; and, coming in, I find my wife plainly dissatisfied with me that I can spend so much time with Mercer, teaching her to sing, and could never take the pains with her. Which I acknowledge; but it is because the girl do take music mighty readily, and she do not, and music is the thing of the world that I love most, and all the pleasure almost that I can now take. So to bed in some little discontent, but no words from me.'

Samuel Pepys had always an eye for 'mighty pretty women,' and Mrs Knipp, the actress, he especially admired. This aroused the 'green-eyed monster' in Mrs Pepys, and sometimes she made things rather warm for her husband, not only metaphorically but literally. One night when he had gone to bed—his wife not being induced to follow his example—and awaking suddenly, he found her standing by his bedside, like an avenging angel, with 'the tongs red-hot at the ends,' as if, he quaintly adds, 'she did design to punish me with them.' What summary vengeance she was about to inflict we do not learn, for the adroit Samuel, stepping out of bed, disarmed her and arranged the articles of a truce.

In 1752 Howard, the prisoner's friend, married his landlady because he was grateful for the way she nursed him during a severe illness. She was sickly, considerably older than himself, and of a different social position, but they lived very harmoniously together until her death, which took place in three years' time.

Then he entered upon that 'circumnavigation of charity' which did so much good and made his fame. Returning to England he married again and retired to his estate, where he employed himself promoting the comfort of his tenantry. After some time there his beloved wife died, but Howard's loss was the world's gain, because it was to relieve his sorrow that he undertook two more tours to visit the prisons of Europe.

One night in the year 1795 the great Greek scholar, Porson, suddenly said to a friend named George Gordon, with whom he was smoking a pipe : 'Friend George, do you not think the Widow Lunan an agreeable sort of personage as times go?' Gordon answered in the affirmative, whereupon Porson added: 'You must meet me to-morrow morning at —— church at eight o'clock'; and without saying more, he went away.

At the wedding service no one was present except the bride and a lady friend and Porson and his friend. After the ceremony, to keep up the secrecy that had been maintained throughout, the two former went out by one door and the two latter by another. Dinner over Porson sought other company, and finished up at the Cider Cellar tavern, where he stayed till eight o'clock next morning.

In a ship in which he sailed to India, Warren Hastings had for fellow-passengers a German, Baron Imhoff, a portrait painter and his wife. When the latter had nursed Hastings through an illness which he had contracted on board, he became attached to her and she to him. What was to be done? Summon the Baron to our aid, thought the lovers, and they did so. It was proposed that the Baroness should seek for a divorce, that the Baron should help her to get one, and that Hastings should marry his wife and support his children—all which things were done. When on account of her health Hastings sent the lady back to England, he fitted up the round-house of an Indiaman for her accommodation with a profusion of sandal-wood and carved ivory, and expended thousands of rupees to secure her an agreeable female companion during the voyage.

When Sir Joshua Reynolds—himself a bachelor—met the sculptor Flaxman shortly after his marriage, he said to him :—

'So, Flaxman, I am told you are married; if so, sir, I tell you you are ruined for an artist.'

Flaxman went home, sat down beside his wife, took her hand in his, and said :—

'Ann, I am ruined for an artist.'

'How so, John? How has it happened, and who has done it?'

'It happened,' he replied, 'in the church, and Ann Denman has done it.'

He then told her of Sir Joshua's remark—whose opinion was well known, and had often been expressed, that if students would excel they must bring the whole powers of their mind to bear upon their art, from the moment they rose until they went to bed; and also, that no man could be a *great* artist unless he studied the grand works of Raphael, Michael Angelo, and others, at Rome and Florence.

'And I,' said Flaxman, drawing up his little figure to its full height, '*I* would be a great artist.'

'And a great artist you shall be,' said his wife, 'and visit Rome, too, if that be really necessary to make you great.'

'But how?' asked Flaxman.

'*Work and economise*,' rejoined the brave wife; 'I will never have it said that Ann Denman ruined John Flaxman for an artist.'

And so it was determined by the pair that the journey to Rome was to be made when their means would admit.

'I will go to Rome,' said Flaxman, 'and show the President that wedlock is for a man's good rather than his harm; and you, Ann, shall accompany me.'

After working for five years, aided by the untiring economy of his wife, Flaxman actually did accomplish his journey and studied at Rome for seven years.

For thirty-eight years Flaxman lived wedded. His wife, to whom his fame was happiness, was always at his side. She was a cheerful, intelligent woman; a collector, too, of drawings and sketches, and an admirer of Stothard, of whose designs and prints she had amassed more than a thousand. Her husband paid her the double respect due to affection and talent; and when any difficulty in composition occurred, he would say, with a smile, 'Ask Mrs Flaxman, she is my dictionary.' She also possessed strong sense, and a business capacity —the very wife for an artist. Without her Flaxman, who was a very child in all the concerns of life, would not have been able to manage his affairs. She died in the year 1820; and from the time of this bereavement, something like a lethargy came over his spirit. He survived her six years.

The famous sculptor, Joseph Nollekens, married a certain Mary Welch, a lady whose charms, it is said, made such an impression on Doctor Johnson, that long afterwards he was heard to say, 'Yes, I think Mary would have been mine if little Joe had not stept in.'

Mary was rather handsome, though her looks were proud, or, as her husband called them, *scorney*, and she paid great attention to dress, her marriage wardrobe costing as much as two hundred pounds. Mr and Mrs Nollekens agreed to differ about religion. They used to walk lovingly together every Sunday morning as far as a certain corner, where they parted—Joseph going to a Roman Catholic chapel, and his wife to the parish church.

Disagreeing seriously in nothing, they were particularly agreed in their desire to save—a desire which became sordid avarice as life advanced. After some years an ailment of the spine confined Mrs Nollekens to a couch, and what she regretted most in the affliction was that she could no longer go to the markets and get the 'bargains' in which she delighted.

When Lord Castlereagh was sitting for his bust coals were high in price, the weather extremely cold, and the sculptor's wife, sitting bolstered up by the fire, seemed shivering. His lordship rose when Nollekens went out for more clay, and good-naturedly threw some coals on the fire.

'Oh, my good lord,' croaked the dame, 'I don't know what Mr Nollekens will say !'

'Tell him, my good lady,' said he, smiling, 'to put them into my bill.'

They had no children, and when the pair, who had denied themselves ordinary comforts, died at an advanced age, they 'cut up' very rich indeed for the benefit of comparative strangers.

'Only a face at the window' of the sentimental song describes the one and only love affair of John Leech, the famous etcher. He was walking one day with a Mr Orrinsmith, in whose house he lived, through Hunter Street, Brunswick Square, when at a dining-room window there appeared the face of a young lady. It was a beautiful face, and attracted Leech's attention. He seemed to be immediately overcome by a most lively emotion—evidently love at first sight. His admiration was unbounded, his talk was of nothing else, and he ended by avowing his determination, should it be possible, to marry the owner of that face. 'The young artist,' adds Mr Orrinsmith, 'left no stone unturned to obtain an introduction to the family. Once introduced, his handsome face, winning manners, and his then rapidly growing fame, made the way easy, and he very shortly married the lady of his sudden choice.'

The last days of the wife of the sculptor, Sir Edgar Boehm, were clouded by terrible physical suffering; but this did not prevent her from being her husband's best and most far-sighted critic. Her judgment was sound, and she had a wonderful power of gauging the popularity any work was likely to have. 'If my wife approve, the public will,' remarked Sir Edgar, on one occasion; 'but if she condemn I may as well give the thing up.'

The wife of the celebrated architect, Sir Gilbert Scott, also greatly encouraged and helped her husband in his work. He used always to follow her criticisms, which were invariably true. How deeply he respected her is told by her son, who thus writes : 'My father, after her death, made it a practice, so often as the thought of her recurred to his mind, to pray silently for her; and whenever, being out of doors, he had occasion to mention her name, he was accustomed to raise his hat while he offered this tribute of natural piety.'

When George Moore, who became such a successful merchant and generous philanthropist, first came to London, he was employed by Flint Ray & Co., at thirty pounds a year. One day he observed a bright little girl tripping into the warehouse, accompanied by her mother.

'Who are they?' he asked of one of those standing near.

'Why, don't you know?' said he; 'that's the governor's wife and daughter !'

'Well,' said George, 'if I ever marry, that girl shall be my wife !'

Such a remark naturally aroused attention, and soon went the round of the house. The other lads laughed at George as another Dick Whittington.

When Moore resolved to marry Miss Ray he had an object for which to work, and the thought of her cheered him in difficulties and enabled him to resist temptation. On obtaining a higher position in the business and becoming a friend of the girl's father, he ventured to ask if he might woo her. This was denied and Moore went on for five years in patient well-doing. Then he asked again for the girl's hand and got it. He said that he had served for her, with an aching heart, nearly as long as Jacob had served for Rachel, but she only lived a few years after her marriage.

Great then was the loneliness of Moore, and he used to envy every man whom he saw with a happy family Years passed and he began to think of another helpmate, and at the same time received a letter from a friend advising him to wait until a suitable partner fell in his way and not to look out for one. Agnes Breeks fell in his way, but as at first he had not much hope of winning, he called her his 'Castle in the air.' The castle, however, in the shape of Agnes and her friends, was not long besieged before it surrendered, whereupon Moore said that he never felt so grateful to God in his life.

CHAPTER XXVII

HENPECKED

Cecilia, the wife of the great painter Titian, is said to have been a domineering, dictatorial woman, who insisted that her husband should render an account to her of every item of his expenditure. The painter was very wealthy, but we are told that the poor man was often put to the sorest straits to buy a glass of wine without letting his wife know anything about the transaction. But this discipline no doubt was good for Titian, and he himself seems to have felt this to be the case, for when his wife died he was 'utterly disconsolate.' They had four children.

The wife of Wycherley, the dramatist of the Restoration, kept an equally tight hand on her husband, who was all the better for it. She wished him always to be within her reach, and objected even to his visiting the Cock Tavern, which was exactly opposite their house, 'whither, if Mr Wycherley at any time went, he was obliged to leave the window open that his lady might see there was no woman in his company.'

Andrea Del Sarto was continually vexed by the unreasonable jealousy of the young widow whom he married. All who knew his case felt compassion for him, and blamed the simplicity which had reduced him to such a condition. He had been much sought after by his friends before he married, but afterwards they were afraid to visit him. Though his pupils stayed with him hoping to learn something from him, there was not one great or small who did not suffer from his wife's words or blows during the time he was there. When Andrea was seized by the sickness that carried him off, this rather ignoble specimen of a wife kept away from him for fear of infection.

'If you want a thing well done, do it yourself.' This maxim is especially true in reference to the choice of a life-partner, as that 'judicious' divine, Richard Hooker, discovered from bitter experience when he was injudicious enough to allow Mrs Churchman to select a wife for him. Having been appointed to preach at Paul's Cross in London, he put up at a house set apart for the reception of the preachers. On his arrival there from Oxford, he was wet and weary, but received so much kindness and attention from the hostess that, according to Isaac Walton, his biographer, he thought himself bound in conscience to believe all that she said. So the good man came to be persuaded by her 'that he was a man of a tender constitution; and that it was best for him to have a wife that might prove a nurse to him—such an one as might prolong his life, and make it more comfortable; and such an one she could and would provide for him, if he thought fit to marry.' The wife she provided was her own daughter Joan, who brought him neither beauty nor portion, and was like that wife 'who is by Solomon compared to a dripping-house.' With this 'silly, clownish Zantippe' he lived a very uncomfortable life.

When visited by Sandys and Cranmer at a rectory in Buckinghamshire, to which he had been presented in 1584, he was found by them reading Horace, and tending sheep in the absence of a servant. In his house the visitors received little entertainment, except from his conversation; and even this Mrs Hooker did not fail to disturb, by calling him away to rock the cradle. 'Their welcome was so like this that they stayed but next morning, which was time enough to discover and pity their tutor's condition. At their parting from him, Mr Cranmer said : "Good tutor, I am sorry your lot is fallen in no better ground as to your parsonage; and more sorry your wife proves not a more comfortable companion, after you have wearied your thoughts in your restless studies." To whom the good man replied, "My dear George, if saints have usually a double share in the miseries of this life, I, that am none, ought not to repine at what my wise Creator hath appointed for me; but labour, as indeed I do daily, to submit to His will, and possess my soul in patience and peace.'"

With indecent haste on Hooker's death this unamiable woman married again, and at first refused to give any account of the literary remains of her deceased husband. She afterwards confessed that she had allowed various Puritan ministers to have access to them; and it is to their tampering that we ought doubtless to attribute not only the destruction of many of these papers, but also alterations which have apparently been made in the text.

In a former chapter we spoke of the love which the great Duke of Marlborough had for his wife, but it certainly was not a love that cast out fear. In one of his letters from the Low Countries he writes : 'I have before me at this moment sixty thousand of the best soldiers in the world, commanded by the best General in Europe, and I am not half so much afraid of them as I am of you when you are angry.'

It would have been a great benefit to the Duchess if she had had a husband who would have curbed and corrected her temper, but Marlborough suffered without rebellion. When he left England for the campaign which was to culminate in Blenheim, there had been between him and the Duchess 'some petty bickerings,' if this expression may be used where the violence was solely on one side. The Duchess, however, wrote to him in terms of reconciliation, and Marlborough answered as follows : 'If you will give me leave it will be great pleasure to me to have it in my power to read this dear, dear letter often and that it may be found in my strong box when I am dead. . . . You have by this kindness preserved my quiet, and I believe my life, for till I had this letter I have been very indifferent what should become of myself.'

The Duchess approved as much as any modern army reformer of promotion by selection, but the selection had to be by herself. She tried to interfere in all the appointments made by her husband, and once wrote to The Hague about some trifling appointment in such an angry tone as to render him miserable. 'I do assure you, upon my soul,' he answered, 'I had much rather the whole world should go wrong than you should be uneasy; for the quiet of my life depends only upon your kindness.' Sometimes even the Duke's good temper would be too much tried, and then he would write to her very penitently, as thus : 'However unhappy my passion and temper may make you, when I have time to re-collect I never have any thought but what is full of kindness for you.'

'This year (1716),' writes Dr Johnson, 'he (Addison) married the Countess Dowager of Warwick, whom he had solicited by a very long and anxious courtship, perhaps with behaviour not very unlike that of Sir Roger to his disdainful widow; and who, I am afraid, diverted herself often by playing with his passion. . . . His advances at first were certainly timorous, but grew bolder as his reputation and influence increased; till at last the lady was persuaded to marry him, on terms much like those on which a Turkish princess is espoused, to whom the Sultan is reported to announce, "Daughter, I give thee this man for thy slave." '

'It was a splendid but dismal union,' and it has been said of Lady Warwick's place, where she and Addison resided : 'Holland House, although a large house, could not contain Mr Addison, the Countess of Warwick, and one guest, Peace.'

In a letter to Pope about Addison's appointment as Secretary of State, Lady Mary Wortley Montagu wrote: 'Such a post as that, and such a wife as the Countess, do not seem to be, in prudence, eligible for a man that is asthmatic; and we may see the day when he will be heartily glad to resign them both.'

If Addison had been happier in his home he might not have acquired the habit of staying late at taverns and drinking too much wine.

Sir Richard Arkwright, the inventor of the spinning-jenny, separated from his wife because she used to break models of the machines he contrived. Many of these were in connection with his search for perpetual motion, and indeed a wife may be excused for not wishing time and money that might have got her husband on in his business and enabled him to provide for the family to be expended upon perpetual motion. What was perpetual motion in comparison to a new pair of boots for the eldest hope?

James Watt, the inventor of the steam-engine, married, when very poor, Margaret Miller, his cousin, whom he had long tenderly loved. Their home was plain and small; but she had the sweetest of dispositions, was always happy, and made his life sunny even in its darkest hours of struggling.

Years passed, and when he was away from home on business his wife died suddenly. He was completely unnerved. Who would care for his little children, or be to him what he had often called her, 'the comfort of his life'? After this he would often pause on the threshold of his humble home to summon courage to enter, since she was no longer there to welcome him. She had shared his poverty, but was never to share his fame and wealth.

His second wife, who did this, was a very different woman. She so detested dirt, and so hated the sight of her husband's leather apron and soiled hands, that he built for himself a 'garret,' where he could work unmolested by his wife, or her broom and dustpan. She never allowed even her two pug dogs to cross the hall without wiping their feet on the mat. She would seize and carry away her husband s snuffbox wherever she found it, because she considered snuff as dirt. At night, when she retired from the dining-room, if Mr Watt did not follow at the time fixed by her, she sent a servant to remove the lights. If friends were present, he would say meekly, 'We must go,' and walk slowly out of the room. Such conduct must have been almost as trying as were his engine models, which caused him for days together to stay in his garret, not even coming down to his meals, cooking his food in the frying-pan and Dutch oven which he kept by him.

There were few men whose lives were more influenced by women than Abraham Lincoln, President of the United States. His first love was a Miss Rutledge, but no sooner had she begun to listen to his suit than she died. She asked for Lincoln several times when dying, and he was with her at the last. He was very much distressed, and it was thought at the time that he would lose his reason. He said, 'I can never be reconciled to have the snow, rains, and storms beat upon her grave.' Years after he was heard to say, 'My heart lies buried in the grave of that girl.'

Some time afterwards, however, Lincoln paid his addresses to a Miss Mary Owen, of Kentucky. She refused him, because, in her opinion, he was 'deficient in those little links which make up the chain of woman's happiness.'

When, at last, Lincoln did get married, it was to a Miss Mary Todd. Whether he suspected that she had a temper, or whether his heart was buried in Miss Rutledge's grave, as he said himself, the future President was not very keen for the marriage. On the day when the wedding should have taken place the groom failed to appear. The bride in grief vanished to her apartment; the wedding feast was left untouched; the guests quietly and wonderingly withdrew. Even after this a well-intentioned but mistaken woman succeeded in bringing the couple together again. On his second wedding-day a boy, seeing Lincoln dressing for the ceremony, asked him where he was going. 'To hell, I suppose,' was the reply. And as he stood before the clergyman he was 'as pale and trembling as if being driven to slaughter.'

A convincing proof of Mrs Lincoln's temper was that she was never able to keep a servant for any length of time, except one, who received secretly from the husband, as he knew what she had to endure, a dollar a week 'to keep up her courage.'

Lincoln obeyed his wife with almost slavish docility. One day a gardener asked Mrs Lincoln if he could cut down a certain tree, and she consented. Before carrying out the order, however, the man went to Lincoln's office to ask him.

'What did Mrs Lincoln say?' inquired he.

'That it should be taken away.'

'Then, in God's name,' exclaimed Lincoln, 'cut it down to the roots !'

On another occasion a man had called to discuss with Mrs Lincoln her unceremonious dismissal of his niece. He was received with gestures so violent and language so emphatic that he was glad to beat a hasty retreat. He went and told his story to the unfortunate husband. Lincoln replied: 'I regret to hear this, but let me ask you in all candour, cannot you endure for a few moments what I have had as my portion for the last fifteen years?' These words were accompanied with such a look of distress that the man was completely disarmed. He expressed his deepest sympathy, and even apologised for having approached him.

These tantrums, it appears, were due to 'cerebral disease,' but this did not make them less unpleasant. Still, there are those who maintain that Lincoln's wife was the real though unintentional cause of his political greatness. She drove him out into the world, and the acquaintance he thus formed with the people around him helped to make him what he was.

No doubt some of the stories about Mrs Lincoln's temper were the concoctions of her enemies, of whom she had many. That she tried in every way to help her husband cannot be denied. Whenever she was absent from home, Lincoln kept her informed by telegraph of important events, especially military successes. This shows his high esteem for her, as well as her intelligent interest in what was going on. When Washington was threatened in 1864 she accompanied her husband to the front, and both were under fire in the Confederate attack on Fort Stevens.

When Lincoln heard that he had been elected President, though he could scarcely help being moved by it, he was very calm. After he had received the congratulations of the many friends who had rushed to offer them, all he said was : 'Well, gentlemen, there is a little woman at our house, who is probably more interested in this despatch than I am; and if you will excuse me, I will take it up and let her see it.' The 'little woman' was his wife.

No queen could have comported herself with more dignity than did Mrs Lincoln at all public functions. She dressed well, even extravagantly, and her dressmaker has told the public that in three or four months she has made for her fifteen gowns.

Whatever may be thought of Mrs Lincoln, there was something which prevented her husband from being unhappy in domestic life, and that was the society of Tad and Willie, his children. To them he turned aside from the mob of office-seekers and others who daily afflicted him, and found refreshment of spirit in so doing. Tad and Willie were afraid of no one, and when their father was discussing difficult problems with statesmen and generals, they would come into the room and climb all over him.

CHAPTER XXVIII

NOTABILITIES WHO NEVER MARRIED

WHEN Michael Angelo was asked why he did not marry, he replied: 'I have espoused my art; and it occasions me sufficient domestic cares, for my works shall be my children. What would Lorenzo Ghiberti have been had he not made the gates of St John? His children consumed his fortune, but his gates, worthy to be the gates of Paradise, remain.'

There was a lady of the name of Western, who would gladly have become the wife of Sir Joshua Reynolds; but the painter would not marry for fear he might be withdrawn from his studies. Angelica Kauffmann and he used to paint each other's portraits, and this was sufficient for society to couple their names together. He was also a great friend of Miss Burney, and of course given to her also by gossip, never tired of marrying the bachelor.

So, too, the late Lord Leighton told the Princess of Wales, who with the Prince was inspecting the artist's pictures, that he had never married because he could not find sufficient leisure to devote to a wife.

The story goes that Sir Isaac Newton once went a wooing, and began to smoke, and, in absence of mind, attempted to use the forefinger of the lady as a pipe-stopper. This unfortunate act brought his courtship to an abrupt termination, and he never had another, or certainly not one that brought him to matrimony.

It was for a not less trifling reason, as most people would think, that Beau Brummell broke off the engagement to marry that was his nearest approach to that state of life. When asked why, 'What could I do, my dear fellow,' he replied, 'but cut the connection? I discovered that Lady Mary actually ate cabbage.'

Pope fell in love with a young lady of the name of Withenburgh, and in spite of his distortion and diminutiveness, she returned the compliment. Indeed, she did this so seriously that when her guardian, disapproving, removed her to the Continent and prevented all communication between the lovers, she killed herself.

The poet's celebrated friendship for Martha Blount began early in his life, and continued to his death on his part in spite of the fact that she heartlessly neglected him at the last. When sent for to see him she said to the messenger, 'What, is he not dead yet?' He left to her nearly all his property.

During one part of his life the poet was desperately in love with Lady Mary Wortley Montagu, but at the period to which the following story relates there existed between them the most rancorous hatred, covered with a flimsy veil of politeness. Lady Mary went one day to Lord Burlington's, in Piccadilly, and inquired if his lordship were at home. The servant replied that he was not, but that Mr Pope was in one of the drawing-rooms. 'Oh,' said Lady Mary, 'I wish to see him; show me the room.' The servant accordingly showed her upstairs, opened the drawing-room door, and having announced her name, retired. After a short time, however, hearing the drawing-room bell ring, he returned and met Lady Mary, who had just left the apartment. 'You told me,' said she, 'that Mr Pope was in the drawing-room; I saw nothing there but a great baboon asleep in an armchair.' This story was told by the servant to Lord Burlington, and, in the usual course of such reports, was whispered by some good-natured friends to Pope himself. The indignant poet shortly afterwards called in his carriage upon Lady Mary, whom he entreated to accompany him, in order, as he said, to show her the excellent effect produced by the substitution of iron rails for the dead brick wall which had intercepted, from the road, the view of Kensington Gardens. She accepted the invitation, and, notwithstanding the great imperfection of her sight, which she was extremely averse to acknowledge, but which prevented her distinguishing objects at the distance of twenty feet, most politely acquiesced in all the extravagant praises lavished on the beautiful scenery which everywhere struck the view through the pretended iron rails. The exhibition ended, Pope took an early opportunity of communicating to his friends the success with which he had retorted on Lady Mary's satire on his personal defects.

Cowper loved his first cousin, Theodora Jane Cowper, and she loved him, but her father forbade marriage on account of the relationship. It is said that this disappointment was what first deranged the poet's mind. The lady remained constant to him, preserving with tender care all the love poems he had written to her under the name of Delia.

The house of Cowper was 'a perfect seraglio of virtuous women.' Mrs Unwin, the 'Mary' of his poems, devoted her life to wait on this man, with his dark soul, his fitful temper, and who had at times nothing to give her but a perverted hatred. By-and-by Lady Austin took her place, who was brilliant and fascinating until she became tiresome. Her tiresomeness consisted in this, that she loved Cowper a great deal more than she was loved by him, and she was always calling for those little demonstrations that women delight in. Southey thought that it was not probable that a lady would fall in love with Cowper at the age of fifty. Every one knows the poet's portrait, and his muslin nightcap, and his passion for hares. But Cowper had the faculty of flattering a woman by lifting the commonplaces of her life into sweetness and nobleness. His weakness, too, may have been attractive, for a woman likes nothing better than to have a good deal to do for the man she loves.

The 'Jessamy Bride' (Miss Mary Horneck) was the

friend but not the sweetheart of Goldsmith. He never married, though on one occasion he was with difficulty dissuaded from uniting himself to a needlewoman whom he wished to oblige.

That quaint divine, John·Berridge, was not so good-natured. Even to oblige a rich lady he would not enter the holy estate. She wrote to him that it had been revealed to her that she should marry him. Berridge replied that if this were the case the Lord would have made a similar revelation to him, and that, on the contrary, he had been distinctly warned not to take to himself a Jezebel.

Thomson, the poet of *The Seasons*, had not sufficient money to marry the Miss Young whom he celebrated as 'Amanda,' so the lady was lost to poetry in all senses, and gained by the navy, for she married a vice-admiral.

When Keats was a schoolboy he thought a fair woman a pure goddess, ethereal, above any man. Afterward he came to the conclusion that women were only equal to men, or if 'great by comparison, very small.' He became indifferent to and suspicious of their society, finding that it aroused in him evil thoughts, malice, spleen. All this was changed when he met a certain Fanny Brawne. At first the impression she made was not altogether favourable, as may be seen from the following description which he wrote to his brother : 'Shall I give you Miss Brawne? She is about my height, with a fine style of countenance of the lengthened sort. She wants sentiment in every feature. She manages to make her hair look well; her nostrils are very fine, though a little painful; her mouth is bad and good; her profile is better than her full face, which is indeed not "full," but pale and thin, without showing any bone; her shape is very graceful, and so are her movements; her arms are good, her hands bad-ish, her feet tolerable.

She improved so much upon further acquaintance that the poet became completely fascinated and engaged himself to her. But love-making was not to him a happy operation. He fretted if the lady's manner was not always the same, and tortured himself with all kinds of fancies about her. When, owing to his failing health, it was decided he should winter abroad, the thought of leaving her was, 'beyond everything, horrible.' And when he became worse, and knew that death was fast approaching, he wrote: 'I cannot bear to die and leave her. Oh, God! God! God! Everything that I have in my trunks that reminds me of her, goes through me like a spear.' Miss Brawne was unworthy of such love, for ten years after Keats's death she could write of him to a friend : 'The kindest act would be to let him rest for ever in the obscurity to which circumstances have condemned him.'

Samuel Rogers did not marry, though he was fond of the society of ladies, and a favourite with them. In his latter years he used to regret not having done so. 'If I had a wife,' he would say, 'I should have somebody to care about me'; to which Lady Jersey on one occasion replied, 'How could you be sure that your wife would not care more about somebody else than about you?'

Rogers's 'nearest approximation to the nuptial tie' was with a girl whom he thought the most beautiful he had ever seen. At the end of the London season, she said to him at a ball: 'I go to-morrow to Worthing. Are you coming there?' He did not go. Some months afterwards, being at Ranelagh, he saw that the attention of every one was drawn towards a large party that had just entered, in the centre of which was a lady leaning on the arm of her husband. Stepping forward to see this wonderful beauty, he found it was his love. She merely said, 'You never came to Worthing.'

It is recorded of David Hume, the historian, that he once made an offer of marriage to a lady who refused him, but whose friends shortly afterwards conveyed to him the intelligence that she had changed her mind.

'So have I,' replied David, laconically, 'so have I,' and he lived and died in single blessedness.

Though by no means handsome, Hume was very successful with the fair sex. This was especially the case when he visited Paris, owing to his being introduced by the Comtesse de Boufflers, who had corresponded with him. The French beauties were amused when in a *tableau vivant* he was placed as a sultan between two slaves, represented by the prettiest of them. He could find nothing to do except smite his stomach, and repeat for a quarter of an hour, '*Eh bien, mesdemoiselles, eh bien, vous voilá donc!*'

The friendship between the philosopher and the countess lasted until the death of the former. In one of his letters to her, he says : 'Three months are elapsed since I left you; and it is impossible for me to assign a time when I can hope to join you. I still return to my wish, that I had never left Paris, and that I had kept out of the reach of all other duties, except that which was so sweet and agreeable to fulfil—the cultivating your friendship and enjoying your society. Your obliging expressions revive this regret in the strongest degree.'

On another occasion the philosopher assured her that she had 'saved him from a total indifference towards everything in human life.'

When living at Lausanne, in Switzerland, Gibbon, who narrated the decline and fall of the Roman Empire, fell in moderate love with Susanna Curchod, daughter of a Protestant pastor. She was 'learned without pedantry; lively in conversation; pure in sentiment; elegant in manners.' Nevertheless, the social position of the lady was objected to by the historian's father, who, as Carlyle expresses it, 'kept a gig.' At the time the lover lived upon a paternal allowance. So he 'sighed as a lover and obeyed as a son.' He left Lausanne, and his wound was healed by absence, time, and the habits of a new life, the cure being accelerated by a faithful report of the tranquillity and cheerfulness of the lady herself. She married Necker, a famous banker of Paris, and when Gibbon's love had subsided to friendship and esteem, he paid her a visit. So conceited was he, however, about his power to fascinate, that he expressed surprise to a friend that M. Necker—whose public duties took him away in the course of the evening—'should care to leave them alone together.'

Buckle, who wrote the *History of Civilisation*, missed himself the civilising influence of matrimony. 'I expect so much in my wife,' he used to say, 'that I cannot look for money,' yet his ideas about education and other domestic matters were so exalted that he considered he would not be justified in marrying on less than £3000 a year. At the age of seventeen he bestowed his affections on a cousin, but found that she was engaged to another cousin. The fortunate rival was challenged to a personal combat, but the girl's matrimonial prospects do not appear to have been altered thereby. He next fell in love with another cousin, above the common in understanding, with a very large fortune, and with a liking for him. The mothers of the young people prevented them from marrying because they were cousins.

In after years Buckle was often rallied by his friends for not taking to himself a wife, and he went so far as to acknowledge his mistake, for he was alone in the world. 'If at least my little nephew had lived,' he said, 'I should have had a friend in time; I would have made something of him. But what I love I lose; and now that I am nearly forty, I am alone.'

One morning Theodore Hook drove a friend home from a party, in his cab, between four and five o'clock. 'Ah,' said he, as the cool air blew freshly against his hot cheeks, 'you may depend upon it, my dear fellow, that there is nothing more injurious to health than *the night air*. I was very ill some months ago, and my doctor gave me particular orders not to expose myself to it.'

'I hope,' observed his friend, 'you attended to them.

'Oh, yes,' was the reply, 'strictly. I came up every day to Crockford's or some other place to dinner, and I made it a rule on no account to go home again till about this hour in the morning.'

This reckless mode of living, which injured his health, would most likely have been avoided had he married in his youth, instead of forming in after life a connection that ruined him.

Though Hook knew his health was failing, and that death was not to be driven away by a cannonade of champagne corks, he made no provision for the poor girl whose virtue he had ruined, or for her five children, of whom he was the father.

It was not altogether his own fault that he did not marry. Once he proposed, but he was like the physician who ordered ice, and then said that perhaps it would be better to have it warmed. After sending to be posted the letter in which he made his proposal, suddenly repenting, he went in haste to the office, and on authenticating his writing and transmission of the epistle, it was returned to him. Notwithstanding this eccentric indecision, but for the intervention of death, which suddenly snatched the object of his affections away, it is not at all improbable that a match might have been finally made.

On being reminded one day in after years, when he had concluded a laboured invective against matrimony, 'that if a certain lady had been alive he would at that moment have been the *slave of a woman!*' he replied: 'A woman ! No, no; she was not a woman, but an angel!'

His friends tried to make him take a more genial view of the fair sex, and once a gentleman seriously advised him 'to settle and take a wife.' He replied in his dry, sarcastic manner: 'With all my heart; and pray, whose wife would you advise me to take?'

In 1795 Charles Lamb was for six weeks in an asylum for some form of mental derangement. The immediate cause may have been a love disappointment. Certainly in a sonnet he distinctly reveals an attachment to a 'gentle maid' named Anna, with whom 'in happier days' he had held free converse, days which, however, 'ne'er must come again.' The girl's name was Simmons. With the heroism of a martyr, Lamb resisted all temptations to marry, because he had devoted himself to his sister, who was always on the verge of insanity.

James Smith of the *Rejected Addresses* never married. 'I have had a horrid dream,' he wrote in his journal—'viz. that I was engaged to be married. Introduced to my bride, a simpering young woman with flaxen hair, in white gloves. Just going to declare off—*coûte que coûte*—when to my inexpressible relief I awoke.'

Washington Irving always remained single because Matilda Hoffman, the beautiful girl to whom he was engaged, died of consumption in her seventeenth year. He says : 'I was by her when she died, and was the last she ever looked upon.' He took her Bible and prayer book away with him, sleeping with them under his pillow, and in all his subsequent travels they were his inseparable companions. Not until thirty years after her death did any one venture to speak of her to him. He was visiting her father, and one of her nieces, taking some music from a drawer, brought with it a piece of embroidery. 'Washington,' said Mr Hoffman, 'this was from Matilda's work.' The effect was electric. He had been talking gaily the moment before, but became quite silent, and soon left the house. It was to Matilda that he alluded when he wrote in *Bracebridge Hall:* 'I have loved as I never again shall love in the world—I have been loved as I never again shall be loved'; and in a notebook : 'She died in the beauty of her youth, and in my memory she will ever be young and beautiful.'

The reason Pitt used to give for remaining single was that he was married to his country, and his opponents asserted that his country had made a bad match. It has been said that he did not care for women, but according to Lady Hester Stanhope this was not the case, for 'Mrs B——s, of Devonshire, when she was Miss W——,was so pretty that Mr Pitt drank out of her shoe. Nobody understood shape and beauty and dress better than he did.' Lady Hester, who was the great statesman's niece, relates how one day when she was going out very nicely dressed, as she thought, Pitt called her back and suggested some slight changes in her toilet, which were just what were required to make it complete.

The story runs that Walpole tried to get up a match between Pitt and Necker's daughter—afterwards the celebrated Madame de Staël—the father of the latter promising to endow her with fourteen thousand pounds a year. But his real love was probably Lady Eleanor Eden, a famous beauty, whom, we are told, he gave up with a hard struggle.

Horace Walpole never married, but he was always fond of female society, and the most faithful friends and correspondents of his later years were women. With the Countess of Ossory he had been on friendly terms from the time when gambling was his nightly occupation, and she was the 'Duchess of Grafton and Loo.' To her and Mary and Agnes Berry and several other ladies, he gossipped on paper for many years of everyday chit-chat, politics, literature, and the scandal which was so dear to them all. People might say that he was in love with Mary and Agnes Berry, but he was too old to care what they said. He was proud of his 'partiality for them. It was as much with both as with either. They are exceedingly sensible, unaffected, and able to talk on any subject. They are of pleasing figures; Mary, the elder, with fine dark eyes. Agnes is hardly handsome, but almost.' When Mary was absent from London Walpole was inconsolable, or else anticipating her return with almost the ardour of a youthful lover.

With another woman very different from these, and one with whom it might have seemed he had nothing in common, Walpole corresponded for some twenty years. This was Hannah ('St Hannah') More. This friendship, in her earlier years at any rate, was fully appreciated by Miss More, and Walpole took pleasure in her quickness and honesty, and in the freshness of her feelings. She presented her poem of *Bas Blue* to him, and was invited to Strawberry Hill, an invitation which, as Mr Walpole was said to be 'a shy man,' she considered 'a great compliment.'

The two friends frequently discussed serious subjects. 'On one occasion,' the lady writes, 'we parted mutually unconvinced, he lamenting that I am fallen into the heresy of Puritanical strictness, and I lamenting that he is a person of fashion for whom the Ten Commandments were not made.' The 'person of fashion,' however, so much respected the lady 'of Puritanical strictness' that he presented her with a magnificent Bible, adorned with an admiring inscription. Miss More showed her gratitude by remarking that she wished 'he would himself study that blessed book.'